Test-Driven Development

T0254122

Lech Madeyski

Test-Driven Development

An Empirical Evaluation of Agile Practice

 Springer

Lech Madeyski
Wrocław University of Technology
Institute of Informatics (I-32)
Software Engineering Department
Wybrzeże Wyspiańskiego 27
50-370 Wrocław
Poland
lech.madeyski@pwr.wroc.pl
http://madeyski.e-informatyka.pl/

ISBN 978-3-642-42526-4   ISBN 978-3-642-04288-1 (eBook)
DOI 10.1007/978-3-642-04288-1
Springer Heidelberg Dordrecht London New York

ACM Computing Classification (1998): D.2, K.6

© Springer-Verlag Berlin Heidelberg 2010
Softcover re-print of the Hardcover 1st edition 2010
This work is subject to copyright. All rights are reserved, whether the whole or part of the material is
concerned, specifically the rights of translation, reprinting, reuse of illustrations, recitation, broadcasting,
reproduction on microfilm or in any other way, and storage in data banks. Duplication of this publication
or parts thereof is permitted only under the provisions of the German Copyright Law of September 9,
1965, in its current version, and permission for use must always be obtained from Springer. Violations
are liable to prosecution under the German Copyright Law.
The use of general descriptive names, registered names, trademarks, etc. in this publication does not
imply, even in the absence of a specific statement, that such names are exempt from the relevant protective
laws and regulations and therefore free for general use.

Cover design: KuenkelLopka GmbH

Printed on acid-free paper

Springer is part of Springer Science+Business Media (www.springer.com)

To Iwona, Lech, Natalia, Judyta and Małgorzata

Foreword

This book makes an important and timely contribution. Agile methods are gaining more and more interest both in industry and research. Many industries transform their way of working from traditional waterfall projects with long duration to more incremental, iterative and agile practices. Furthermore, the need to evaluate and to obtain evidence for different processes, methods and tools has been emphasized in research in particular over the last decade. The main contribution comes primarily from combining agile methods (or more precisely XP and test-first programming) with empirical evaluation.

The book's contribution is important since it evaluates empirically a way of working which is more and more embraced by companies developing software or software-intensive systems. Thus, it evaluates new way of working which is a challenge given the pace in which new technologies evolve, and in particular it provides evidence in relation to test-first programming or test-driven development. However, this is not the sole contribution. The book presents three experiments in much more depth than normally is possible in a research article. This means that it provides readers with in-depth insights into experimental methods in the context of agile development. This includes presentation of statistical methods having concrete examples of how to conduct the statistical analysis with SPSS and a thorough discussion about the different validity threats in empirical studies. Furthermore, the book presents how meta-analysis can be conducted when having several separate experiments.

In summary the book provides many valuable insights both to practitioners in terms of the evidence for test-first programming and to researchers in terms of clear illustrations of how new processes, methods and tools can be evaluated using experimentation in software engineering. It is pleasure to recommend this book to practitioners and researchers being interested in agile methods or empirical evaluation or both of them.

Karlskrona, Sweden
Professor Claes Wohlin
Blekinge Institute of Technology

Preface

There is strong shadow where there is much light.
–Johann Wolfgang von Goethe

Following the recent recommendations in medicine and psychology [21, 98], as well as the guidelines offered by the empirical software engineering community [109, 127, 140, 141, 227], this preface takes the form of a structured abstract.[1] For the sake of clarity, statistical results are not included in the preface itself but they may be found in Appendix.

Background

The quality of the methods used to evaluate new software development techniques, practices, processes, technologies, tools, etc., indicates the maturity of the software engineering research discipline. Consequently, experimentation, as a systematic, disciplined, quantifiable and controlled way of evaluation becomes a fundamental part of both research and practice in software engineering. The importance of properly conducted and replicated experiments has become widely accepted in the software engineering community. Owing to the empirical studies and their analysis or meta-analysis, industry may take advantage of the already accumulated knowledge. The roots of that fundamental shift in software engineering research can, to a large extent, be found in evidence-based medicine. Controlled experiments, quasi-experiments and case studies become the primary research methods by which the choice of software development techniques should be justified. Systematic reviews and meta-analyses are gaining increasing acceptance as the methods of summarizing

---

[1] Structured abstracts organize the summaries of publications with the following common headings: background or context, objective or aim, method, results, limitations and conclusions [127]. Several researchers who compared structured abstracts with traditional ones support the claim that structured abstracts are an improvement over traditional ones. Not only is more information presented, which is helpful for the reader, but also the format requires that the authors organize and present their findings in a systematic way, easier to read [109].

the results of a number of empirical studies. Evidence-based software engineering (EBSE) undermines anecdotal evidence and unsystematic experience as sufficient grounds for decision making while stressing instead the empirical evidence from software engineering research.

Another interesting shift in software engineering has been created by the agile movement in general, and eXtreme Programming (XP) in particular. Agile teams shape software systems using a collaborative process, with executable software and automated tests at its heart, whilst marginalising the documents. That creates a shift away from tools for managing requirements to tools (originating from the XP values, principles and practices) supporting collaboration and the gradual distillation of requirements into automated test suites [58]. The Test-First Programming (TF) practice, also called Test-Driven Development, is considered the flagship and one of the most influential practices of the XP methodology [15, 23, 144], as well as the one of the most controversial ones [179].

Both the experimentation in software engineering and the agile movement influenced this book. The latter attracted the attention of the author to the agile methodologies, XP and then the flagship XP practice, i.e. TF. The former influenced the way the research was conducted and reported (e.g. the stress on the effect size estimates and meta-analysis).

Objective

The purpose of this book was to evaluate the effects of the TF agile software development practice with respect to the percentage of acceptance tests passed (considered an external code quality indicator [87, 88]), design complexity metrics (that have been found significant for assessing fault proneness by several researchers [19, 32, 33, 95, 200, 238]) and the number of acceptance tests passed per development hour (which is an indicator of development speed). Moreover, the aim is to present the preliminary evaluation of the impact of the TF practice on mutation score indicator and branch coverage, the indicators of the fault detection effectiveness and the thoroughness of unit tests, respectively.

An additional (but auxiliary) objective of the book was to present how to perform an analysis of experiments in software engineering using the Statistical Package for the Social Sciences (SPSS). Conference or even journal papers usually present short and thus superficial descriptions of the performed analyses, while the existing excellent books [131, 227, 259] cover a wide range of topics related to Empirical Software Engineering (ESE) and, therefore, do not focus on the joint analysis of closely related experiments.

Method

The effects of the TF programming practice were evaluated by conducting three experiments named ACCOUNTING (experiment on the development of an accounting system), SUBMISSION (experiment on the development of a paper submission and review system), and SMELLS&LIBRARY (experiment on the development of both a tool for identifying bad smells in Java source code through the use of a set of software metrics and a library application). Those experiments, described in Chap. 4, were carried out in academic setting with over 200 graduate MSc students, using both between-groups (in Experiments ACCOUNTING and SUBMISSION) and repeated measures (in Experiment SMELLS&LIBRARY) experimental designs. Furthermore, the Pair Programming (PP) practice was used along with the TF programming practice in the first experiment to check whether there is a synergy between both XP practices. The data were collected with the help of different measurement tools. Some of them (Judy, Aopmetrics, ActivitySensor and SmartSensor Eclipse plugins) have been developed especially for the sake of the experiments. The statistical analysis of experiments has been described in Chaps. 5, 6 and 7, while the meta-analysis has been performed in Chap. 9. A selective analysis and selective meta-analysis have been carried out to minimize threats to the validity (e.g. process conformance threat). Effect sizes were reported and interpreted with respect to their practical importance.

Results

The main result observed on the basis of the meta-analysis of Experiments ACCOUNTING, SUBMISSION and SMELLS&LIBRARY is that programmers using Test-First Solo Programming (TFSP) technique produce a code that is significantly less coupled than that produced by programmers using Test-Last Solo Programming (TLSP) technique. This finding has also been confirmed by the selective analysis of Experiments SUBMISSION and SMELLS&LIBRARY. Furthermore, the mean effect size represents a medium (but close to large) effect on the basis of meta-analysis of all the experiments, as well as selective meta-analysis, which is a substantial finding. It suggests a better modularization (i.e. a more modular design), easier reuse and testing of the developed software products [43] due to the TF programming practice.

However, the superiority of the TF practice in the investigated context was not confirmed with respect to the two remaining areas of investigation. The mean value of weighted methods per class (WMC_{Mean}) was not significantly affected by the TF programming practice according to the meta-analysis, as well as selective meta-analysis, while the mean effect size represents a small effect according to the meta-analysis, as well as the selective meta-analysis.

The mean value of response for a class (RFC_{Mean}) was not significantly affected by the TF practice based on Fisher's method of combining p-values. The mean effect size represents a small effect according to meta-analysis as well as selective meta-analysis.

Moreover, the results revealed that the TF practice does not have a statistically significant impact, neither on the percentage of acceptance tests passed (PATP), which is an indicator of external code quality, nor on the number of acceptance tests passed per development hour (NATPPH), which is an indicator of development speed. The mean effect size of TF on the percentage of acceptance tests passed (PATP) represents a small effect. The mean effect size of TF on the number of acceptance tests passed per hour (NATPPH) represents a small effect, too.

Furthermore, the effect of the TF practice on unit tests was measured by branch coverage (BC) and mutation score indicator (MSI), which are indicators of the thoroughness and the fault detection effectiveness of unit tests, respectively. Relying on the preliminary results, BC was not significantly higher in the TFSP than in the TLSP group. However, the effect size was medium in size and therefore the effect of TF on branch coverage is a substantive effect. TLSP and TFSP did not significantly differ in MSI and the effect size was small.

Limitations

The threats to the validity of the conducted experiments (e.g. relevance to industry) are thoroughly discussed in Sect. 10.5. The generalization of results is limited, since the analysed TF practice was applied to develop systems smaller than 10,000 lines of code. Further experimentation (e.g. in industrial context) is needed to establish evidence.

Conclusions

The results reinforced the evidence regarding the superiority of the TF practice over the Test-Last Programming (TL) practice, with respect to the lower coupling between objects (CBO_{Mean}). However, the superiority of the TF programming practice in the investigated context was not supported with respect to the percentage of acceptance tests passed (PATP), the number of acceptance tests passed per development hour (NATPPH), weighted methods per class WMC_{Mean}, and response for a class (RFC_{Mean}).

Wroclaw, Poland   Lech Madeyski

Acknowledgements

The movement called Extreme Programming is to my mind the most encouraging trend in software development today. It focuses us all on the real essentials: talent, discipline without dogma, teamwork, risk-taking, and light process. It poses a particular challenge to the manager, since it pushes control downward (managing people who are empowered to make decisions and even make their own mistakes is a lot harder than managing people who are obliged to shut up and do what you tell them to). I think XP will be a new generation's answer to the mindless regimentation embodied in the C.M.M. and other fat-book methodologies.

Tom DeMarco

First of all, I would like to thank the head of my institute, Prof. Zbigniew Huzar, for a friendly atmosphere, making an excellent environment to work in, and for supporting me during my post-doctoral research. In 2007 I was invited to take part in XP, PROFES, ENASE, EuroSPI and CEE-SET conferences, either to present accepted papers or as an invited speaker. Without his support and encouragement, I would not have been able to manage that. I would also like to thank my Ph.D supervisor, Prof. Zygmunt Mazur, especially for introducing me to the Polish Information Processing Society, and Prof. Adam Grzech for his encouragement to start my Ph.D at the Wrocław University of Technology. Also, I would like to thank Prof. Janusz Górski, who confirmed my intuition about the importance of experimentation for software engineering research during our short, but fruitful discussion in 2003. That conversation had serious consequences and this book is one of them. I would also like to thank Prof. Jerzy Nawrocki, who taught me that valuable research results should be presented at major international conferences and published in recognized international journals. I hope I followed his advice. Furthermore, I would like to thank Prof. Leszek Maciaszek with whom I had an opportunity to come up with the idea of a new series of ENASE (Evaluation of Novel Approaches to Software Engineering) conferences. He encouraged me to play the role of devil's advocate at ENASE conferences in 2006 and 2007, along with top-ranked software engineering researchers (e.g. Prof. Mehmet Aksit, Prof. Brian Henderson-Sellers, Prof. Ulrich Eisenecker, Dr Giuseppe Berio, Prof. Stefan Kirn). In fact, challenging the basic XP assumptions and practices and presenting the available empirical evidence and lessons learnt was an exciting experience. I would also like to thank the co-authors of my research papers, i.e. Marcin Kubasiak, Wojtek Biela, Michał Stochmiałek, Łukasz Szała, Norbert Radyk and all the other people who have contributed to my understanding of the topics presented in this book (e.g. Dr Małgorzata Bogdan, Dr Andy Field and Prof. Scott B. Morris for helpful suggestions concerning statistical analysis). Thanks to my MSc students (e.g. Marcin Kubasiak, Nicos Karagieorgopulus, Wojtek Biela, Michał Stochmiałek, Adam Piechowiak, Łukasz Szała, Tomasz Poradowski, Bartłomiej Bogaczewicz, Norbert Radyk, Piotr Przybył and Piotr Wójcicki). Without you, my research would not have been performed or would not have been so interesting.

If I were to point out only one book that influenced the way this research was conducted, it would be "Experimentation in Software Engineering" by Wohlin et al. [259]. I was lucky when I came across that book one day in the library of the Royal Institute of Technology (KTH) located in Stockholm. The International Conference on Product Focused Software Process Improvement (PROFES), led by the people from Fraunhofer Institute for Experimental Software Engineering (IESE) (e.g. Dr Jürgen Münch and Andreas Jedlitschka) and VTT (e.g. Prof. Pekka Abrahamsson), has to be mentioned as an extremely friendly empirical software engineering community to grow up in. Therefore, it was an exceptionally pleasant occasion for the author to become the member of that community and the winner of the "Best Paper and Best Presentation Award" at the PROFES conference in 2007.

I would also like to thank anonymous reviewers, as well as Prof. Zbigniew Huzar, Marian Jureczko and Wojciech Biela, for their valuable comments. Special thanks go to Ralf Gerstner of Springer Germany for providing professional advice during the publishing process and Małgorzata Rybak for assisting with proofreading.

Last but not least, I do like to express gratitude to my family and friends. Nothing would have happened without you – Iwona and Lech. Nothing would have been so colourful without you – Natalia, Judyta and Małgorzata.

Wrocław, Poland   *Lech Madeyski*

Contents

Acronyms

ANOVA	Analysis of Variance
ANCOVA	Analysis of Covariance
APA	American Psychological Association
BC	Branch Coverage
CBO	Coupling Between Objects (CK metric)
CK	Chidamber–Kemerer [44]
CVS	Concurrent Versions System
DevTech	Development Technique (e.g. TFSP)
DV	Dependent Variable
EBT	E-Business Technologies
EO	Effort Overhead
ES	Effect Size
ESE	Empirical Software Engineering
IDE	Integrated Development Environment
IV	Independent Variable
MSI	Mutation Score Indicator
NATP	Number of Acceptance Tests Passed
NATPPH	Number of Acceptance Tests Passed Per Hour
PATP	Percentage of Acceptance Tests Passed
PIJ	Programming in Java
PP	Pair Programming
RFC	Response for a Class (CK metric)
SbS	Side-by-Side Programming
SE	Software Engineering
SP	Solo Programming
SPSS	Statistical Package for the Social Sciences
SR	Speedup Ratio
SVN	Subversion (successor to the widely used CVS)
TDD	Test-Driven Development (also known as Test-First Programming)
TF	Test-First Programming (also known as Test-Driven Development)
TFSP	Test-First Solo Programming
TFPP	Test-First Pair Programming
TL	Test-Last Programming (also known as Test-Last Development)

TLD	Test-Last Development (also known as Test-Last Programming)
TLSP	Test-Last Solo Programming
TLPP	Test-Last Pair Programming
TVL	Test-Very-Last
VE	Virtual Enterprise
WMC	Weighted Methods per Class (CK metric)
WUT	Wroclaw University of Technology
XP	eXtreme Programming

Chapter 1
Introduction

When defects in an existing paradigm accumulate to the extent
that the paradigm is no longer tenable, the paradigm is
challenged and replaced by a new way of looking at the world.
Dawn Freshwater and Gary Rolfe

Bauer coined the term "software engineering" (SE) forty years ago at a NATO Software Conference, expressing a need: "What we need is software engineering". In the last decade, an incredible impact on research and practice in SE has been made by the agile movement. Under this broad umbrella of the agile methodologies sit specific approaches such as eXtreme Programming (XP) [23, 25, 129, 247], Scrum [220, 221], Lean Software Development [206], etc. They share similar values and beliefs, which have been documented in the "agile manifesto" [24]. Among the agile methodologies, XP is probably the most prominent one and an empirical evaluation of one of its key practices, called Test-First Programming (TF), is a general aim of this book.

1.1 Test-First Programming

According to DeMarco, "XP is the most important movement in our field today." [25]. This statement emphasizes the importance of XP as a new software development methodology.

XP can be seen from various perspectives, such as: a mechanism for social change, a software development methodology, a constant path to perfection, and an attempt to bring together humanity and productivity in software development [248]. XP is founded on five abstract but universal values (communication, simplicity, feedback, courage, respect) and tangible practices (e.g. test-first programming, pair programming) that are bridged together by certain principles (e.g. mutual benefit) [23]. According to Beck [23], values are the large-scale criteria we use to judge what we see, what we think and what we do; values also underlie our immediate and intuitive recognition of what we accept and what we reject in a given situation. Making values explicit is important, as, without values, practices (which are extremely situated) lose their purpose and direction. However, there is a gap between values and practices, since values are too abstract to directly guide development. Therefore,

L. Madeyski, *Test-Driven Development*,
DOI 10.1007/978-3-642-04288-1_1, © Springer-Verlag Berlin Heidelberg 2010

principles act as a bridge between values and practices. A detailed description of XP, its values, principles and practices is given by Beck [23].

This book focuses on one agile software development practice promoted by XP, i.e. Test-First Programming (TF) [23], also known as Test-Driven Development (TDD).[1] However, the impact of another XP practice, called pair programming (PP), is also taken into account in the first experiment to uncover possible interaction between both XP practices. TF and PP are considered not only the flagship and the most influential practices of XP methodology [15, 23, 144] but also the most controversial ones [179]. Classic development techniques, to which TF and PP are often compared, are Test-Last Programming (TL), also known as Test-Last Development (TLD) and Solo Programming (SP).

The key characteristic of TF is that programmers write tests before related pieces of the production code (i.e. before they change the behaviour of the production code, they must have a failing test) [22, 23, 72, 179]. The main characteristic of PP is that two programmers work on the same task using one computer and one keyboard [14, 23, 252, 254]. Both practices are presented in detail in Sects. 3.3.1.1 and 3.3.1.2 along with graphical process models that allows developers to apply the techniques. Of all of the practices of XP, TF is perhaps the most counterintuitive [179]. On the other hand, TF is, according to McBreen [179], the most powerful of XP practices for promoting the necessary paradigm shift for understanding and benefiting from XP.

TF has gained recent attention in professional settings [15, 22, 23, 97, 144, 195] and has made initial inroads into software engineering education [66, 67]. A wide range of empirical studies on the impact of both the TF and the PP practice in industrial [14, 28, 40, 56, 57, 87, 88, 126, 174, 192, 196, 217, 254, 255, 268] and academic environments [72, 79, 89, 91, 94, 111, 126, 157–161, 185, 187, 193, 194, 201, 252, 254, 257] give compelling evidence of their popularity.

1.1.1 Mechanisms Behind Test-First Programming that Motivate Research

Literature presents several interesting mechanisms behind TF adoption. The search for the possible consequences of those mechanisms underlies the empirical investigation carried out and expanded in this book.

TF provides instant feedback as to whether new functionality has been implemented as intended and whether it interferes with previously implemented functionality [72]. TF encourages developers to dissect the problem into small, manageable programming tasks to maintain focus and to provide steady, measurable progress [72]. Maintaining up-to-date tests gives courage to refactor [81] mercilessly in order to keep the design simple and to avoid needless clutter and

---

[1] According to Koskela [144], TDD and TF are just different names for the same practice and both may be used interchangeably.

complexity. Up-to-date and frequently run tests written for any piece of the production code that could possibly break [129] help to ensure a certain level of quality [72] and an acceptable level of test coverage as a side effect.[2] Moreover, tests provide the context for the making of low-level design decisions (concerning how classes and methods are named, what interfaces they provide and, consequently, how they are used) [72]. Tests are also perceived as another form of communication and documentation. Since unit tests exercise classes and methods, the source code of the tests becomes the critical part of system documentation. Unit tests communicate the design of a class because they show concrete examples of how to exercise the class's functionality [36]. A noteworthy aspect of TF is that it addresses the fears about staff turnover in a complementary way to the PP practice. The suite of unit tests is a safety net and repository of design decisions, so even if a new team member makes a coding mistake, it is highly likely that the suite of unit tests will detect the error [179]. Therefore, TF supports the refactoring and maintenance activities. Without the safety net, the developers would be very reluctant to change the design of the existing code [179].

A similar set of influential mechanisms behind PP adoption can also be presented. Therefore, synergy between both the TF and the PP practice will be investigated as well. Some researchers argue, two distinct roles (i.e. the role of a driver and a navigator) may be recognized when using the PP practice [14, 161, 254, 258]. The limited ability to think simultaneously at both the strategic and the tactical level can be easily addressed by the aforementioned distinct roles focused on different thinking levels. Furthermore, two distinct roles contribute to a synergy of the individuals in the pair [14, 161] as "two heads are better than one". PP also turns out to be a way of coping with the risks associated with bringing new programmers into the team [179]. The problem of the limited spread of knowledge inside the team may be dealt with by rotating pairs frequently [153, 253], as active pairing requires every pair to talk about the design, the requirements, the tests and the code. Also, active pairing ensures compliance with the rest of the programming practices, because the entire team can see who does not really comply with the rules [179]. Furthermore, one can try to reduce the risk of a high-defect rate because pairing acts like a continuous code review [179, 183–185]. Last but not least, PP has an effect on how programmers work, since it requires that all production code is written with a partner [23].

The aforementioned mechanisms behind TF and PP may affect many aspects of the software development, which includes code quality (e.g. percentage of acceptance tests passed, design complexity measures) or development speed (e.g. the number of acceptance tests passed per development hour). On the other hand, sceptics argue that such approaches to programming would be counterproductive. Managers sometimes feel they get two people to simply do the same task, thus wasting valuable "resources". At the same time, some programmers are long conditioned to working alone and resist the transition from solo programming (SP) to

---

[2] Code coverage analysis is sometimes called test coverage analysis but both terms are synonymous [53] and will be used interchangeably.

the PP practice [258]. Therefore, convincing all the members of development teams (e.g. programmers, managers) to accept the pair programming work culture may be a difficult task. TF is also not without difficulty to start with. Developers sometimes resent having to change their habit and to follow strict rules of the TF practice [162] instead of the TL (test-last) practice or even "code and fix" chaotic programming [80]. Furthermore, continuous testing and refactoring does not extend functionality. Better code or tests quality, as well as higher development speed, might be good counter-arguments in such situations. Therefore, this research objective is to empirically evaluate the hypothesized effects of the TF practice.

After this brief introduction to the agile movement in general and TF, PP as well as XP in particular, the rest of this chapter is structured as follows: general introduction to empirical research methodology is given in Sect. 1.2; the fundamentals of software measurement with respect to software quality and software development productivity are presented in Sect. 1.3; research questions are introduced in Sect. 1.4, while book organization and claimed contributions of the book are presented in Sects. 1.5 and 1.6, respectively.

It is worth mentioning that topics related to both research methodology and software measurement, if easily available and thoroughly addressed by existing books or research papers, have been dealt with briefly and corresponding references have been given, while more specific aspects of the conducted experiments and their analysis are covered in detail in other chapters.

1.2 Research Methodology

Research methodology presented in this section starts with a short introduction to the empirical software engineering movement in Sect. 1.2.1, while empirical methods are discussed in Sect. 1.2.2.

1.2.1 Empirical Software Engineering

The quality of the methods used to evaluate new methods, processes, technologies etc. indicates the maturity of the SE research discipline. Although the term SE was coined 40 years ago, the SE discipline is as yet not mature enough because there is still the need to make a transition from the software development based on presumptions, speculations and beliefs, to that based on facts and empirical evidence [132].

SE was formally defined by IEEE as "the application of a systematic, disciplined, quantifiable approach to the development, operation, and maintenance of software" [113]. Consequently, experimentation, as a systematic, disciplined quantifiable and controlled way of evaluating new techniques, methods, practices, processes, technologies or tools [259], has become a fundamental part of research and practice in SE [227] and lays the foundation for this book.

Empirical software engineering (ESE) requires the scientific use of quantitative and qualitative data to understand and improve software development products and processes. ESE can be viewed as a series of actions to obtain evidence and a better understanding about some aspects of software development. An experiment can be performed to prove or disprove stated hypotheses. Software development practices, processes, technologies and tools have to be empirically evaluated in order to be better understood, wisely selected (among different alternatives) and deployed in appropriate contexts. Higher quality or productivity in SE would not be possible without well-understood and tested practices, processes etc. Recognizing that need, top level SE journal editors and conference organisers tend to expect empirical results to back up the claims or even select overtly empirical papers (e.g. *Empirical Software Engineering* journal by Springer, *International Symposium on Empirical Software Engineering and Measurement, International Conference on Software Engineering, International Conference on Product Focused Software Process Improvement*).

1.2.2 Empirical Methods

Empirical research methods in SE are used to explore, describe and explain phenomena. The empirical methods presented in this section encompass introduction to qualitative and quantitative research paradigms, fixed and flexible research designs, empirical strategies (e.g. experiments, case studies, surveys), as well as between-subjects and repeated measures experimental designs.

1.2.2.1 Qualitative and Quantitative Research Paradigms

A distinct feature that marks qualitative research is that it does not seek to produce quantified answers to posed research questions but can substantially contribute to the understanding of the subjects' perspective and a particular context within which the subjects (or participants) act (and the influence of that context), when developing explanations, generating theories etc. [175].

Quantitative research is often based on initial qualitative work (e.g. once research objectives are defined). That research consists in the systematic collection of data, which results in the quantification of relationships or characteristics of groups. Hence, it is particularly useful for finding quantitative answers and is well suited for testing hypotheses.

1.2.2.2 Fixed and Flexible Research Designs

Two main types of research designs are the fixed and the flexible design. The fixed research design typically involves a substantial amount of pre-specification about what should be done and how it should be done (e.g. the collection of quantitative data from two or more compared groups) [210]. The flexible research design, also called qualitative, relies on qualitative data (in many cases in the form of words) and requires less pre-specification [210]. Mixed-method designs are also possible.

1.2.2.3 Empirical Strategies

The three most common empirical methods (or strategies) used in ESE are experiments, case studies and surveys. They have been discussed in detail by several researchers [181, 210, 267] and presented briefly in the forthcoming sections.

Experiments

A formal experiment is a controlled, rigorous investigation of an activity, where independent variables (IVs) are manipulated to document their effects on dependent variables (DVs). Formal experiments require a great deal of control, and therefore they tend to be small (so-called "research in the small"), i.e. involving small numbers of subjects or events [74].

Experiments are viewed by many as the "gold standard" for research [210] and are particularly useful for determining cause-and-effect relationships. Experiments provide a high level of control and are usually done in a laboratory environment [259]. In a true experiment, the experimenter has a complete control over the independent variable, e.g. the timing of the experimental manipulations, measurements of the dependent variable etc. Furthermore, in a true experiment there is a random allocation of subjects to the groups (two or more) and different groups get different treatments (e.g. development techniques). The objective is to manipulate one or more variables and to control the other variables that can influence the outcome (dependent variables). The effect of the experimental manipulation is measured and analysed by means of statistical techniques with the purpose of showing which technique is better.

Sometimes, especially in (close to) real-world situations, it is not feasible to conduct true experiments, and we have to accept a quasi-experimental design. In a quasi-experimental empirical study, the experimenter does not have complete control over manipulation of the independent variable as well as over the assignment of the subjects to the treatments. For example, it may be impossible to allocate the subjects randomly to the treatment groups (i.e. to different levels of the independent variable) for practical or ethical reasons. Although the same statistical tests can be applied, the conclusions from quasi-experimental studies cannot be drawn with as much confidence as from the studies employing true experimental designs (e.g. due to the lack of random allocation of the subjects to the treatments).

Single case experiments (labelled commonly as "small-N experiments" or "single subject experiments") focus on the effects of a series of experimental manipulations on the individuals who act as their own control. Experiments are prime examples of fixed research design [210].

Case Studies

A case study is, as suggested by its name, a study of a case (project, individual, group, organization, situation etc.), or a small number of related cases, taking its context into account [210, 267]. A case study is a research technique that makes it possible to identify the key factors that may affect the outcome of an activity, and to document the activities (their inputs, outputs, resources and constraints).

In case studies, one usually investigates a typical project (so-called "research in the typical"), rather than trying to capture information about a wide range of possible cases [74]. This research strategy involves the collection of qualitative data but may also include quantitative data [210]. Case studies are examples of flexible research design [210].

Surveys

A survey is an investigation in which data are collected from a population, or a sample from that population, through some form of interviews or questionnaires aimed at describing accurately the characteristics of that population (e.g. to describe the subjects' background, experience, preferences). The results from the survey are analysed in order to make generalisations, validate the effects of experimental manipulation etc. It is possible to poll over large groups of subjects or projects (so-called "research in the large") but it is not possible to manipulate variables as in case studies and experiments [74].

Surveys fall into two categories of research design: flexible and fixed, depending on degrees of pre-specification (e.g. open-ended interviews are usually flexible, while questionnaires with closed questions are typically fixed).

1.2.2.4 Between-Groups and Repeated Measures Experimental Designs

Between-groups (independent groups or between-subjects) experimental designs take advantage of separate groups of subjects for each of the treatments in the experiment and each subject is tested only once. There are some benefits from between-groups designs. Firstly, it is their simplicity. Secondly, their usefulness when it is impossible for a subject to participate in all treatments (e.g. when sex or age is one of the independent variables or when treatments alter the subjects irreversibly). Thirdly, the effect of the subjects' fatigue in course of the subsequent treatment occasions (e.g. when the subjects become bored or tired) is reduced, as the subjects participate in only one treatment occasion. However, there are also serious disadvantages of between-groups designs, mainly the following: a lower ability to detect cause–effect relationships (i.e. insensitivity to experimental manipulations) and expense in terms of the number of subjects, effort and time. Therefore, repeated measures (i.e. within-subjects) experimental designs are often preferred.

In repeated measures (within-subjects) experimental designs, each subject is exposed to all of the treatments in the experiment, so that two or more measures are collected for each subject. In consequence, the number of subjects, effort and time are minimized, while sensitivity is increased due to the fact that variability in individual differences between the subjects is removed. In fact, each subject serves as his own control in the repeated measures design. On the other hand, treatments have to be reversible which is a kind of limitation. Moreover, carry-over effects from one condition to another have to be taken into account. The issues related to carry-over effects are discussed further in Sect. 4.7.3.

Mixed or hybrid experimental designs involve a combination of both of the aforesaid experimental designs.

1.3 Software Measurement

This section presents the fundamentals of software measurement, while more details can be found in [74].

Measurement is defined as "a mapping from the empirical world to the formal, relational world. Consequently, a measure is the number or symbol assigned to an entity by this mapping in order to characterize an attribute" [74]. This definition encompasses attributes of entities. An entity is an object (e.g. a developer, a software product) or an event (e.g. the maintenance phase of a project) in the real world, while an attribute is a property of an entity (e.g. active development time spent on the production code) [74].

Measurement helps us to understand the current situation and to establish baselines useful to set goals for the future behaviour. By measuring the inputs and the outputs of an object under study we are able to investigate and understand the effects of an experimental manipulation. Thus measurement is a crucial activity in empirical studies. Moreover, before we can expect to improve software processes and products, we must measure them. So measurement is important for understanding, control and improvement or corrective activities [74]. DeMarco emphasizes in his famous statement: "You can't control what you can't measure." [59].

Kan classifies software metrics into the following three categories: product metrics, process metrics and project metrics [135]. He also argues that software quality metrics are more closely associated with product and process metrics than with project metrics.

A short introduction to measurement levels is given in Sect. 1.3.1. The issues of software product quality and software development productivity are discussed in Sect. 1.3.2 and 1.3.3, respectively. Both sections are an introduction to research questions formulated in Sect. 1.4.

1.3.1 Measurement Levels

There are four levels at which variables can be measured: nominal (categorical), ordinal, interval and ratio levels. All that may be said about nominal data is that things with the same number are equivalent, while things with different numbers are not equivalent [76]. Consequently, nominal data should not be used for arithmetic; however, it is possible to compute frequencies.

Ordinal data offer more information than nominal data, as the ordinal scale allows us to imply order or rank. For example, the best subject, who has a rank of 1, is better than the next best subject, who has a rank of 2. However, ordinal data tell us nothing about the relative differences, e.g. how better one of the subjects performed than the other one. Consequently, ordinal data need to be analysed with non-parametric tests. It is worth mentioning that a lot of data from questionnaires are ordinal.

Interval and ratio data are even more useful than ordinal data. For interval data, it is required that equal intervals between different points on the scale represent the same difference in the property being measured at all points along the scale. Ratio data have the same properties as interval data, but in addition, the ratios of values along the scale are meaningful. For example, the temperature scale in Celsius is an interval scale, since $2°C$ is not twice as hot as $1°C$, in opposite to, for example, development time (something that lasts, say, 2 minutes is twice as long as something that lasts 1 minute). The difference between those two measurement levels is not critical. For example, the statistical package SPSS version 14.0 (SPSS Inc., Chicago, IL, USA), used for analysis, does not attempt to distinguish between them, and it employs, instead, the term "scale" to describe both measurement levels. Interval and ratio data can be analysed with parametric tests.

1.3.2 Software Product Quality

There is a wide range of views of what "software quality" is. A famous statement, attributed to Kitchenham (confirmed in personal communication from Barbara Kitchenham, July 2006), is that software quality is hard to define, impossible to measure and easy to recognize. Another famed statement concerning quality is that "quality, like beauty, is very much in the eyes of the beholder" [74].

Unfortunately, as for the measuring software quality, we have neither an accepted understanding of what quality is, nor commonly accepted software quality measures [130], even though a lot of quality standards and models have been proposed [80, 130]. The software quality standard ISO 9000-3 states that: "There are currently no universally accepted measures of software quality..." but "the supplier of software products should collect and act on quantitative measures of the quality of these software products."

1.3.2.1 ISO/IEC 9126

One of the most widely known software quality standards is the ISO/IEC 9126 standard. It is divided into four parts [121–124]. The first part [121] presents product *quality model*, explains the relationships between the different approaches to software quality and presents the quality characteristics and sub-characteristics that influence the quality of software products. The ISO/IEC 9126 standard provides different views of product quality which are closely related. According to the Quality

Model Framework Lifecycle of ISO/IEC 9126 [121], process quality influences internal quality which in turn influences external quality, which influences quality in use [30]. If experimental treatment (e.g. the TF practice) influences process quality, then it also affects *internal metrics*, *external metrics* and then *quality in use metrics*, as maintained by the aforementioned Quality Model Framework Lifecycle.

External Metrics of Product Quality

The second part of the standard [122] describes *external metrics* of product quality used to measure the characteristics (i.e. functionality, reliability, usability, efficiency, maintainability an portability) and related sub-characteristics (e.g. interoperability) identified in the aforementioned quality model. This external view of software quality focuses on the software dynamic aspect and is concerned with the completed software executing on the computer hardware, with real data [30]. The percentage of acceptance tests passed (PATP), called "reliability" by Müller and Hagner [187], can be considered an example of an *external metric* and is used in this book. *External metrics* of product quality can indicate the *quality in use* (e.g. if the percentage of acceptance tests passed is low, then expected end-user satisfaction and effectiveness is likely to be low). Research question related to the external view of software quality is posed in Sect. 1.4, while related research goal is formulated in Sect. 3.1. PATP is presented in Sect. 3.3.2.1, while the impact of TF on that *external metric* is analysed in Chap. 5.

Internal Metrics of Product Quality

The third part of the standard [123] presents the *internal metrics* used to measure the same collection of characteristics and sub-characteristics as in the second part of the standard [122]. However, the internal view of software quality concerns mainly static properties of the software product individual parts, including complexity and structure of the design and code elements. The advantage of *internal metrics* is that they can be used to measure quality properties in the early stages of development. Moreover, *internal quality metrics*, as opposed to *external quality metrics* as well as *quality in use metrics*, are meaningful on their own, i.e. do not depend on the hardware, the data etc. Class-level metrics proposed by Chidamber and Kemerer (hence labelled as CK metrics) [43] are, as mentioned by Bøegh [30], commonly used *internal metrics*. Higher level design quality metrics, proposed by Martin [171, 172], and the CK metrics may complement each other to spot weaknesses in the software architecture. *Internal metrics* can act as early indicators of external quality. Research question related to the internal view of software quality is posed in Sect. 1.4, while the related research goal is formulated in Sect. 3.1. Both internal quality metrics suites (i.e. the CK metrics and Martin's metrics) as well as the references to the underlying theory about the relationship between the OO metrics and some quality characteristics (e.g. maintainability) are presented in Sect. 3.3.2.2. However, it is worth mentioning that only some of the proposed *internal metrics* have been empirically confirmed as very significant for assessing maintainability or fault proneness [19, 32, 33, 95, 200, 238]. The impact of TF on those *internal metrics* is analysed in Chap. 7.

Quality in Use Metrics

The fourth part [124] describes *quality in use metrics* and embraces the metrics used to measure the effects on the user, i.e. end-user productivity, effectiveness, satisfaction and safety. The *quality in use* view refers to the final product used in the real environment and conditions. That view is out of the scope of the empirical evaluation presented in this book, since the subjects used in the conducted experiments were developers, and not end-users, of the software products.

1.3.2.2 Test Code Metrics

Test code quality may be considered as a new perspective on software product quality. The quality of tests can indicate the quality of the related production code [201], especially when writing tests is a part of the development practice. Therefore, the goal is to shed light on the effects of the experimental manipulation from a different, test code, perspective. Consequently, research question related to this view of software product quality is posed in Sect. 1.4, while the related research goal is formulated in Sect. 3.1. The thoroughness and the fault detection effectiveness of unit tests are described in Sect. 3.3.2.4, while the impact of the TF practice on unit tests characteristics is analysed in Chap. 8.

1.3.2.3 Validity of Software Quality Standards

The ISO/IEC 14598 series [114–116, 118–120] defines a software product evaluation process, based on the ISO/IEC 9126. Both the ISO/IEC 9126 and the ISO/IEC 14598 series share a common terminology. The SQuaRE (Software Product Quality Requirements and Evaluation) project has been created to make them converge into the ISO/IEC 25000 series [125], as an attempt at eliminating the existing gaps, conflicts or ambiguities.

Several doubts concerning software quality standards have been raised by researchers. Pfleeger et al. [203] suggested that "standards have codified approaches whose effectiveness has not been rigorously and scientifically demonstrated. Rather, we have too often relied on anecdote, 'gut feeling', the opinions of experts, or even flawed research rather than on careful, rigorous software engineering experimentation." Al-Kilidar et al. [9] conducted a large experiment with 158 subjects and concluded that ISO/IEC 9126 is not suitable for measuring design quality of software products which casts serious doubts on the validity of the standard as a whole. Also, Kitchenham [139] argues that the selection of quality characteristics and sub-characteristics seems to be rather arbitrary and not clear (e.g. "it is not clear why portability is a top-level characteristic but interoperability is a sub-characteristic of functionality."). Also Arisholm [13] called the ISO/IEC 9126 quality model into question (e.g. "why is adaptability not a sub-characteristic of maintainability when changeability is?", "most of the characteristics have not been defined at an operational level").

Although the ISO/IEC 9126 quality model has been brought into question by the aforementioned researchers, the principle that within a predefined context, the quality of a software product "can be evaluated by measuring internal attributes (typically static measures of intermediate products), or by measuring external attributes (typically by measuring the behaviour of the code when executed), or by measuring quality in use attributes" [121], is generally accepted and will be followed in this book. However, according to Jørgensen [130], one should avoid considering the measures of the software quality-related attributes (i.e. software quality indicators or factors) as the equivalent of software quality measures.

1.3.3 Software Development Productivity

Munson [190] argues that one of the greatest problems of measurement in SE is the lack of standards for anything we wish to measure e.g. there are no standards for measuring the productivity of programmers. Productivity is usually defined as the output divided by the effort (e.g. measured in hours) required to produce that output [176, 177]. However, the question is how to translate the output into a reasonable measure. According to Maxwell and Forselius [176], output measurement should be based on a project's size, functionality and quality but, unfortunately, such measurement does not yet exist and lines of code (*LOC*) and function point (*FP*) counts are currently the most widely used output measurements. However, *LOC* per unit of effort tends to value longer rather than efficient or high-quality programs. In Object-Oriented (OO) development, a class or method may stand for the unit of output, thus the number of classes per person-year (*NCPY*) and the number of classes per person-month (*NCPM*) are also used as productivity metrics [135]. The number of acceptance tests passed (NATP) was used as an indicator of external code quality by George and Williams [87, 88], Pančur et al. [201], Madeyski [157], as well as Gupta and Jalote [94]. In contrast to some productivity measures (e.g. *LOC* per unit of effort), NATP per unit of effort (e.g. the number of acceptance tests passed per hour) takes into account the functionality and quality of software development products [157, 168] and thus seems to be an interesting productivity indicator. Poppendieck [205] goes even further and argues that to measure the real productivity of software development, we need to look at how efficiently and effectively we turn ideas into software; she proposes to measure the revenue generated per employee. However, we cannot use that measure in non-commercial, academic projects.

The term "software development speed" is sometimes used to avoid misunderstandings related to different meanings of productivity. The research question related to software development speed is posed in Sect. 1.4, while the related research goal is formulated in Sect. 3.1. Software development speed indicators are described in Sect. 3.3.2.3, while the impact of TF on development speed indicator is analysed in Chap. 6.

1.4 Research Questions

The aim of this book is to present the results of an empirical evaluation of the effects of the TF practice on different indicators of software quality, as well as software development speed based on a series of closely related empirical studies. The aim is to shed light on the effects of the TF practice, based on different views, in order to embrace a wider perspective of the possible effects of the TF practice.

Because the readers may benefit from the understanding, at some level, of what is being investigated before they can read how it relates to the already existing work presented in Chap. 2, the research questions are introduced here:

RQ1 What is the impact of TF on external code quality indicator(s)?
RQ2 What is the impact of TF on development speed indicator(s)?
RQ3 What is the impact of TF on internal quality indicator(s)?
RQ4 What is the impact of TF on indicators of the fault detection effectiveness and the thoroughness of unit tests?

As mentioned before, a possible interaction between the TF and the PP practice is also investigated in the first experiment. Hence, the following development techniques are considered: Test-Last Solo Programming (TLSP or TL for short), Test-Last Pair Programming (TLPP), Test-First Solo Programming (TFSP or TF for short) and Test-First Pair Programming (TFPP). The differences between the TF and the TL practices are described in depth in Sect. 3.3.1. Research questions RQ1–RQ4 correspond to Chaps. 5, 6, 7, and 8, respectively.

1.5 Book Organization

This book is divided into ten chapters. The book also contains references to the cited works, glossary, lists of figures, tables, and acronyms, as well as the index of terms.

Chapter 1 starts with an introduction to the investigated TF programming practice and presents the mechanisms behind that practice that motivate empirical investigation. The first chapter also provides background information on research methodology and software measurement used in empirical software engineering. Furthermore, it presents research questions addressed in this book, and gives an overview of the book and its main contributions.

Chapter 2 describes the most important findings from empirical studies concerning the TF and PP software development practices, since both are sometimes used simultaneously.

Chapter 3 presents research goals refined from research questions with the help of a goal definition template, the high level conceptual model that guides the research, the independent, dependent and possible confounding variables.

Chapter 4 focuses on the planning and execution of the three experiments that have been carried out at Wroclaw University of Technology (WUT). The chapter gives details about the context of the experiments, research hypotheses, experimental materials, tasks and designs. Moreover, there is also a short overview of the new measurement tools (Aopmetrics, Judy, ActivitySensor and SmartSensor plugins) developed for the sake of the experiments carried out.

Chapters 5, 6, 7 and 8 describe the results of the statistical analysis of the impact of the TF practice on the indicators of external code quality, development speed, design complexity, the fault detection effectiveness and the thoroughness of unit tests, respectively.

In order to get more reliable and unbiased conclusions from the merged results of the three performed experiments that address the same research questions, a meta-analysis of the experimental results is presented in Chapter 9. The meta-analysis is based not only on combining p-values, but also on combining effect sizes using fixed, as well as random, effects model.

Chapter 10 provides a summary of the results, presents plausible mechanisms behind the results, main contributions of the book, possible threats to the validity of the results, conclusions and future work.

1.6 Claimed Contributions

The main contribution of this book to the body of knowledge in software engineering consists in the increased understanding of the impact of TF on the percentage of acceptance tests passed PATP (an external code quality indicator), a number of acceptance tests passed per development hour NATPPH (the development speed indicator), internal code quality indicators (i.e. the mean value of: coupling between object classes CBO_{Mean}, weighted methods per class WMC_{Mean} and response for a class RFC_{Mean}), as well as indicators of the fault detection effectiveness (i.e. mutation score indicator MSI) and the thoroughness of unit tests (i.e. branch coverage BC).

Furthermore, practical contributions are related to new measurement tools (ActivitySensor and SmartSensor Eclipse plugins, Judy and Aopmetrics) which have been developed to support the experiments. ActivitySensor and SmartSensor Eclipse plugins contributed to reducing and monitoring several threats to the validity of the results. Judy mutation testing tool contributed greatly to the obtaining of the unique results concerning the impact of the TF practice on mutation score indicator (an indicator of the fault detection effectiveness of unit tests). Aopmetrics helped to collect internal metrics (sometimes labelled as design complexity metrics [238]) from a large number of software projects.

Additional contribution consists in the overview of the state-of-the-art of the empirical studies concerning the effects of the TF and PP practices.

Chapter 2
Related Work in Industrial and Academic Environments

> *Design and programming are human activities; forget that and all is lost.*
>
> Bjarne Stroustrup

This chapter presents the overview of the majority of empirical studies that have investigated the TF (Test-First) and PP (Pair Programming) practices versus the TL (Test-Last) and SP (Solo Programming) practices or closely related treatments. Some empirical studies were excluded due to the toy size of the delivered software products [266], or treatments loosely related to TF or PP [17]. The effects of the TF practice are discussed in Sect. 2.1, while the effects of the PP practice are presented in Sect. 2.2.

2.1 Test-First Programming

The fact that programmers end up with a comprehensive set of unit tests, eventually, is a nice bonus of the TF practice. However, writing comprehensive suites of tests, and, in particular, writing unit tests for any piece of the production code that could possibly break [129], is time consuming, even though it sometimes may help in reaching the desired code quality. It is also worth mentioning that poorly organized or highly coupled tests make code changes difficult, which would be exactly the opposite of what is expected. Every change to the code requires changes to the tests. If the change is simple, it is usually not a noticeable overhead to maintain the tests, but when the test scenario is more complex (e.g. requires multiple mock objects to be set up for the test), the change might demand more time so that the tests remain valid and useful. Therefore, both quality and development speed-related effects of the TF practice are presented in this section, which provides a summary of many empirical studies conducted so far.

Empirical results in industrial, quasi-industrial and academic environments are presented in separate Tables (2.1, 2.2 and 2.3, respectively) in order to highlight the impact of the TF practice in different environments, as well as for the sake of clarity. The tables report, from left to right, the references for each study, the number of subjects involved in each empirical study, and textual descriptions of the

L. Madeyski, *Test-Driven Development*,
DOI 10.1007/978-3-642-04288-1_2, © Springer-Verlag Berlin Heidelberg 2010

Table 2.1 Industrial empirical studies on the effects of Test-First (TF) programming

Studies	Subjects	TF effects
Ynchausti [268]	5	• 38–267% increase in the quality test pass rate
		○ 60–187% longer development time
Williams et al. [255]	9	• reduced defect rate by 40% [255]–50% [174]
Maximilien and		○ minimal [174] or no difference [255] in *LOC /*
Williams [174]		*person-month*
George and	24	○ 16% longer development[a]
Williams [87, 88]		• 18% more functional tests passed[a]
Geras et al. [89]	14	○ little or no difference in developer productivity
Canfora et al. [40]	28	○ required more time per assertion, more overall
		and average development time ⓢ
		• no evidence of more assertions or more assertions
		per method
Bhat and	6 (A)	• 15%(project B)–35%(project A) longer
Nagappan [28]		development time
	5–8 (B)	• decreased *defects/KLOC* by 62%(project A)–76%
		(project B)
Damm and	100	• 5–30% decrease in fault-slip-through rate[b]
Lundberg [56, 57]		• 60% decrease in avoidable fault costs[b]
		• total project cost became less by 5–6%[b]
		• the ratio of faults decreased by from 60–70%
		(release 5) to 0–20% (release 7)[b]
		• cost savings in maintenance are up to 25% of the
		development cost[b]
Sanchez et al. [217]	9–17	○ it took on average 15% or more[c] of overall time to
		write unit tests ("moderate perceived productivity
		losses")
		• reduced internal defect rate
Nagappan et al. [192][d]	9,6,	• decreased defects rate by 40–90%
	5–8,7	○ 15–35% longer development time
Slyngstad [232]		• mean defect density reduced by 36%
		• mean change density reduced by 76%

○ denotes the effect on development speed or effort.
• denotes the effect on software quality factors.
ⓢ means statistically significant result at the 0.05 level.
[a] TF pairs vs. TL pairs.
[b] Combined effect of introducing component-level test automation together with TF.
[c] Calculated based on questionnaires.
[d] Builds up on the prior empirical work [28, 174, 255].

findings. Significant results are marked by "ⓢ", while effects on development speed and software quality factors are marked as "○" and "•", respectively.

Empirical studies on the effects of the TF practice in an industrial setting are summarized in Table 2.1. Several case studies have been performed in well-known, large companies such as Microsoft [28, 192], IBM [174, 192, 217, 255], Ericsson AB [56, 57], Soluziona Software Factory [38, 40], StatoilHydro ASA (Statoil merged with Hydro creating StatoilHydro ASA in 2007) [232]. The promising results of the aforementioned industrial empirical studies are discussed in

Table 2.2 Quasi-industrial empirical studies on the effects of Test-First (TF) programming

Studies	Subjects	TF effects
Abrahamsson et al. [8]	4[a]	• little or no added value to a team (according to developers) ○ team used 0%(iteration 5)–30%(iteration 1) of effort for TF
Siniaalto and Abrahamsson [230]	4,5,4[b]	• slightly less coupled code (based on CBO metric) but results are dispersed • high *LCOM* metric (lack of cohesion) • *WMC, DIT, NOC* and *RFC* metrics did not reveal significant differences • higher method, statement and branch coverage levels
Madeyski [167]	1[c]	○ higher ratio of active to passive development time[d] ○ increased *LOC/h*[e] ○ increased *number of user stories/h*[e] ○ increased *number of acceptance tests/h*[e]
Janzen and Saiedian [126]	Industrial: 1,2,2,5/ Academic: 3,7	• size metrics point to a possible tendency to write smaller, simpler classes and methods[f] • a tendency to write simpler classes and sometimes simpler methods (usually lower WMC)[f] • coupling analysis (*CBO*) does not give a clear answer • cohesion analysis does not reveal improved cohesion

○ denotes the effect on development speed or effort.

• denotes the effect on software quality factors.

[a] Three students with industrial experience and one industrial developer.

[b] Undergraduates but usually having some industrial experience and working on real projects.

[c] An experienced programmer, with recent industrial experience, classified as E4 according to Höst et al. [106]; developed a web-based system for academic institution.

[d] The active time may be described as typing and producing a code, while the passive time is spent on reading the source code, looking for a bug etc.

[e] Not only TF, but also experience and knowledge of the application domain gained during the course of the project seem to drive productivity.

[f] In the case of some studies, differences were statistically significant.

subsequent paragraphs of this section, as they may encourage practitioners to use the TF practice in other companies as well.

A crucial question is whether the TF practice drives the development to a better code quality. Neither a wide range of quality indicators, nor some elusiveness of the notion of software quality mentioned in Sect. 1.3.2, makes it easier to answer that question. Fortunately, some useful findings can be derived from the empirical research presented in this section.

For example, Finding 2.1 concerns the impact of the TF practice on defect rate, as there is some empirical evidence based on industrial case studies (conducted in Microsoft, IBM, and StatoilHydro ASA) that the TF practice reduces defect rate [28, 174, 192, 217, 232, 255]. In particular, researchers reported that defect rate decreased due to the TF practice by 40–50% in IBM [174, 192, 255] (it was reduced even further in subsequent releases [217]), 60–90% in Microsoft [28, 192] and 36% in StatoilHydro [232].

Table 2.3 Academic empirical studies on the effects of Test-First (TF) programming

Studies	Subjects	TF effects
Müller and Hagner [187]	19	• does not accelerate the implementation • lower reliability after the implementation phase ⓢ (*reliability = passed assertions / all assertions*) • slightly lower code coverage • does not aid the developer in a proper usage of the existing code • seems to support better program understanding
Pančur et al. [201]	38	• slightly lower external code quality (the number of external tests passed) • slightly lower code coverage
Erdogmus et al. [72]	24	• on average 52% more tests per unit of programming effort ⓢ ○ on average 28% more delivered user stories per total programming effort[a] • on average 2% less assertions passed in acceptance tests[a]
Melnik and Maurer [91]	240	• 73% of students perceived that TF improves quality
Madeyski [157, 159]	188	• significantly less acceptance tests passed ⓢ • significantly less acceptance tests passed ⓢ[b] • package dependencies were not significantly affected
Flohr and Schneider [79]	18	○ 21% decrease in development time[b] • small difference in code coverage[b] • no difference in number of assertions written[2]
Gupta and Jalote [94]	22	• improves external code quality in one of the two programs ⓢ[c] ○ reduces overall development efforts ⓢ[c] ○ slightly improves developer's productivity
Huang and Holcombe [108]	39	• does not influence external clients' assessment of quality • more effort on testing ($p < 0.1$) ○ 70% higher productivity (*LOC / person-hour*) but the improvement is not statistically significant

○ denotes the effect on development speed or effort.
• denotes the effect on software quality factors.
ⓢ means statistically significant result at the 0.05 level.
[a] Only USs that passed at least 50% of the assert statements from the acceptance test suite were considered.
[b] TF pairs vs. TL pairs.
[c] Affected by the actual testing efforts.

Finding 2.1: Industrial empirical studies in Microsoft, IBM and StatoilHydro ASA reported a positive impact of the TF practice on defect rate.

Furthermore, mean change density was 76% lower for the TF than for the TL development in the industrial case study performed in StatoilHydro [232].

There is also preliminary evidence that fault-slip-through rates, fault cost, total project cost [56] and maintenance cost [57] have been reduced as a result of introducing both component-level test automation and the TF practice in Ericsson AB.

Experimental trials with eight-person groups of programmers at three companies (John Deere, RoleModel Software and Ericsson) showed a positive effect of the TF practice on the number of acceptance tests passed (NATP) [87, 88]. Empirical studies of the effects of TF practice in a quasi-industrial and an academic setting are summarized in Tables 2.2 and 2.3. Partial support for the positive effect of the TF practice on NATP in an academic environment can be found in [94]. On the other hand, some empirical studies lead to the conclusion that the TF practice has no significant impact on NATP [201], or that NATP is significantly lower if the TF practice is used by solo programmers ($p = 0.028$) and pairs ($p = 0.013$) [157], assuming the same development time. Moreover, the programs developed according to the TF rules are significantly less reliable after the implementation (but not acceptance test) phase [187], where *reliability = passed assertions / all assertions* is, in fact, equal to the percentage of acceptance tests passed (PATP). In conclusion, the impact of the TF practice on PATP, which can be seen as the external code quality indicator, needs further investigation and will be examined in this book (RQ1).

Another crucial question is whether or not the TF practice speeds up development in comparison with the TL practice (RQ2). Several empirical findings in an industrial environment [28, 38, 40, 87, 88, 157, 192, 217, 268] indicate that the answer to that question might be negative or neutral. There is statistical evidence from a controlled experiment performed in Soluziona Software Factory [38, 40] that TF requires more time than TL. In particular, there is an empirical evidence that TF requires more time per assertions than TL ($p < 0.05$), TF requires an overall amount of time longer than TL ($p < 0.01$) and TF requires more time in average than TL ($p < 0.05$). Researchers also reported about 16% longer development time in John Deere, RoleModel Software and Ericsson [87, 88], 15–35% increase in the development time because of TF in Microsoft [28, 192, 217] and 15–20% in IBM [192, 217]. Also, Ynchausti [268] reported 60–187% longer development time due to the TF practice. Little or no difference in development speed owing to the TF practice is reported by some researchers in an industrial setting as well [89, 174, 255]. More or less positive impact of the TF practice on development speed [72, 79, 94, 108, 167], or the conclusion that TF does not accelerate the implementation [187], is reported in an academic and quasi-industrial environments. As a result, industrial empirical studies suggest a negative impact, or lack of impact of the TF practice on development speed, while academic and quasi-industrial studies exhibit more positive or neutral conclusions. It would be thus advisable to take into account differences between the subjects and minimize process conformance threats to get more reliable results [160, 161, 167, 188, 234, 251].

Package level design quality indicators (package dependencies) are not significantly affected by TF [159]. However, the TF practice seems to have an effect on LCOM class-level metric (a high value of LCOM, i.e. low cohesion, has been reported) [230]. Furthermore, a tendency to write simpler classes and sometimes simpler methods due to the TF practice has been mentioned [126]. The impact of TF on class-level design complexity metrics is one of the least studied effects and will be examined in this book (RQ3).

The controlled experiment with professionals in Soluziona Software Factory has led to the conclusion that there is no statistical evidence that TF brings about more accurate and precise unit tests [40]. Researchers reported higher [230], similar [79] or slightly lower [187, 202] code coverage as a result of the TF practice. Another interesting and entirely new area of empirical research concerns the impact of the TF practice on the fault detection effectiveness of unit tests [162]. Hence, the impact of TF on mutation score indicator (an indicator of the fault detection effectiveness of unit tests) and the impact of TF on code coverage (an indicator of the thoroughness of unit tests) will be examined in this book (RQ4).

Another interesting question – whether the TF practice leads to "better testable programs" – was investigated by Müller [186]. He studies "the concept of the controllability of assignments" to measure testability of programs and concludes that the number of methods in which all assignments are completely controllable is higher for the TF projects than for conventional projects.

A relatively new area of empirical research concerns a detailed analysis of the TF programmers' behaviour and process conformance threat mitigation [167, 188, 251]. Process conformance threat is a serious risk, and, therefore, it will be further discussed in Sect. 4.7.7. An interesting observation, reported by Madeyski and Szała [167], related to the TF programmers' behaviour, is that TF exhibits a higher ratio of active development time (defined as typing and producing a code) to passive development time (spent on reading the source code, looking for a bug etc.).

Finally, it is worth mentioning that a large portion of students strongly agree (29%) or somewhat agree (44%) with the opinion that TF improves quality [91].

2.2 Pair Programming

Pair programming (PP) may interact with TF to create synergy between both practices. Therefore, the effects of the PP practice are included in this study. PP means that all the production code is written by two people sitting at one computer [23]. However, this key feature of the PP practice is sometimes seen as one of its greatest problems, as two people are doing the same thing. On the other hand, it is not uncommon for people to solve complex problems in pairs (in any team, not necessarily an XP one).

Empirical studies focus on different kinds of the effects of the PP practice:

1. Development speed (the calendar time required to produce a given part of a system) or project duration (the calendar time required to produce a final system). Speedup Ratio (SR) based on the difference in completion times between solo programmers and pairs is defined as follows:

$$SR = \frac{\text{Completion Time Of Solo Programmer} - \text{Completion Time Of Pair}}{\text{Completion Time Of Solo Programmer}} \times 100\%$$

2. Effort (the person-hours required). Effort Overhead (EO) is defined as follows:

$$EO = \frac{2 \times \text{Completion Time Of Pair} - \text{Completion Time Of Solo Programmer}}{\text{Completion Time Of Solo Programmer}} \times 100\%$$

because for a pair the effort is twice the completion time.
3. Quality (how good the product is). Quality indicators of the production code, as well as test code, are reported in a similar manner as in the case of the TF practice.

Table 2.4 provides a summary of some empirical studies concerning the effects of PP on software development speed, effort and quality indicators. The table reports, from left to right, the references for each study, the environment (e.g. academic, industrial) in which the empirical study was conducted, the number of subjects involved in each empirical study and textual descriptions of the findings. As mentioned before, statistically significant results are marked by "Ⓢ", while "○" denotes the effect on development speed or effort, and "•" represents the effect on software quality indicators. Presented studies compare solo programming and collocated pair programming, if not mentioned otherwise.

Beck and Andres argue that a pair is even more than twice as effective as the same two people programming solo [23]. However, the empirical studies concerning the effort overhead and speedup ratio of the PP practice are inconclusive [14, 111, 185, 193, 194, 196, 254]. According to the empirical results, the effort overhead varies between 7% (13%, excluding rework), if pairs and solo students are forced to produce programs of similar correctness [185], and 84% (obtained in a large one day experiment in 29 international consultancy companies) [14]. Speedup ratio associated with PP ranges from 8% [14][1] to almost 47% [185]. The results obtained by other researchers [111, 193, 194, 196, 254] are somewhere between the above extremes. As a result, one of the key findings related to the effort overhead and speedup ratio associated with pair programming is Finding 2.2.

Finding 2.2: The effort overhead associated with pair programming varies between 7% and 84%, while speedup ratio is between 8 and 47%.

Another important question concerning the PP practice is whether it improves the quality of software products. According to the empirical results [14, 111, 157, 159, 183, 184], PP may not lead to the improvement of software quality factors. However, it is worth mentioning that positive effects are also reported [29, 185].

---

[1] 3% was as obtained in the 2nd run of the experiment performed by Canfora et al. [39].

Table 2.4 Empirical studies on the effects of Pair Programming (PP)

Study	Environment	Subjects	PP effects
Nosek [196]	Industry	15 (5PP/5SP)	○ SR = 29%, EO = 42%
Williams et al. [254]	Academic	41(14PP/13SP)	○ SR = 20%–42.5%, EO = 15%–60%
			• pairs always passed more automated post-development test cases ⑤
Nawrocki and Wojciechowski [194]	Academic	21 (5PP/5+6SP)	○ SR = 20%, EO = 60%
Nawrocki et al. [193]	Academic	25 (5PP/5SbS/5SP)	○ EO = 50%, EO = 20% for SbS programming (when each developer in a pair has his own PC and works on each subtask individually) ⑤
Hulkko and Abrahamsson [111]	Quasi-Industrial	4/5.5/4/4–6 (4 case projects)	○ neither PP nor SP had consistently higher productivity
			• lower level of defect density in the case of PP was not supported
Müller [185]	Academic	38 (2 experiments)	○ SP is as costly as PP if similar level of correctness is required (EO = 7%)
			• pairs developed programs with a higher level of correctness after implementation phase
Canfora et al. [39]	Academic	24	○ SR = 38% (1st run)–3% (2nd run) ⑤
Vanhanen and Lassenius [244]	Academic	6 (2PP/2SP)	○ SR = 28%, EO = 44% (for use cases 1–10)
Arisholm et al. [14]	Industry	295 (98PP/99SP)	○ PP in general did not reduce the time needed to solve tasks correctly
Heiberg et al. [101]	Academic	84 (phase 1) 66 (phase 2)	• pairs and solo programmers performed with similar final results
Müller [184]	Academic	37 (10PP/17SP)	• PP did not produce more reliable code than SP whose code was reviewed
Madeyski [157]	Academic	188 (28TLSP/ 28TFSP/ 31TLPP/	• there was no difference in NATP (Number of Acceptance Tests Passed) when PP was used instead of SP
Madeyski [159]		35TFPP)	• package dependencies were not significantly affected by P
Madeyski [160, 161]		63 (28TFSP/ 35TFPP)	• PP did not significantly affect branch coverage and mutation score indicator
Arisholm et al. [14]	Industry	295 (98P/99S)	• PP in general did not increase the proportion of correct solutions
Bipp et al. [29]	Academic	25 (phase 1) 70 (phase 2)	• lower *LCOM*, RFC and WMC metrics

○ denotes the effect on development speed or effort.
• denotes the effect on software quality factors.
⑤ means statistically significant result.
Explanations: Solo/Pair Programming (SP/PP), Side-by-Side (SbS), Test-First/Test-Last (TF/TL) Programming, Effort Overhead (EO), Speedup Ratio (SR).

The results of meta-analysis [65] demonstrate that PP leads to reduction of the time needed to deliver the finished product, in comparison with SP (medium effect size $g = 0.40$)[2] Furthermore, there is a general agreement that PP shows rather negative effect regarding effort (medium effect size $g = -0.57$), whilst positive effect regarding quality (medium effect size $g = 0.38$) [65]. In consequence, another key finding may be formulated (Finding 2.3).

> **Finding 2.3: Pair programming has a medium and positive impact on development time, medium and negative impact regarding effort, while medium and positive effect regarding quality [65].**

However, the aforementioned meta-analysis [65] combined different quality indicators together. In fact, that is the commonly raised argument against meta-analysis, vividly characterized as "combining apples and oranges" [152]. Therefore, it is important to conduct more focused and separate meta-analyses for each software quality indicator to avoid combining different indicators of software quality in one meta-analysis. Actually, this book can be seen as a step in that direction with respect to the TF practice: focused meta-analyses are carried out in Chap. 9.

A new area of research investigation related to the effects of PP on software quality is the impact of the PP practice on developed tests. As suggested by Langr [147], the synergy between the individuals in a pair working together on the same unit tests may have a positive impact on unit test characteristics (e.g. code coverage). However, the impact of pair programming on test code was not empirically investigated in depth beyond code coverage. Preliminary results obtained by Madeyski [160, 161] do not confirm the anecdotal opinion regarding the positive impact of the PP practice on the thoroughness or the fault detection effectiveness of unit tests measured by branch coverage and mutation score indicator, respectively.

2.3 Summary

Tables 2.1, 2.2, 2.3 and 2.4 summarize diverse effects of TF and PP in different environments. Empirical findings are often inconclusive and the contradictory results may be explained by the differences in the contexts in which the studies were conducted, the difficulty in isolating the TF effects from other variables (e.g. programmers expertise), incomparable measurements etc. In addition, generalization of the obtained empirical findings may be hindered due to different threats to the validity of the results, as discussed in Section 10.5. So, the readers should judge the empirical findings within the specific context of each study [128]. Furthermore, many of the above-mentioned studies do not apply statistical analysis,

---

[2] For studies in SE, Hedges' g effect sizes of 1.00–3.40, 0.38–1.00 and 0–0.37 are considered large, medium and small, respectively, according to Kampenes et al. [134].

do not report effect sizes and do not discuss threats to the validity of each study to allow generalizations.

According to reviewing guidelines by Tichy [242], no empirical study may be found flawless. Hence, we should not expect perfection or decisive answers, and neither should we reject negative results [242]. However, on the basis of our review, conducted in this section, several interesting areas of empirical research have been pointed out and will be further investigated in this book. They correspond to research questions RQ1–RQ4 addressed in Chaps. 5–8, while the need for focused meta-analyses to ensure more reliable conclusions is met in Chap. 9. As a result, the aim of the book is to extend the body of knowledge in software engineering by means of analyses (and also meta-analyses) of important characteristics of developed software products on the basis of experiment conducted at WUT.

Chapter 3
Research Goals, Conceptual Model and Variables Selection

> *If we knew what we were doing, it wouldn't be called research, would it?*
>
> Albert Einstein

This chapter presents research goals and the high level conceptual model used to guide the research along with the independent, the dependent and possible confounding variables.

3.1 Goals Definition

The purpose of this section is to refine the high-level research questions (posed in Sect. 1.4) by means of a goal definition template [20, 233, 259]. It is helpful, as it allows traceability down to hypotheses [227].

> **Goal 1 Analyse the** TFSP and TLSP software development techniques
> **for the purpose of** their evaluation
> **with respect to** external code quality indicator
> **from the viewpoint of** the researcher
> **in the context of** Experiment ACCOUNTING, SUBMISSION as well as SMELLS&LIBRARY[1] run with the help of M.Sc. students as subjects involved in the development of a Java-based application.

> **Goal 2 Analyse the** TLSP and TFSP software development techniques
> **for the purpose of** their evaluation
> **with respect to** the development speed
> **from the viewpoint of** the researcher
> **in the context of** Experiment ACCOUNTING, SUBMISSION as well as SMELLS&LIBRARY run with the help of M.Sc. students as subjects involved in the development of a Java-based application.

---

[1] Experiments are named ACCOUNTING (the experiment on the development of an accounting system), SUBMISSION (the experiment on the development of a paper submission and review system) and SMELLS&LIBRARY (the experiment on the development of both a tool for identifying bad smells in Java source-code through the use of a set of software metrics and a library application).

L. Madeyski, *Test-Driven Development*,
DOI 10.1007/978-3-642-04288-1_3, © Springer-Verlag Berlin Heidelberg 2010

Goal 3 Analyse the TLSP and TFSP software development techniques
for the purpose of their evaluation
with respect to internal code quality indicators of the production code
from the viewpoint of the researcher
in the context of Experiment ACCOUNTING, SUBMISSION as well as
SMELLS&LIBRARY run with the help of M.Sc. students as subjects involved
in the development of a Java-based application.

Goal 4 Analyse the TFSP and TLSP software development techniques
for the purpose of their evaluation
with respect to the thoroughness and the fault detection effectiveness of unit
test suites
from the viewpoint of the researcher
in the context of Experiment SUBMISSION run with the help of M.Sc.
students as subjects involved in the development of a Java-based application.

3.2 Conceptual Model

After the first Experiment ACCOUNTING, focused on the effects of both the TF and
PP practices, further experiments (SUBMISSION and SMELLS&LIBRARY) focused
strictly on the TF practice. The experiments based on a conceptual model underlying
the research. The conceptual model assumes that there are two separate effects on
the dependent variables. On the one hand, the effect of the independent variable
(IV), and, on the other, the confounding effect of, e.g., pre-existing differences
between subjects. This section discusses variables in the high-level conceptual
model: the main experimental manipulation, called an "independent variable" or
a "factor", with treatments related to development techniques applied (e.g., test-
first solo programming – TFSP), dependent variables (e.g., branch coverage) and
variables that can influence the outcome but are not part of the main experimental manipulation (e.g., pre-test result). The high-level conceptual model used to
guide the research is shown in Fig. 3.1. This model can be further specified by the
dependent variables considered in the successive chapters. Such conceptual models

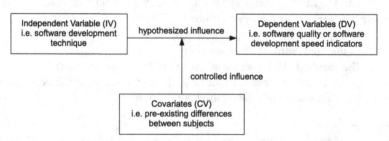

Fig. 3.1 High-level conceptual research model of the hypothesized effects of development
techniques

can be seen as parts of a larger model as, for example, unit tests (and their measures) constitute only a part of a larger puzzle.

According to Maxwell and Delaney, pre-existing differences among the subjects are at least as important in predicting their scores on the dependent variable as any independent variable [178]. Furthermore, the purpose of including covariates in experimental designs is to increase power and precision. Therefore, it may be justified to take into account another variable or variables (called covariates in the analysis of covariance) that are not part of the main experimental manipulation (described in Sect. 3.3.1) but have an influence on the dependent variables. So-called pre-test results are often used as covariates, because the way the subjects score before treatments generally correlates with how they score after treatments [235]. As a result, the analysis of covariance (ANCOVA) is considered a helpful statistical technique that takes advantage of information concerning the individual differences between the subjects that were present at the beginning of the studies. By getting rid of the effects due to covariates, the error variance (i.e. the variance brought by other "nuisance variables", such as individual differences) can be reduced. Since the analysis of covariance may compensate, to some extent, for pre-existing differences between groups, it is suggested as a means of addressing the internal validity threats that arise in studies with selection differences between groups [52]. As a result, when reasonable, the effect of covariates that are not part of the main experimental manipulation but can influence the dependent variables is controlled by means of the analysis of covariance. It is noteworthy that in the analysis of Experiment SMELLS&LIBRARY, a repeated measures experimental design was used. Hence, each subject serves as his own control and covariates are not included in analysis. In fact, the repeated measures design reduces random "noise", produced by differences between subjects, much more effectively but has some disadvantages as well (see Sect. 1.2.2.4).

The independent variable (IV) and related treatments (i.e. the software development techniques under investigation) are presented in detail in Sect. 3.3.1. The dependent variables (DVs), which depend on the measurement goals, are described in Sect. 3.3.2, while covariates (CVs) are discussed in Sect. 3.3.3. Some guidelines concerning the number of covariates to include in a specific model are given in Box 3.1.

Box 3.1 Number of covariates in a model

It is difficult to determine how many covariates should be included in a specific model (e.g., related to the effect of TF on the number of acceptance tests passed). Fortunately, some guidelines are given by Huitema [110] and Raab et al. [209]. Huitema [110] recommends limiting the number of covariates according to the following inequality:

$$c < 0.1 * N - k + 1 \qquad (3.1)$$

where c is the number of covariates, N is the total sample size and k is the number of groups.

Raab et al. [209] present a more sophisticated guideline for comparing two groups with equal sample sizes. According to Raab et al., larger experiments are more likely to benefit from covariate adjustment [209]. Stevens [235] suggests to consider two or three covariates in studies with small or relatively small group sizes to reduce the error variance as much as possible and to obtain a more powerful test.

3.3 Variables Selection

When conducting empirical studies, we are interested in how variables change and what causes the changes. However, to draw meaningful conclusions about the relationships between the independent and the dependent variables, we have to measure them.

3.3.1 Independent Variable (IV)

In a series of experiments the effects of the development technique alteration are studied. The idea is that the other independent variables are controlled at a fixed level during experiments.

3.3.1.1 Test-First and Test-Last Programming

TF constitutes an incremental development, design and coding practice which is based on taking a requirement,[2] specifying a piece of functionality as a test, ensuring that the test can fail, then writing the production code that will satisfy the test condition, refactoring (if necessary) to improve the internal structure of the code and iterating the process, as shown in Fig. 3.2.

TF provides feedback through tests, and ensures simplicity through rigorous refactoring. The tests are run frequently while writing the production code, thus driving the development process. The technique is usually supported by frameworks for writing and running automated tests, e.g., JUnit [85, 246].

As suggested by Erdogmus et al. [72], writing tests before the related production code has been isolated in this investigation, since that characteristic is most central

---

[2] Sometimes refactoring (i.e. improving an internal structure of the existing code without altering its external behaviour) is necessary to enable the new requirement to be implemented properly.

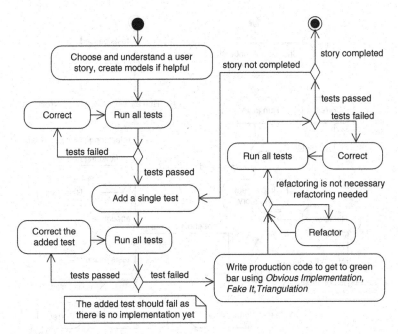

Fig. 3.2 Test-First Programming (TF) activities

to TF. Therefore, the reference TL development method, that represents a classic (control) approach, for the purpose of the investigation also involves common characteristics, i.e. incremental development, writing tests by the programmer and regression testing, but the programmer writes all the tests for a new system feature after, instead of before, the corresponding piece of the production code for that feature, as shown in Fig. 3.3. The investigated technique is labelled as TF, while the reference, classic technique is marked as TL.

There are several green bar patterns (sometimes called strategies) used in the TF practice (see Fig. 3.2) for getting to a green bar. A description of these green bar patterns (i.e. *Obvious Implementation*, *Fake It*, and *Triangulation*) along with code snippets is given by Beck [22]. However, the aforementioned green bar patterns are formalized in this section to allow more precise measurement of development processes. Formalization of the TF and TL practices, as well as *Obvious Implementation*, *Fake It*, and *Triangulation* green bar patterns, facilitated automatic measurement of TF conformance by means of SmartSensor Eclipse plugin (see Sect. 4.7.7).

When a developer knows what to type, he uses the *Obvious Implementation* strategy (i.e. type in the real implementation). It is worth mentioning that, in accordance with the regression testing rule, the tests are run all the time to ensure that what is obvious to the programmer is still obvious to the compiler. As soon as the developer gets an unexpected red bar, he backs up, and shifts to the *Fake It* strategy. The name of this pattern comes from the fact that, in the simplest case, the developer

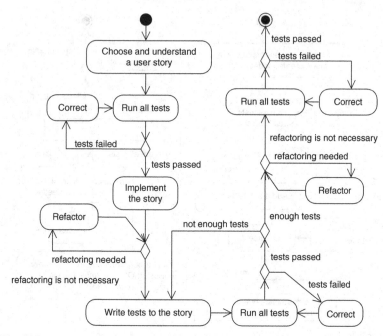

Fig. 3.3 Test-Last programming (TL) activities

returns a constant (thus faking implementation) and gradually replaces constants with variables until he has the real code. Sometimes the developer returns a mock object or provides a quick stubbed implementation. When confidence is back, the developer goes back to the *Obvious Implementation* pattern. However, if the right design is not clear, the third strategy, called *Triangulation*, is used. Triangulating to the right design is based on a rule that we only generalize code when we have two or more examples. The detailed flow of these green bar patterns is shown in Figs. 3.4, 3.5 and 3.6.

The TF practice is not a testing or quality assurance practice per se, as it may appear. It is primarily, and very intentionally, a development, design and coding practice (guided by tests), with possible quality side effects. By writing the test first, you ensure that you write the code that embodies the requirements. Refactorings are suggested in both the TF and TL practices. Refactorings are secured by tests which are required in both treatments.

3.3.1.2 Pair Programming and Solo Programming

PP is a software development practice in which two distinct roles are usually identified by researchers, i.e. the role of a driver and a navigator [14, 161, 254, 258]. They contribute to the synergy of the individuals in a pair working together at one computer and collaborating on the same development tasks (e.g., design, test, code). The driver types on the keyboard and focuses on the details of the production code

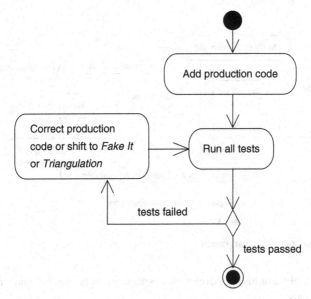

Fig. 3.4 *Obvious implementation* green bar pattern

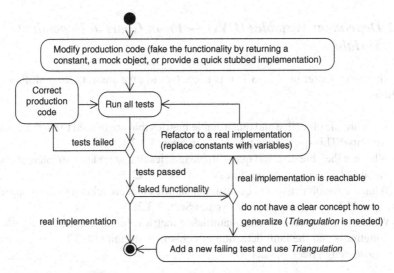

Fig. 3.5 *Fake it* green bar pattern

or tests. The navigator observes the work of the driver, reviews the code, proposes test cases, considers the strategic implications [254, 258] and looks for tactical and strategic defects or alternatives [14]. In the case of solo programming, both activities are performed by a single programmer. Convincing all programmers and managers to accept pair programming work culture may be a difficult task because people sometimes feel as if they wasted valuable "resources". Empirical evidence of a better

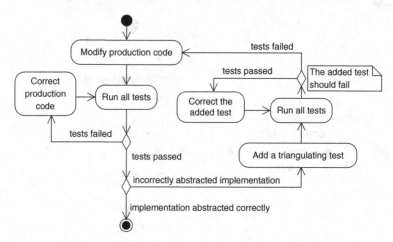

Fig. 3.6 *Triangulation* green bar pattern

code or tests quality, or higher development speed might be good counter-arguments
in such situations.

3.3.2 Dependent Variables (DVs) — From Goals to Dependent Variables

To attain the goals set in Sect. 3.1, it is necessary to give answers to the following
questions:

Q1 What are the objective and quantifiable metrics that are related to external code
    quality? This question is addressed in Sect. 3.3.2.1.
Q2 What are the objective and quantifiable metrics that are related to internal code
    quality? This question is addressed in Sect. 3.3.2.2.
Q3 What are the objective and quantifiable metrics that are related to development
    speed? This question is addressed in Sect. 3.3.2.3.
Q4 What are the objective and quantifiable metrics that are related to the thor-
    oughness and the fault detection effectiveness of unit tests? This question is
    addressed in Sect. 3.3.2.4.

3.3.2.1 External Code Quality

The aim of this section is to select one or more external code quality indicators. The
selection is based on the introduction to *external metrics* of software product quality
[122] presented in Sect. "External Metrics of Product Quality" (p. 10).

As mentioned before in Sect. 1.3.3, the number of acceptance tests passed
(NATP) was used as an indicator of external code quality by several researchers
[87, 88, 94, 157, 201]. The percentage of acceptance tests passed (PATP) is NATP

normalized by the number of acceptance tests (NAT), i.e. PATP=NATP/NAT. PATP was mentioned by Cohn and Ford [48] as a key metric of the project's current state. Moreover, this metric, called reliability, was used by Müller and Hagner [187]. Therefore, PATP is selected as an external quality indicator investigated in this book.

3.3.2.2 Internal Code Quality

The aim of this section is to select one or more internal code quality indicators. The selection is based on the introduction to *internal metrics* of software product quality [123] presented in Sect. "Internal Metrics of Product Quality" (p. 10).

As suggested by Bøegh [30], commonly used *internal quality metrics* are class-level metrics proposed by Chidamber and Kemerer [43] labelled as CK metrics. Subsystem (package) level design quality metrics proposed by Martin [171, 172] seem a useful higher level complement to the CK metrics.

As mentioned in Sect. 1.3.2.1, *internal quality metrics* (e.g., CK and Martin's metrics) may act as early indicators for external quality. For example, if the complexity of code (indicated by *WMC*) [43], the coupling between objects (*CBO*) [43] and the balance between abstractness and stability, denoted as normalized distance from the main sequence (*Dn*) [171, 172], are high, the software will likely be difficult to maintain.

Underlying theory about a relationship between the OO metrics and fault-proneness as well as maintainability due to the effect on cognitive complexity has been developed by Briand et al. [34] and El Emam et al. [71].

Empirical analyses of object-oriented metrics and their suitability for assessing fault-proneness have been performed by numerous researchers [19, 33, 34, 95, 200, 238, 270]. According to the latest results obtained by Pai and Dugan [200], *WMC*, *CBO* and *RFC* have been found very significant for assessing fault content (the number of errors in a software artefact) and fault-proneness (the probability that an artefact contains a fault). Furthermore, the aforementioned authors concluded that neither *DIT* nor *NOC* are significant [200]. Zhou and Leung empirically validated the use of the same CK metrics suite [270]. Their study also finds that *DIT* is not sufficiently significant for fault-proneness analysis, whereas in the case of *NOC* their results were inconclusive. Zhou and Leung reviewed the related work concerning the relationships between OO design metrics and fault-proneness and concluded that *WMC*, *RFC* and *CBO* were almost consistently found to be statistically significant to fault-proneness of classes, but the other metrics were not [270]. Hence, *WMC*, *CBO* and *RFC* seem to be worth further investigation whether they are influenced by TF.

Selected CK metrics have been used by many researchers [10, 19, 32, 33, 71, 95, 150, 200, 238] and are defined as follows [43]:

- Weighted Methods per Class (*WMC*) measures the complexity of an individual class. In accordance with [43], we consider all methods of a class to be equally complex, i.e. *WMC* is simply the number of methods defined in each class. This approach is commonly adopted for the sake of simplicity, and in order to avoid being somewhat arbitrary, since the choice of a method complexity metric is not fully specified in the metrics suite [19].

- Coupling Between Object classes (*CBO*) is the number of classes to which a class is coupled. Two classes are coupled when methods declared in one class use methods or instance variables defined by the other class.
- Response For a Class (*RFC*) is the number of methods that can potentially be executed in response to a message received by an object of that class.

3.3.2.3 Development Speed

Bearing in mind the line of reasoning in Sect. 1.3.3, the following indicators of software development speed are considered:

- Non-Commented Lines of Code (*NCLOC*) per hour, denoted as *NCLOCPH*, is currently one of the most widely used metrics. Unfortunately, it exhibits serious limitations. For example, it tends to value longer rather than efficient or high-quality programs. Moreover, refactoring effort may result in negative productivity measured by *NCLOCPH*.
- Number of Classes (*NOC*) per hour, denoted as *NOCPH*, is one of productivity metrics used in the OO development, as mentioned by Kan [135]. However, *NOCPH* has similar limitations as *NCLOCPH*.
- The Number of Implemented User Stories (*NIUS*) per hour, denoted as *NIUSPH*.
- The Number of Acceptance Tests Passed (NATP) per hour, denoted as NATPPH.

In order to choose between the two last mentioned indicators, it is indispensable to scrutinize their properties. User stories have different sizes and different numbers of associated acceptance tests. NATP metric is a more accurate indicator of system completion (i.e. "output" in the software development productivity definition [176]) than $NIUS$, as NATP is more fine-grained than $NIUS$. Therefore, NATPPH was selected to measure development speed in the conducted experiments.

3.3.2.4 Thoroughness and Fault Detection Effectiveness of Unit Tests

Programmers who follow the TF or the TL practice and thus write unit tests would benefit from measures indicating whether their software was thoroughly and effectively tested. Accordingly, thoroughness is discussed in Sect. "Thoroughness of Unit Tests" (p. 34), while effectiveness is covered in Sect. "Fault Detection Effectiveness of Unit Tests" (p. 35).

Thoroughness of Unit Tests

Code coverage tools measure how thoroughly tests exercise programs [170]. Code coverage measures are sometimes misused, but they still remain helpful when used to enhance thought, not to replace it [170]. There is a number of code coverage measures. Kaner [134] presents many of them. It is essential to choose the proper code coverage measure. Cornett [53] presents a number of useful insights into this question, explaining key differences between code coverage measures. For example, statement coverage (or line coverage) reports whether each executable statement is encountered, but it is insensitive to some control structures. Branch coverage, devised to avoid this problem, makes it possible to evaluate if the decision points (e.g., if statements) assume true or false values, as, during the test, this method is capable of exercising both execution paths accordingly. Branch coverage includes statement (line) coverage because the exercising of every branch leads to the exercising of every statement [53]. A disadvantage of branch coverage measure is that it ignores branches within Boolean expressions due to short-circuit operators (e.g., || and && available in Java). The second argument of these operators is only evaluated or executed if the first one does not suffice to determine the value of the expression. Hence, when calculating branch coverage, control structures could be considered completely exercised even without calls to all methods. Unfortunately, more powerful measures such as Modified Condition/Decision Coverage (used in aviation software) or Condition/Decision Coverage are not offered by available code coverage tools in Java. Therefore, branch coverage, as the best among the available code coverage measures, was used in the analyses of the thoroughness of unit tests. It is worth mentioning that branch coverage is measured by several measurement tools (e.g., Clover, Cobertura).

Fault Detection Effectiveness of Unit Tests

Code coverage measures can be useful as indicators of the thoroughness of test suites but it remains a controversial issue if code coverage measure is a good indicator for the fault detection capability of test cases [136]. In fact, Cai and Lyu [37] found that code coverage is a good estimator for fault detection in exceptional test cases, but a poor one for test cases in normal operations. Therefore, a measure of the fault detection effectiveness of test suites, based on the mutation testing technique, is considered. Mutation testing is a fault-based technique proposed by DeMillo et al. [61] and Hamlet [96]. It can be seen as a method to measure the quality of test cases, while the actual testing of the software product can be seen as a side effect [198]. The effectiveness of test suites for fault localization is estimated on seeded faults inserted into a program by creating a collection of mutants, i.e. faulty versions of the original program. Mutants are produced on the basis of the original program by using mutation operators that describe syntactic changes to the programming language. The tests are used to execute mutants, while the goal is to find incorrect output. Although mutation testing is powerful, it is not meant as a replacement for code coverage, but as a complementary approach useful in detection of a code that is executed by tests, but not really tested.

Mutation score (also called mutation adequacy) is a kind of quantitative measurement of test quality [271] and is defined as the ratio of the number of killed mutants to the total number of non-equivalent mutants. The total number of non-equivalent mutants results from a difference between the total number of mutants and the number of equivalent mutants. The latter always produce the same output as the original program, so they cannot be killed. Determining which mutants are equivalent to the original program is a very tedious and error-prone activity, so even ignoring equivalent mutants is sometimes advised [198]. In such case, we accept the lower bound on mutation score, called "mutation score indicator" [160, 161]. The acceptance of that results in the cost-effective application of a mutation testing while it still provides meaningful information about the fault detection effectiveness of unit tests.

Several empirical studies indicated the effectiveness of mutation testing. For example, mutation testing appeared to be more powerful than statement and branch coverage [250], as well as more effective at finding faults than data-flow [82, 197]. Furthermore, some practitioners (e.g., Fowler [245]) found that the support of mutation testing tool can be useful in practice, but there is a need for faster tools.

Mutation testing of real-world software would be extremely difficult without a reliable, fast and automated tool that generates mutants, runs the mutants against a test suite and reports the mutation score of the test suite. Unfortunately, to date, proposed mutation tools for Java exhibit several limitations that may prevent practitioners from using them [163]. Therefore, a new mutation testing tool, called "Judy", has been developed [163, 164]. Judy makes use of an aspect-oriented approach to speed up mutation testing and has a build-in support of JUnit and Ant. A short introduction to Judy is presented in Sect. 4.3.3.

In conclusion, branch coverage and mutation score indicator serve as complementary measures which indicate the thoroughness and the fault detection effectiveness of unit tests.

3.3.3 Confounding Variables

Variables that are not part of the main experimental manipulation (e.g., TF or TL) but have the influence on the dependent variables can be taken into account as covariates (CVs). In experiments, subjects are assigned to treatments at random, so that any pre-existing differences between subjects are randomly distributed. Unfortunately, randomization does not guarantee that subjects are equal in all treatments, but only avoids systematic biases.

The so-called pre-test result is often used as a covariate, because how the subjects score before treatments generally correlate with how they score after treatments [235]. By getting rid of the effects due to the covariate, the error variance (e.g., the variance brought by individual differences) can be reduced. *Grade* is a pre-test result which may be employed as a covariate. It takes into account the number of acceptance tests passed and development time. A traditional 2–5 grade system was used if not mentioned otherwise.

There is an assumption that a covariate should be a continuous or discrete variable. Categorical covariate can be applied in the analysis of covariance (ANCOVA) if you dummy code it into binary variables (personal communication from Andy

Field, August 2007). However, if the pre-test covariate is a kind of discrete but quantitative variable and there is a linear relationship between the covariate and the dependent variable, then dummy coding may be omitted (personal communication from Małgorzata Bogdan, April 2008).

Independent variable, dependent variables and covariates are components of the conceptual model presented in Sect. 3.2.

Chapter 4
Experiments Planning, Execution and Analysis Procedure

A theory is something nobody believes, except the person who made it. An experiment is something everybody believes, except the person who made it.

Albert Einstein

This chapter describes experiments conducted at Wroclaw University of Technology since 2004. The description of the experiments contains the information on the context of the experiments, subjects (i.e. participants), experimental materials and tasks, hypotheses and variables and experimental designs and procedures chosen.

It is worth mentioning that the first Experiment ACCOUNTING investigated not only TF and TL but also the PP and SP practices, as TF and PP are sometimes used together. In fact, the results of Experiment ACCOUNTING did not confirm the benefits of PP, and the next Experiments, SUBMISSION and SMELLS&LIBRARY, were focused on TF vs. TL empirical investigation.

The first Experiment (ACCOUNTING) was the largest (with a large sample size, i.e. 188 developers), but also the least focused one (four techniques: TFSP, TLSP, TFPP and TLPP were investigated). Also, the measurement infrastructure was not so sophisticated as in Experiments SUBMISSION and SMELLS&LIBRARY when ActivitySensor and SmartSensor Eclipse plugins collected interesting data concerning development processes. Furthermore, Experiment SMELLS&LIBRARY (as opposed to Experiments ACCOUNTING and SUBMISSION) employed repeated measures experimental design and improved Eclipse plugin.

4.1 Context Information

The description of the context of the experiments is essential for practitioners, as well as for researchers, to understand whether the research relates to a specific situation or environment. Researchers need context information to replicate experiments, aggregate results in course of meta-analyses, etc. Practitioners need context information to see if the techniques under study would be applicable in their own organizations. Both researchers and practitioners need context information to

Table 4.1 Context factors

Context factor	Experiment ACCOUNTING	Experiment SUBMISSION	Experiment SMELLS&LIBRARY
Treatments:	TLSP (28 projects) TFSP (28 projects) TLPP (31 projects) TFPP (35 projects)[c]	TL (11 projects) TF (13 projects)[a]	TF-TL (13 projects) TL-TF (14 projects)[b]
M.Sc. students:	188	24	27
• Second year students	108	0	0
• Third year students	68	16	0
• Fourth year students	10	8	27
• Fifth year students	2	0	0
Subjects background before experiments: Students with recent industrial/ non-academic experience	33	9	23
Average programming experience in years	3.79	5.54	5.37
Average size $NCLOC_{Mean}$[d] of the largest software component written individually	4714	9575	8415
$NCLOC_{Mean}$[d] of the largest software component written individually in Java	411	8812	4746
Preparation time in weeks	7	6	5
The experiment: Duration of the experimental task(s) in weeks	8	9	4+4
Number of user stories	27	23	27+23
$NCLOC_{Mean}$[d]	687	4976	1879+2344
Software system built	Accounting	Paper submission	Bad smells detector, Library application[e]
Software platform	Java SE	Java EE	Java EE
IDE	Eclipse	Eclipse	Eclipse

[a] Four TF projects did not, in fact, follow TF and have been excluded from further, selective analysis based on the analysis of developers' activities collected by means of ActivitySensor Eclipse plugin. Furthermore, in the case of one TLSP project, as well as one TFSP project, tests were written in such a way that metrics calculation was not possible.

[b] According to the analysis of developers' activities collected by means of SmartSensor Eclipse plugin, five TF projects did not, in fact, follow TF and have been excluded from further, selective analysis.

[c] Nine TFSP and eight TFPP projects have been excluded from further, selective analysis due to the fact that criterion C1 presented in Sect. 4.7.7 was not satisfied.

[d] Average size ($NCLOC_{Mean}$) is measured as an average of Non-Commented Lines Of Code (NCLOC) across developed systems.

[e] The software was produced for an external company.

determine to what extent the results are generalizable. Basic context factors that might affect generality and utility of conclusions are summarized in Table 4.1.

The context of Experiments ACCOUNTING, SUBMISSION and SMELLS& LIBRARY (presented in Table 4.1) was Programming in Java (PIJ), E-Business

Technologies (EBT) and Virtual Enterprise (VE) course, respectively. Hence, all the experiments were run offline (i.e. it was not an industrial software development) [259]. Moreover, Java was the programming language and the software platform, while Eclipse was the Integrated Development Environment (IDE) in all the experiments. Additionally, Java Enterprise Edition (Java EE) technologies, e.g. servlets, JSPs were used in the two latter experiments. Different subjects were involved in consecutive experiments. Their experience before the experiments is presented in Table 4.1. It is worth mentioning that the subjects in Experiments SUBMISSION and SMELLS&LIBRARY had longer programming experience. Moreover, over 85% of the subjects in Experiment SMELLS&LIBRARY had recent industrial experience.

Experimental hypotheses are formulated in Sect. 4.2, the new measurement tools which have been developed to support the experiments are introduced in Sect. 4.3, while further details of the experiments are presented in Sects. 4.4, 4.5 and 4.6.

4.2 Hypotheses

The crucial aspect of the experiments is to know and formally state what we intend to evaluate.

Research questions formulated in Sect. 1.4 and refined into goals in Sect. 3.1 lead us to the following null hypotheses, denoted $H_{0,j,k}$, where j corresponds to the dependent variable and k corresponds to the investigated development techniques (e.g. TLSP/TFSP):

- $H_{0,\text{PATP,TLSP/TFSP}}$ – There is no difference in the percentage of acceptance tests passed (PATP) between the projects using the TLSP and TFSP software development techniques.
- $H_{0,\text{NATPPH,TLSP/TFSP}}$ – There is no difference in the number of acceptance tests passed per hour (NATPPH) between the projects using the TLSP and TFSP software development techniques.
- $H_{0,\text{CBO}_{\text{Mean}},\text{TLSP/TFSP}}$ – There is no difference in the mean values of coupling between object classes (CBO_{Mean}) between the projects using the TLSP and TFSP software development techniques.
- $H_{0,\text{WMC}_{\text{Mean}},\text{TLSP/TFSP}}$ – There is no difference in the mean values of weighted methods per class (WMC_{Mean}) between the projects using the TLSP and TFSP software development techniques.
- $H_{0,\text{RFC}_{\text{Mean}},\text{TLSP/TFSP}}$ – There is no difference in the mean values of response for a class (RFC_{Mean}) between the projects using the TLSP and TFSP software development techniques.
- $H_{0,\text{MSI,TLSP/TFSP}}$ – There is no difference in MSI between the projects using the TLSP and TFSP software development techniques.
- $H_{0,\text{BC,TLSP/TFSP}}$ – There is no difference in BC between the projects using the TLSP and TFSP software development techniques.

The aforementioned hypotheses (e.g. $H_{0,\text{PATP,TLSP/TFSP}}$) can be tested in a specific context of a particular experiment or a series of experiments. For example, in the analysis of Experiment SUBMISSION we may accept or reject the hypothesis $H_{0,\text{PATP,TLSP/TFSP}}^{\text{SUBMISSION}}$, while in the meta-analysis of Experiments ACCOUNTING, SUBMISSION and SMELLS&LIBRARY we may accept or reject the hypothesis $H_{0,\text{PATP,TLSP/TFSP}}^{\text{ACCOUNTING,SUBMISSION,SMELLS&LIBRARY}}$.

In Experiment ACCOUNTING additional specific comparisons (contrasts) are as follows:

- Contrast 1 – TLSP vs. TFSP,
- Contrast 2 – TLPP vs. TFPP,
- Contrast 3 – TLSP vs. TLPP,
- Contrast 4 – TFSP vs. TFPP,
- Contrast 5 – TF vs. TL (TFSP&TFPP vs. TLSP&TLPP),
- Contrast 6 – PP vs. SP (TFPP&TLPP vs. TFSP&TLSP).

4.3 Measurement Tools

For the sake of the experiments several measurement tools have been developed with the invaluable help of my M.Sc. students (e.g. Michał Stochmiałek, Norbert Radyk, Adam Piechowiak and Piotr Wójcicki). The most interesting measurement tools are presented in this section. It should also be mentioned that server side development and measurement infrastructure (e.g. versioning control system) were maintained during the experiments.

4.3.1 Aopmetrics

Aopmetrics [3] is a tool that calculates a collection of object-oriented metrics (as well as some of their aspect-oriented extensions), e.g. the CK metrics and Martin's metrics for programs written in Java. This tool uses the AspectJ [4, 146] compiler to compile the entire source code of the analysed application and then computes the metrics based on the application's syntax tree.

The objectives of the AOPmetrics project were twofold: the automated (and fast) metrics collection of a large number of software projects (as there were 122 projects to analyse in Experiment ACCOUNTING) and the collection of aspect-oriented extensions of classic OO metrics (as there was no measurement tool able to do it).

The project was made available [3] to other practitioners and researchers and became a great success. Aopmetrics was used and cited by several researchers (e.g. Munnelly et al. [189], Cazzola and Marchetto [42], Filho et al. [78], Hoffman and Eugster [103] to recall a few) as well as by the author [159, 166]

The tool was created by Michał Stochmiałek as a part of his M.Sc. thesis supervised by the author. More information about the project can be found on the project's web site [3].

4.3.2 ActivitySensor and SmartSensor Plugins

ActivitySensor and SmartSensor (which can be seen as an enhanced version of ActivitySensor) are Eclipse plugins. The primary objective of the plugins is to monitor developer's activities related to the writing of the production code and tests, performed refactorings and JUnit test executions. Each activity is described by many parameters: start and end time of the activity, type of the activity (e.g. typing, refactoring and test execution), related artefact, i.e. its name, type (e.g. class, interface and method), file path, etc. Refactoring type, test execution result, the number of typed or deleted characters are collected as well [260].

The first version of the plugin (ActivitySensor) was created by Adam Piechowiak, while the second version (SmartSensor) was developed by Piotr Wójcicki as a part of their M.Sc. theses supervised by the author. As mentioned in Sect. 2.1, the ActivitySensor plugin allowed to collect unique research results concerning the ratio of active to passive development times [167].

4.3.3 Judy

Judy is a mutation testing tool developed in Java (with AspectJ extension). Some basic concepts related to mutation testing, the fault detection effectiveness and mutation score indicator are presented in Sect. "Fault Detection Effectiveness of Unit Tests" (p. 35).

The aim of the tool was to get, in a cost-effective and reliable manner, meaningful information about the fault detection effectiveness of unit tests written using JUnit testing framework. The total mutation testing time is equal to the sum of the mutants generation time and the mutants execution time [154]. Mutants execution time is unaffected by the mutation testing tool being used. Therefore, the aim of Judy is to minimize mutants generation time. Judy presents an innovative approach to mutation testing that takes advantage of a novel aspect-oriented programming mechanism, called pointcut and advice, to avoid multiple compilation of mutants and, therefore, speed up mutation testing. Moreover, Judy offers a unique combination of features which may be useful for practitioners (e.g. JUnit [85] and Ant [2] support, command line interface which supports running in batch mode, cost-effective and reliable calculation of mutation score indicator). The tool was created by Norbert Radyk as a part of his M.Sc. thesis supervised by the author. More details concerning interesting mechanisms used in Judy mutation testing tool and an empirical evaluation of the tool have been presented by Madeyski and Radyk [163]. As mentioned in Sect. 2.2, Judy allowed to collect unique research results concerning the impact of the PP practice on mutation score indicator [160, 161]. Latest empirical results concerning the impact of the TF practice on mutation score indicator are presented in this book in Chap. 8.

4.4 Experiment ACCOUNTING

Experiment labelled ACCOUNTING was conducted in 2004 within the period of 15 weeks.

4.4.1 Goals

Goals *1, 2*, and *3*, formulated in Sect. 3.1, relate to Experiment ACCOUNTING.

4.4.2 Subjects

The choice of subjects was based on convenience. The subjects participating in the study were mainly second- and third-year (and few fourth- and fifth-year) graduate M.Sc. computer science students[1] taking the PIJ course. They earned educational credits for taking part in the experiment. It is worth mentioning that all the subjects had prior experience in C and C++ programming (using the OO approach), 7 weeks of programming in Java as a minimum, and almost 4 years of programming experience on average. The ability to generalize from this context is further elaborated when discussing threats to the validity of the experimental results.

4.4.3 Experimental Materials

The materials for the experiment [227, 259] were prepared in advance and consisted of requirements artefacts (user stories) available via a dedicated, WIKI-based [6] web site, pre-test and post-test questionnaires, Eclipse project framework, a detailed description of software development techniques, subjects' duties, instructions how to use the experiment infrastructure (e.g. CVS version control system) and examples (e.g. sample applications developed using the TF practice) etc. Wherever possible, data were collected by means of measurement infrastructure consisting of a collection of tools. With respect to Goal 3, the CK metrics were collected by means of Aopmetrics [3, 159]. As a result, it was possible to collect interesting data from a large number of projects with a minimal effort. More information concerning tools developed at WUT is presented in Sect. 4.3.

---

[1] The M.Sc. programme of Wroclaw University of Technology (WUT) was a 5-year programme after high school.

4.4.4 Experimental Task

The experimental task, i.e. the development of the finance accounting system, was as close to a real one, as it is possible in an academic environment. The requirements came from an external client and were introduced in the form of 27 user stories. The accounting system developed by the subjects was aimed to support a small Internet provider company in the collecting of data about clients and requested services, accounts monitoring and the history of all financial requests.

4.4.5 Hypotheses and Variables

Hypotheses $H_{0,\text{PATP,TLSP/TFSP}}$, $H_{0,\text{NATPPH,TLSP/TFSP}}$, $H_{0,\text{CBO}_{\text{Mean}},\text{TLSP/TFSP}}$, $H_{0,\text{WMC}_{\text{Mean}},\text{TLSP/TFSP}}$ and $H_{0,\text{RFC}_{\text{Mean}},\text{TLSP/TFSP}}$, formulated in Sect. 4.2, relate to Experiment ACCOUNTING.

The independent variable (IV) is the software development technique used by the experimental groups (TLSP, TFSP, TLPP, TFPP). Development techniques are presented in Sect. 3.3.1. The dependent variables (DVs), defined in the hypotheses formulated in Sect. 4.2, are as follows:

- The percentage of accepted tests passed (PATP), see Sect. 3.3.2.1.
- The number of acceptance tests passed per development hour (NATPPH), see Sect. 3.3.2.3.
- The mean values of Coupling Between Object classes (CBO_{Mean}), Weighted Methods per Class (WMC_{Mean}), Response For a Class (RFC_{Mean}), see Sect. 3.3.2.2.

4.4.6 Design of the Experiment

The design of the experiment is an independent groups (i.e. between-groups) design with one factor (the software development technique) having four treatments (alternatives), i.e. TLSP, TLPP, TFSP and TFPP. It can be argued that an alternative design with independent groups and two factors (labelled as, e.g. collaboration and programming technique), each having two treatments (SP, PP and TL, TF, respectively), would be valid as well. All treatments used by the experimental groups are described in Sects. 3.3.1.1 and 3.3.1.2.

The assignment to PP teams took into account the subjects' preferences (i.e. they were allowed to suggest partners), as it seemed more natural and close to real-world practice. Therefore, that was a quasi-experiment [225]. However, it is worth noting that the assignment to the TF and TL groups was randomized. The design resulted in an unbalanced design, with 28 solo programmers and 31 pairs using the classic TL approach, 28 solo programmers and 35 pairs using the TF development practice. In total, 188 subjects were involved in the experiment. Therefore, Experiment ACCOUNTING was one of the largest experiments ever carried out to measure the impact of the TF and PP practices.

4.4.7 Experiment Operation

The experiment was conducted within 15 weeks with 7 lectures and 15 laboratory sessions (90 min each) to learn and practice programming in Java using different development techniques. The experiment consisted of both the preparation and the execution phases.

4.4.7.1 Preparation Phase

The preparation phase of the experiment embraced lectures and training exercises, given directly before the experiment in order to improve skills and to give practice in the areas of PP, TF and unit testing using JUnit. The goal of this preparation phase was to train student subjects sufficiently well so that they would be able to perform the experimental tasks required of them. Therefore, it took seven laboratory sessions (over 10 hours) to attain the goal. Prior to the execution phase of the experiment, the students filled in a pre-test questionnaire. The aim of the questionnaire was to get the picture of the students' background before the experiment (see Table 4.1).

4.4.7.2 Execution Phase

The execution phase of the experiment took place during the last 8 laboratory sessions (12 hours). The subjects were given an introductory presentation of a finance accounting system and were asked to implement it during eight laboratory sessions of the execution phase. Both the preparation phase and the execution phase were conducted in classroom settings under continuous supervision of assistant lecturers.

The subjects were divided into groups as described in Sect. 4.4.6. Up-to-date development environment composed of Java development Kit, Eclipse IDE, JUnit testing framework and CVS repository were used in the experiment. At the end of the experiment the subjects were asked to fill in post-test questionnaires, to obtain their opinions, as well as to enable qualitative validation of the results. The subjects were not aware of the actual hypotheses formulated.

It is also noteworthy that tests were often deferred or even neglected by the subjects in the TL projects in Experiment ACCOUNTING. Therefore, one may argue that the TL practice in Experiment ACCOUNTING can be called Test-Very-Last (TVL) practice rather than TL. That was, in fact, the reason of selective meta-analysis performed in Sect. 9.3.

4.5 Experiment SUBMISSION

Experiment labelled SUBMISSION was conducted in 2006 within the period of 15 weeks.

4.5.1 Goals

Goals 1, 2, 3 and 4, formulated in Sect. 3.1, relate to Experiment SUBMISSION.

4.5.2 Subjects

The choice of subjects was based on convenience. The subjects were the students taking the EBT course. The subjects participating in the study were third-year (16 of 24 subjects) and fourth-year (8 of 24 subjects) graduate M.Sc. software engineering students. They earned educational credits for taking part in the experiment. The subjects had over 5 years of programming experience on average (see Table 4.1). Almost 38% of the subjects (9 of 24 subjects) had recent industrial or non-academic experience in programming. It is also worth mentioning that all the subjects had prior experience in programming in C, C++ (using object-oriented approach), .NET and Java programming and had completed various software engineering and programming courses (including algorithms and data structures, C language, concurrent programming, object-oriented programming in C++, C#, .NET, Java and web applications development) totalling over 450 h. The ability to generalize from this context is further elaborated, when discussing threats to the validity of the experimental results.

4.5.3 Experimental Materials

The materials for the experiment [227, 259] (user stories, questionnaires, a detailed description of software development techniques, subjects' duties, instructions how to use the experiment infrastructure, e.g. SVN version control system) were prepared in advance in a similar manner as in Experiment ACCOUNTING. The experimental materials were available to the subjects via a WIKI-based [6] web site dedicated to the experiment and assigned SVN accounts. To achieve Goal 4, branch coverage (BC) and mutation score indicator (MSI) were collected by means of Clover [16] and Judy [163, 164], respectively. With respect to Goal 3, the CK metrics were collected by means of Aopmetrics [3]. To enable better measurement of the developments time (necessary to attain Goal 2) and of the development process (especially of how the development techniques were carried out and whether tests were written before related pieces of the production code) the ActivitySensor plugin [1], integrated with the Eclipse IDE, has been tested beforehand [167] and used by the subjects. Some of the aforementioned tools (Aopmetrics [3, 159], Judy [160, 161, 163, 164] and ActivitySensor [1, 167]) were developed at WUT to collect interesting data. More information concerning the tools developed at WUT is presented in Sect. 4.3.

4.5.4 Experimental Task

The experimental task, i.e. the development of the paper submission and review web application, was as close to a real one, as it is possible in an academic environment. The requirements description consisted of 23 user stories that reflected the needs of an academic institution [204].

4.5.5 Hypotheses and Variables

Hypotheses $H_{0,\text{PATP,TLSP/TFSP}}$, $H_{0,\text{NATPPH,TLSP/TFSP}}$, $H_{0,\text{CBO}_{\text{Mean}},\text{TLSP/TFSP}}$, $H_{0,\text{WMC}_{\text{Mean}},\text{TLSP/TFSP}}$, $H_{0,\text{RFC}_{\text{Mean}},\text{TLSP/TFSP}}$, $H_{0,\text{MSI,TLSP/TFSP}}$ and $H_{0,\text{BC,TLSP/TFSP}}$, formulated in Sect. 4.2, relate to Experiment SUBMISSION.

The independent variable is the software development technique used by the experimental groups (TFSP or TLSP) and described in Sect. 3.3.1. The dependent variables (DVs), identified in the hypotheses formulated in Sect. 4.2, are as follows:

- The percentage of accepted tests passed (PATP), see Sect. 3.3.2.1.
- The number of acceptance tests passed per development hour (NATPPH), see Sect. 3.3.2.3.
- The mean values of Coupling Between Object classes (CBO_{Mean}), Weighted Methods per Class (WMC_{Mean}), Response For a Class (RFC_{Mean}), see Sect. 3.3.2.2.
- Branch coverage (BC) and mutation score indicator (MSI) are described in Sects. "Thoroughness of Unit Tests" (p. 34) and "Fault Detection Effectiveness of Unit Tests" (p. 35), respectively.

4.5.6 Design of the Experiment

The design of the experiment is an independent groups (i.e. between-subjects or between-groups) design with one factor (the software development technique) having two treatments (alternatives), i.e. TLSP and TFSP. All treatments used by the experimental groups are described in Sects. 3.3.1.1 and 3.3.1.2.

The assignment of subjects to treatments was randomized. Randomization on the allocation of the subjects to the TF and TL groups was used to average out the effect of the factor that may otherwise be present [259]. Moreover, some differences between subjects were controlled by means of the analysis of covariance.

4.5.7 Experiment Operation

The experiment consisted of the *preparation* and *execution* (i.e. the main experimental task) phases preceded by the *pre-study* phase.

4.5.7.1 Pre-study

The *pre-study* was run before the main part of the experiment (i.e. before the *preparation* as well as the *execution* phase) with three subjects in order to check the experimental procedures, infrastructure and instruments (see Sect. 4.5.3) [166, 167].

4.5.7.2 Preparation Phase

The *preparation* phase consisted of exercises prepared to enhance development expertise of the subjects in the areas related to the main experimental task (e.g. web applications development, the TL and TF practices, refactoring). The subjects were given programming assignments concerning the development of three versions of the voter web application using Java EE technologies (servlets, Java Server Pages, JavaBeans) and different web architectures (e.g. Model 1 and Model 2 [224]). It was an opportunity for the subjects to check advantages and disadvantages of different architectural patterns. Web application based on model 2 architecture, which in turn is based on Model-View-Controller (MVC) architectural pattern, was covered by unit tests (using JUnit testing framework) and in-container tests (using Cactus testing framework [5]) using the TL practice. Additional functionalities concerning questionnaire web management capabilities of defining, removing and serving different questionnaires, as well as built-in support for different roles and access rights, were developed by the subjects in accordance with the TF practice.

Requested method coverage for JavaBeans and servlets was about 90–100% level (with exception of getters and setters automatically generated in Eclipse). More advanced architectural frameworks, for example, Presentation-Control-Mediator-Entity-Foundation (PCMEF) [156] and eXtensible Web Architecture (XWA) [165] (combining the strengths of MVC and PCMEF frameworks), were also introduced as convenient ways to deal with applications' complexity.

Refactoring exercises consisted of six practice-oriented refactoring tasks. The subjects had to refactor different samples of the existing code. One of the refactoring tasks was to refactor the code of the voter application developed earlier. The latest (optional) set of exercises concerned aspect-oriented development. Lectures and exercises were given by the author as well as by developers with recent industrial experience.

The goal of the *preparation* phase was to prepare the subjects sufficiently well so that they would be able to perform the tasks required them during the main experimental phase. The aim was that subjects should not be overwhelmed by the complexity of, or unfamiliarity with, the main experimental task [242]. Therefore, the *preparation* phase took 6 weeks.

4.5.7.3 Execution Phase

In the *execution* phase, the subjects were given an introductory presentation of a web-based paper submission and review system's requirements and were asked to implement it during the 9 weeks assigned to that phase. The subjects were randomly divided into the TLSP and the TFSP group. In addition, they filled in pre-test and post-test questionnaires which enabled the author to get to know their experience, opinions and to enable qualitative validation of the quantitative results. The subjects were not aware of the actual hypotheses being tested. Measurements were, to a large extent, collected automatically by the tools mentioned in Sect. 4.5.3. The industry standard for code coverage is in the range 80–90% [53, 255, 256] and the same method coverage level for Java Beans and servlets was suggested, but not required, during the experiment. The main experimental task was not a trivial one and required about 5000 of non-commented lines of code on average.

4.6 Experiment SMELLS&LIBRARY

Experiment labelled SMELLS&LIBRARY was conducted in 2007 and 2008 within the period of 15 weeks.

4.6.1 Goals

Goals defined in Sect. 4.5.1 for Experiment SUBMISSION are also valid in Experiment SMELLS&LIBRARY.

4.6.2 Subjects

The choice of subjects was based on convenience. The subjects were the students taking the VE course. The subjects participating in the study were fourth-year graduate M.Sc. software engineering students. They earned educational credits for taking part in the experiment. The subjects had over 5 years of programming experience on average. Over 85% of the subjects (23 of 27 subjects) had recent industrial experience. Nine subjects can be classified as E2 (i.e. with less than 3 months recent industrial experience), while 18 subjects can be classified as E4 (i.e. recent industrial experience between 3 months and 2 years) in accordance with Höst et al. classification scheme [106]. It is also worth mentioning that the subjects had similar prior academic experience as subjects in Experiment SUBMISSION, i.e. experience in programming in C, C++ (using object-oriented approach), .NET and Java programming and had completed various software engineering and programming courses totalling over 450 h. The ability to generalize from this context is further elaborated when discussing threats to the validity of the experimental results.

4.6.3 Experimental Materials

The experimental materials [227, 259] for the experiment were prepared in advance with the help of software development company and were available to the subjects via a WIKI-based web site dedicated to the experiment and assigned SVN accounts.

Most of the tools needed to collect data were similar to those used in Experiment SUBMISSION and mentioned in Sect. 4.5.3. Some of these tools were developed at WUT and are presented in Sect. 4.3.

4.6.4 Experimental Tasks

The subjects were asked to develop four applications. Two of them (P1 and P2) were developed during the preparation phase of the experiment, while the latter two (P3 and P4) were 4-week projects during the main experimental run.

Project P1 concerned development of an Eclipse plugin which supports the developer during the process of writing unit tests in Java [261]. Project P2 regarded development of a web application, based on the MVC (Model View Controller) design pattern, for transforming HTML 4.01 Strict code into XHTML 1.0 Strict code [262]. The idea was to take any validated HTML 4.01 Strict code as an input and to produce its XHTML 1.0 Strict equivalent as an output. The project was a good opportunity to write a lot of unit tests. The aim of the P3 project was to create a web application (based on the MVC design pattern again) for detecting bad smells [168, 169, 231] in Java code through the use of a set of software metrics [263]. There were 27 functional requirements introduced via user stories as well as five non-functional requirements [264]. Project P4 concerned a web application working as an electronic library. Requirements came from a software development company which was also responsible for code quality audit of the projects. There were 23 functional requirements introduced via user stories and several non-functional requirements [207, 208, 265].

4.6.5 Hypotheses and Variables

Hypotheses $H_{0,\text{PATP,TLSP/TFSP}}$, $H_{0,\text{NATPPH,TLSP/TFSP}}$, $H_{0,\text{CBO}_{\text{Mean}},\text{TLSP/TFSP}}$, $H_{0,\text{WMC}_{\text{Mean}},\text{TLSP/TFSP}}$ and $H_{0,\text{RFC}_{\text{Mean}},\text{TLSP/TFSP}}$, formulated in Sect. 4.2, relate to Experiment SMELLS&LIBRARY.

The independent variable is the software development technique used by the experimental groups (TFSP or TLSP) and described in Sect. 3.3.1. The dependent variables (DVs) are the same as in Experiment ACCOUNTING, see Sect. 4.4.5.

4.6.6 Design of the Experiment

The design of the experiment is a repeated measures (i.e. within-subjects) design
with one factor (the software development technique) having two treatments (alternatives), i.e. TLSP and TFSP. That means that each subject was exposed to all of
the treatments (development techniques). Repeated measures designs have several
advantages in comparison with between-groups designs (e.g. they are economical
in terms of time and effort, as well as more sensitive) but also some disadvantages
(e.g. carry-over effects, the need for conditions to be reversible) [76]. The danger of
the effect of carry over, associated mostly with the repeated measures experimental
design, is discussed further in Sect. 4.7.3.

The assignment of subjects to treatments was randomized. Treatments used by
the experimental groups are described in Sects. 3.3.1.1 and 3.3.1.2.

4.6.7 Experiment Operation

The experiment consisted of both the *preparation* and the *execution* phase.

4.6.7.1 Preparation Phase

The *preparation* phase consisted of two projects (P1 and P2 mentioned in
Sect. 4.6.4) prepared to enhance development expertise of the subjects in areas
related to the main experimental task (e.g. unit testing, TL and TF development
practices, web applications development). Lectures and preparation phase projects
(P1 and P2) were given by the author, as well as by a developer with a recent
industrial experience. Moreover, there was a dedicated TF training given by a professional agile coach with a long TF and XP experience. JUnit tests were requested
for business logic and encouraged for other parts of the developed systems.

The goal of the *preparation* phase was to prepare the subjects sufficiently well
so that they would be able to perform the tasks required of them during the main
experimental phase. Again, the aim was that subjects should not be overwhelmed
by the complexity of, or unfamiliarity with, the main experimental task [242]. The
preparation phase took 5 weeks.

4.6.7.2 Execution Phase

In the *execution* phase, the subjects were randomly divided into TL–TF and TF–TL
groups. In addition, they filled in pre-test and post-test questionnaires which made
it possible for the author to get to know their experience, opinions, and to enable
qualitative validation of the quantitative results. The subjects were not aware of the
actual hypotheses stated.

The measurement data were, to a large extent, collected automatically by tools
mentioned in Sect. 4.5.3. As in the preparation phase, unit tests were requested for
business logic and recommended for other parts of the developed applications. An

introductory presentation of the P3 project mentioned in Sect. 4.6.4 was followed
by a 4-week development. Then an introductory presentation of the P4 project mentioned in Sect. 4.6.4 was given by an external company. It was followed by an over
4-week development cycle.

4.7 Analysis Procedure

Analysis helps us understand how the different treatments affected the software
quality and development speed indicators in Experiments ACCOUNTING,
SUBMISSION and SMELLS&LIBRARY. Key elements of the analysis procedure
are discussed in this section. The procedures of summarizing or describing data
(i.e. descriptive statistics) and the procedures of interpreting data in order to make
estimates, hypotheses testing, predictions or decisions (i.e. inferential statistics) are
introduced.

4.7.1 Descriptive Statistics

Reporting descriptive statistics should include measures of central tendency and
dispersion, e.g. mean (M), standard deviation (SD) [12, 44]. However, there is
sometimes a dilemma regarding whether to report the SD or standard error (SE),
which is the SD divided by the square root of the sample size. Both approaches
have their proponents and critics. Elliott and Woodward [69] suggest that the SD
should be reported if you are describing the variability of the data and the SE if
you are describing the variability of the mean. However, some journals and books
recommend that you always report the SD since the SE can be calculated easily
from the SD and sample size [69], and the SE can be made smaller by increasing
sample size. Both SD and SE are reported for convenience.

Standard deviation and boxplots tell us more about the shape of the distribution
of the results. Boxplots display the distribution of data based on minimum, first
quartile, median, third quartile and maximum. The box represents the range within
which 50% of the data fall. The line within the box is the median. The whiskers
connect the box to upper and lower adjacent values, i.e. the third quartile plus 1.5
times the length of the box and the first quartile minus 1.5 times the length of the
box, respectively. Any value falling outside that interval is considered an outlier.
However, points that extend more than 3 box-lengths from the edge of the box are
called extreme points.

4.7.2 Assumptions of Parametric Tests

The following general assumptions of parametric tests are usually checked:

- Level of measurement (see Sect. 1.3.1) – the dependent variable is measured at
  the interval or ratio level since parametric tests work on the arithmetic mean.

- Independence of observations – the observations that make up the data are independent of one another.
- Homogeneity of variance – there are roughly the same variances between groups or treatments (if different subjects are involved). The equality of variances is usually checked by Levene's test.
- Normal distribution – the collected data come from a population that has a normal distribution. Objective tests of the distribution are the Kolmogorov–Smirnov and the Shapiro–Wilk tests. Fortunately, most of the techniques are reasonably "robust" or tolerant of violations of this assumption. Moreover, the violations of this assumption should not cause any serious problems with large enough sample sizes (e.g. 30+) [235].

Additional specific assumptions are checked if needed.

4.7.3 Carry-Over Effect

Another kind of assumption, usually associated with the repeated measures experimental design, is that a carry-over effect has not seriously distorted obtained results. A carry-over effect may occur when the effect of the first treatment persists and, thus, influences the results of the second treatment. To reduce the potential dangers of practice effects, a counterbalanced repeated measures experimental design was employed in Experiment SMELLS&LIBRARY. As a result, both combinations by which treatments can be ordered (i.e. TL–TF and TF–TL) were used. Moreover, the subjects were randomly assigned to both sequences of treatments. The aim of counterbalancing is to spread the unwanted variance among the different treatments. However, counterbalancing provides a partial solution to this problem, since the interference effects may not be bidirectional. The test for the carry-over effect was originally suggested by Grizzle [93] and was popular for many years. However, as a result of the influential paper by Freeman [83], it is now known to be extremely biased and is not recommended. The fact that the carry-over effect is a potential problem for the repeated measures experimental design is not a reason for not using it [223]. Moreover, the danger of declaring an ineffective treatment effective due to the use of the repeated measures design is minimal, because the carry-over effect, if it occurred, would bias the effect of treatment downwards [223].

Another approach to dealing with the carry-over effect is a wash-out period (i.e. a period during which the effect of a previously given treatment is believed to disappear). Unfortunately, we are never certain if it has worked [222].

Yet another approach to the problem, suggested by Senn [222], is carrying out many studies with different designs. That suggestion was followed, as Experiments ACCOUNTING and SUBMISSION adopted a between-subjects, and Experiment SMELLS&LIBRARY – a repeated measures, experimental design. In conclusion, the findings are true assuming that the carry-over effect has not altered them seriously [222].

4.7.4 Hypotheses Testing

The level of significance for the hypotheses tests was set at $\alpha = 0.05$. However, the reader should bear in mind that multiple tests are performed and, to allow for a stricter and more conservative interpretation of the results (e.g. using the Bonferroni correction), p-values are provided.

A wide range of statistical tests (e.g. t-test, AN(C)OVA, Kruskal–Wallis, Mann–Whitney, Wilcoxon signed-rank test) was used as a result of different experimental designs or violated assumptions of parametric tests, see Sect. 4.7.2. It is worth mentioning that when only two groups are involved (e.g. in Experiments SUBMISSION and SMELLS&LIBRARY), the F statistics used in the one-way ANOVA is simply the square of the t score from the t-test.

4.7.5 Effect Sizes

Effect size (ES) is a name given to indicators that measure the magnitude of a treatment effect. The sizes of any observed effects are reported, as recommended by the American Psychological Association (APA) [12]. Effect sizes are extremely useful as they provide an objective measure of the importance of the experimental effect regardless of the statistical significance of the test statistic. Moreover, the effect size is much less affected by sample size than statistical significance and, therefore, is a better indicator of practical significance [237, 243]. For two treatments and a continuous outcome, the effect size r is called the point–biserial correlation. Furthermore, r^2 is called η^2 and can be interpreted as the proportion of variance in the population that is accounted for by variation in the treatment [92]. The correlation coefficient (r) value of 0 means that the experiment had no effect (i.e. explains none of the variance in the data), while the value of 1 means that the experiment can completely explain all of the variance in the data. Cohen [45, 46] has given some widely used guidelines about what constitutes a small, a medium or a large effect for the behavioural sciences. However, it is worth mentioning that Lipsey and Wilson [151] found these guidelines somewhat arbitrary and presented other interpretations of the magnitude of effect sizes. Furthermore, Kempenes et al. [133] provided recently similar guidelines for studies in software engineering. The aforementioned guidelines are presented in Table 4.2.

It may be misleading to use Cohen's labels, as some areas, like software engineering, are likely to have different effect sizes than others. Therefore, to allow an

Table 4.2 Guidelines for effect size magnitude

Effect	Cohen'88 [45]			Cohen'92 [46]			Kempenes et al. [133]	
Size	d	r	r^2	d	r	r^2	r	r^2
Small	0.20	0.10	0.01	0.20	0.10	0.01	0.09 [0–0.193]	0.008 [0–0.0372]
Medium	0.50	0.243	0.059	0.50	0.30	0.09	0.30 [0.193–0.456]	0.09 [0.0372–0.208]
Large	0.80	0.371	0.138	0.80	0.50	0.25	0.60 [0.456–0.868]	0.36 [0.208–0.753]

independent interpretation of the empirical results, effect sizes are provided along with magnitude labels proposed by Kempenes et al. [133]. As a result, r effect sizes of 0–0.193 are considered small, 0.193–0.456 are considered medium, and effect sizes of 0.456–0.868 are considered large. The transformations between different effect size measures are summarised in Box 4.1.

4.7.6 Analysis of Covariance

The purpose of including covariates in the analysis is threefold. First, to reduce the within-group error variance. In ANOVA we compare the amount of variability explained by the experimental manipulation against the variability that cannot be explained. In the analysis of covariance (ANCOVA or MANCOVA) we hope that we can explain some of that unexplained variance in terms of other variables (covariates) and, consequently, we can reduce the error variance getting a much more sensitive measure of our experimental effect [76, 77].

Second, to eliminate confounds, since in any experiment there may be variables that confound the results (i.e. vary systematically with the experimental manipulation). ANCOVA and MANCOVA are able to remove the bias of these confounding variables (measured and entered into the analysis as covariates) that are known to influence the dependent variable(s) [76, 77].

Third and actually the least important purpose is to be consistent with the conceptual model that guides the research presented in Sect. 3.2.

Box 4.1 Transformations between effect size measures

One class of effect sizes involves standardized mean differences. Effect sizes in this class include indices such as Glass' D, Hedges' g, and Cohen's d. Another class of effect sizes, which can be computed in both experimental and non-experimental studies, includes r^2 (or η^2). The effect sizes in those two classes can be transformed into each others' metrics:
Cohen's d can be converted to an r using Cohen's formula [45]:

$$r = \frac{d}{\sqrt{(d^2 + 4)}} \tag{4.1}$$

When total sample size (N) is small or group sizes are disparate ($n1 \neq n2$), a more complicated but also more general and precise formula proposed by Aaron et al. [7] can be used:

$$r = \frac{d}{\sqrt{(d^2 + \frac{N^2 - 2N}{n_1 n_2}}} \tag{4.2}$$

Friedman's formula [84] may be employed to convert r to a d:

$$d = \frac{2r}{\sqrt{(1 - r^2)}} \qquad (4.3)$$

For usual range (i.e. for $-0.21 < r < 0.21$ and $-0.41 < d < 0.41$) $d \approx 2r$ [112].

The so-called pre-test result is used as a covariate, because how subjects score before treatments generally correlates with how they score after treatments [235].

4.7.6.1 Non-Parametric Analysis of Covariance

When the assumptions of parametric tests are broken, non-parametric tests (e.g. the Kruskal–Wallis and the Mann–Whitney tests) are often performed. To get more sensitive measure of our experimental effect, further analysis can be based on a non-parametric ANCOVA using the rank transformation (formalized by Shirley [226] and Conover and Iman [50, 51]), which has greater power than its parametric analogue in non-normal distributions [199]. The rank transformation refers to the replacement of data by their ranks, with a subsequent analysis using the usual theory procedure, but calculated on the ranks rather than on the original data [51]. Hence, a non-parametric ANCOVA is performed like any ANCOVA except that the ranks of the observations are used as the dependent variable. Therefore, the entire set of observations is ranked from smallest to largest, with the smallest observation obtaining rank 1, the second smallest rank 2, etc., while average ranks are assigned in the case of ties. It is worth mentioning that SPSS provides support for ranking data (see Box 5.9). As with the standard ANCOVA, two models are used. The first model does not include the interactions for tests of the adjusted averages (i.e. the analysis of covariance). The second one is the full model with the interaction between the covariate and the treatment effects as a test of homogeneity of slopes.

4.7.7 Process Conformance and Selective Analysis

Selective analysis is inspired by the intention to minimize the threat of process conformance and relative difficulty of the TF practice. Other threats to validity of the experiments are discussed in Sect. 10.5. However, the process conformance threat is so important that it influenced both prepared measurement tools and analysis procedure. Process conformance threat is a threat to statistical conclusion validity (see Sect. 10.5.1), through the variance in the way the processes are actually carried out, and also to construct validity (see Sect. 10.5.3), through possible discrepancies between the processes, as prescribed, and the processes, as carried out [234]. Unfortunately, the threat of process conformance is often neglected in experimentation in software engineering. It is a serious problem especially in the case of the TF programming practice which can be more difficult to follow than the TL practice (see Box 4.2). Therefore, TF conformance is considered one of the most important threats in TF experimentation. It is also worth noting that Wang and Erdogmus [251], Madeyski and Szała [167], as well and Müller and Höfer [188] raised the issue of process conformance in the context of TF experimentation recently.

An interesting piece of evidence of relative difficulty of TF vs. the TL practice is presented in Box 4.2.

Box 4.2 Relative difficulty of TF vs. TL

Subjects' opinion concerning both techniques was expressed in questionnaires and the TL development practice appeared easier to follow than TF. For example, in the pre-test questionnaire of Experiment SUBMISSION, one subject (4.2%) strongly disagreed, one subject (4.2%) disagreed, eight subjects (41.7%) agreed and ten subjects (41.7%) strongly agreed with the statement "TF development method is more difficult than TL", while two subjects (8.3%) were neutral.

Also, in the pre-test questionnaire of Experiment SMELLS&LIBRARY, one subject (3.7%) strongly disagreed, five subjects (18.5%) disagreed, eight subjects (29.6%) agreed, and nine subjects (33.3%) strongly agreed with the aforementioned statement "The TF development method is more difficult than TL", while four subjects (14.8%) sat on the fence.

Since the subjects consider the TL practice to be easier to follow, the risk that they followed TF instead of TL, when the latter was assigned, seems really unlikely. An opposite situation (i.e. when the subjects follow TL instead of TF) is more probable and, therefore, measurement of TF conformance is crucial.

Process conformance threat was mitigated by taking several precautions during the conducted experiments. The subjects were informed of the importance of the following of the assigned procedures and trained during the preparation phase of each experiment. Regular meetings and discussions about various details (or problems), related to the assigned development techniques, were organized to avoid possible deviations. In the post-test questionnaires, the subjects were asked how strongly they agree with process conformance, with the intention to exclude those who disagreed.

A formal criterion, proposed by Erdogmus et al. [72] to gauge conformance in the TF experimental groups, is that "subjects who did not write any tests for at least half the time (i.e. for half the stories they implemented) were deemed nonconformant". However, this criterion seems to be rather weak as it accepts projects without any single test for a large portion of the developed software which is not in line with the TF guidelines. Hence, a more harsh formal criterion (C1) to gauge conformance in the experiment group was applied: The TF subjects who did not achieve at least 20% branch coverage were deemed non-conformant. That was entirely justified, since in the TF practice tests are considered to be indispensable prerequisites of related pieces of the production code. A more sophisticated criterion (C2) was based on a detailed monitoring of programmers' activities by means of a dedicated plugin integrated with Eclipse IDE in Experiments SUBMISSION and SMELLS&LIBRARY. The programmers' activities were collected in Experiment SUBMISSION with the help of ActivitySensor plugin enabling the analysis of how development techniques were carried out. After the detailed analysis of the subjects' activities with the help of an expert (a developer with recent industrial and test-first programming experience), it was possible to exclude from further, selective analysis the subjects who committed serious deviations from the prescribed TF practice. The subjects were excluded if tests were written after rather than before related pieces of the production code. Thanks to the SmartSensor plugin (which can be seen as an improved ActivitySensor plugin) used in Experiment SMELLS&LIBRARY, it was possible to exclude from the selective analysis the subjects who committed serious deviations from TF, on the basis of the quantitative TF conformance measure.

The TF conformance measure was defined as a ratio of the active development time in which a subject followed the TF flow to the total active development time. However, it is worth mentioning that there are many other activities than TF development (e.g. GUI building as certain things must always be verified visually [144], large refactoring, maintenance or set-up activities related to production code or tests). Hence, TF conformance value, we might expect, is far from 1.

SmartSensor plugin was also used in an industrial environment. Hence, the idea is to determine the TF conformance cut-off value on the basis of industrial data. The lowest TF conformance measured among the professional agile developers (i.e. in industrial context) was 0.05. Therefore, the cut-off value was set at 0.05 as well. It means that if the TF conformance ratio is below 5:100, development technique is considered to be non-TF. The aforementioned professional agile software development team was involved in an industrial JEE (Java Enterprise Edition) project. The agile team members used the TF practice and SmartSensor plugin in several iterations. The average TF experience in the agile team was about 12 months. Software process metrics (e.g. TF conformance) gathered by means of the SmartSensor plugin were compared with the results obtained in Experiment SMELLS&LIBRARY. Interestingly, it turned out that, on average, the TF conformance values in academic projects, before ($M = 0.38$, SD $= 0.20$, Min $= 0$, Max $= 0.74$ 95% CI 0.30–0.46) as well as after ($M = 0.38$, SD $= 0.20$, Min $= 0.10$, Max $= 0.74$, 95% CI 0.29–0.47) the exclusion of the project with TF conformance below the aforementioned cut-off value, were better than in the industrial agile development team ($M = 0.24$, SD $= 0.10$, Min $= 0.05$, Max $= 0.36$, 95% CI 0.14–0.35) using TF as its fundamental software development practice. However, the standard deviation in the academic projects was higher than in the industrial agile development team. That comparison suggests that TF conformance in Experiment SMELLS&LIBRARY is comparable to the one in the aforementioned industrial environment; however, it was a higher mean of the TF conformance measure, but on the other hand greater uncertainty in the academic projects.

In the selective analysis of Experiment ACCOUNTING, nine subjects were discarded from the TFSP group and eight subjects were discarded from the TFPP group due to criterion C1. In the selective analysis of Experiment SUBMISSION, four subjects were discarded from the TFSP group due to criterion C2. In the selective analysis of Experiment SMELLS&LIBRARY, four subjects were discarded from the TFSP group due to criterion C1 and one subject was discarded due to criterion C2.

To illustrate the importance of the selective analysis, the analysis of selected projects is presented along with the complete analysis of all the projects in Chapter 5. To keep the book concise and, simultaneously, to present the most essential results, next chapters include only the final (i.e. selective) analyses.

4.7.8 Combining Empirical Evidence

The basic goal of any empirical work is to produce a single reliable conclusion, which is, at first glance, difficult if the results of several studies are divergent or not statistically significant in each case. Therefore, meta-analysis as a statistical technique has been carried out to combine the results from a series of experiments in a reliable and unbiased manner. The meta-analysis of all three experiments, and the meta-analysis of Experiments SUBMISSION and SMELLS&LIBRARY, which have many characteristics in common (e.g. Experiments SUBMISSION and SMELLS& LIBRARY involved more experienced subjects, on average, than Experiment ACCOUNTING) has been carried out in Chap. 9.

Chapter 5
Effect on the Percentage of Acceptance Tests Passed

> *There is no such thing as a failed experiment, only experiments with unexpected outcomes.*
>
> Richard Buckminster Fuller

Pursuing Goal **3.1**, expressed in Sect. 3.1, and bearing in mind the selection of dependent variables made in Sect. 3.3.2.1, the aim of this chapter is to evaluate the impact of the TF software development practice on PATP (Percentage of Acceptance Tests Passed) which, in turn, is NATP (Number of Acceptance Tests Passed) normalized by the total number of acceptance tests. As mentioned in Sect. 1.3.2.1, PATP may be viewed as an external metric of software product quality. In Experiment ACCOUNTING the effect of TF on PATP is evaluated in the context of both the SP and the PP practice (see Sect. 5.1). The two consecutive Experiments SUBMISSION and SMELLS&LIBRARY (analysed in Sects. 5.2 and 5.3) focused solely on the empirical evaluation of test-first solo programming (TFSP) vs. test-last solo programming (TLSP) technique. It was justified, since PP used instead of SP appeared to have a tiny impact on PATP.

5.1 Analysis of Experiment ACCOUNTING

The preliminary analysis of all 122 projects is conducted in Sect. 5.1.1, while further, selective analysis (based on the selection criteria discussed in Sect. 4.7.7) is presented in Sect. 5.1.2. The aim of the selective analysis is to exclude the subjects who deviated seriously from the TF practice from further analysis.

5.1.1 Preliminary Analysis

The experiment data are analysed by means of descriptive analysis and statistical tests.

L. Madeyski, *Test-Driven Development*,
DOI 10.1007/978-3-642-04288-1_5, © Springer-Verlag Berlin Heidelberg 2010

5.1.1.1 Descriptive Statistics

The descriptive statistics of PATP, when different development techniques ("DevTech") were applied, are summarized in Table 5.1. Standard abbreviations for statistical values are presented in Box 5.1.

> ## Box 5.1 Standard abbreviations for statistical values
>
> "Mean", "Std.Dev.", "Std.Error", "Max", "Median", "Min" and 95% CI (lower and upper bounds) stand for the mean (M), standard deviation (SD), standard error (SE), maximum, median (Mdn), minimum, 95% confidence interval lower and upper bound values. Other commonly used abbreviations are degrees of freedom (df) and statistical significance ($Sig.$).

Table 5.1 Descriptive statistics for the percentage of acceptance tests passed (DV: PATP)

DV	Dev Tech	Mean (M)	Std.Dev. (SD)	Std. Error (SE)	Max	Median (Mdn)	Min	95% CI Lower Bound	Upper Bound
PATP	TLSP	0.469	0.271	0.051	0.974	0.566	0.000	0.364	0.574
	TFSP	0.338	0.211	0.040	0.605	0.408	0.000	0.256	0.420
	TLPP	0.501	0.259	0.047	0.842	0.553	0.000	0.406	0.596
	TFPP	0.351	0.231	0.039	0.842	0.342	0.000	0.272	0.431

Listing 5.1: Related SPSS syntax

```
EXAMINE
    VARIABLES=PATP BY DevTech
    /PLOT BOXPLOT STEMLEAF HISTOGRAM NPPLOT
    /COMPARE GROUP
    /STATISTICS DESCRIPTIVES
    /CINTERVAL 95
    /MISSING LISTWISE
    /NOTOTAL.
```

The first impression is that the TF practice has a negative impact on PATP, as both TF groups (TFSP and TFPP) have lower PATP means, medians and confidence intervals than the TL groups (TLSP and TLPP). Furthermore, a positive effect of PP is not visible, because the TFSP and TFPP results, as well as the TLSP and TLPP results, are similar to a large extent (see PATP means and medians). Bearing that in mind, it seems reasonable to focus further empirical investigation on the impact of the TF practice on PATP, as PP does not influence the results.

The accuracy of the mean as a model of data can be assessed by the standard deviation which is rather large (compared to the mean) in all cases (SD > 0.21). A large SD indicates that the data points are far from the mean, i.e. they are not clustered closely around the mean. A higher SD for the TL groups means that there is a greater uncertainty in the TL projects. It should be noted that the difference in SD between the TL and TF projects is more visible in the solo projects (TLSP vs. TFSP) than in pairs (TLPP vs. TFPP).

The values of SD and boxplots shown in Fig. 5.1 tell us more about the shape of the distribution. In course of the visual inspection of Fig. 5.1, overt differences come to the fore, with the TL groups (TLSP and TLPP) performing better than the TF groups (TFSP and TFPP). Moreover, the whiskers on the TLPP and TFPP boxplots, coming out of the boxes, differ in length. It shows that the distribution is skewed to some extent. Other whiskers on the TLSP and TFSP boxplots, coming out of the top of the boxes, are more or less equal to those at the bottom. Neither extreme points (that extend more than 3 box-lengths from the edge of the box), nor outliers (that extend more than 1.5 box-lengths) can be located in Fig. 5.1.

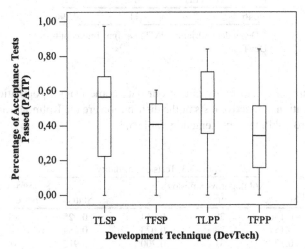

Fig. 5.1 Boxplot for the percentage of acceptance tests passed (DV: PATP) – preliminary analysis of Experiment ACCOUNTING

Listing 5.2: Related SPSS syntax

```
EXAMINE
    VARIABLES=PATP BY DevTech /PLOT=BOXPLOT/STATISTICS=NONE/NOTOTAL.
```

Summarizing the descriptive statistics in APA (American Psychological Association) format [12], we can conclude that PATP in the TFSP projects ($M = 0.34$, SD $= 0.21$) and TFPP projects ($M = 0.35$, SD $= 0.23$) are similar. Somewhat higher levels of PATP are reached in the case of the TLSP projects ($M = 0.47$, SD $= 0.27$) and TLPP projects ($M = 0.50$, SD $= 0.26$).

To answer the question whether the impact of the TF and PP practices on PATP is significant or not, statistical tests must be performed, preceded by the testing of the underlying assumptions.

5.1.1.2 Assumption Testing

The general assumptions of parametric tests are presented in Sect. 4.7.2. The assumption that the dependent variable (i.e. PATP) is measured at the interval or ratio level is met. The assumption that the observations are independent of one another is met as well. The assumption of homogeneity of variance is tested using Levene's test (Table 5.2). Levene's test is not significant ($p > 0.05$), so we accept the null hypothesis that the difference between the variances is roughly zero (the variances are more or less equal). Consequently, the assumption of homogeneity of variance is not violated.

Table 5.2 Levene's test of equality of error variances[1]

F	df1	df2	Sig.
1.246	3	118	0.296

[1] Dependent variable: PATP. Design: Intercept+ DevTech.

The assumption of normality is that our data come from a population that has normal distribution. Objective tests of the distribution are the Kolmogorov–Smirnov and the Shapiro–Wilk tests presented in Table 5.3.

Table 5.3 Tests of normality

DevTech	Kolmogorov–Smirnov[1]			Shapiro–Wilk		
	Statistic	df[2]	Sig.	Statistic	df[2]	Sig.
TLSP	0.186	28	0.014	0.925	28	0.046
TFSP	0.157	28	0.073	0.884	28	0.005
TLPP	0.120	31	0.200[3]	0.912	31	0.015
TFPP	0.111	35	0.200[3]	0.960	35	0.222

[1] Lilliefors Significance Correction.
[2] Degrees of freedom.
[3] This is a lower bound of the true significance.

The significance value is lower than 0.05 for the TLSP group, according to both statistics, as well as for the TFSP and TLPP groups, according to the Shaprio–Wilk statistic (Table 5.3). This finding points to the fact that the data are not normally distributed and the assumption has been broken. Transforming the data did not rectify this problem. Therefore, one solution is to use non-parametric tests. Another solution is to conduct AN(C)OVA, but it must be emphasized that the normality assumption is broken. Such an approach can be justified because, as mentioned in Sect. 4.7.2, the violations of the assumption of normality should not cause any serious problems with large enough sample sizes (e.g. 30+) [235]. The former kind of analysis (i.e. non-parametric analysis) is presented in Sect. 5.1.1.3, while the latter (i.e. parametric analysis) is shown in Sect. 5.1.1.4.

5.1.1.3 Non-Parametric Analysis

The non-parametric analysis presented in this section is based on [157]. The hypothesis $H_{0,PATP,TLSP/TLPP/TFSP/TFPP}^{A}$, regarding the difference in PATP between the projects using TLSP, TLPP, TFSP and TFPP software development techniques, is evaluated by means of the Kruskal–Wallis one-way analysis of variance by ranks. The Kruskal–Wallis test is a non-parametric alternative to the parametric ANOVA and can always be applied instead of ANOVA, if it is not sure that the assumptions of ANOVA are met. The Kruskal–Wallis test is used for testing the differences between the four experimental groups (TLSP, TLPP, TFSP and TFPP) when different subjects are used in each group.

Table 5.4 illustrates a summary of the ranked data and tells us the mean rank in each treatment. The test statistic is a function of those ranks. Table 5.5 shows this test statistic and its associated degrees of freedom (in this case we had 4 groups so $df = 4-1$ degrees of freedom), and the significance.

Table 5.4 Ranks

DevTech	N	Mean Rank
TLSP	28	69.30
TFSP	28	50.77
TLPP	31	74.50
TFPP	35	52.33
Total	122	

Table 5.5 Kruskal–Wallis test statistics[1]

	NATP
Chi-Square	10.503
df	3
Asymp. Sig.	0.015

[1] Grouping variable: DevTech (TLSP, TLPP, TFSP, TFPP).

Listing 5.3: Related SPSS syntax

```
NPAR TESTS
  /K-W=PATP BY DevTech(1  4)
  /MISSING ANALYSIS.
```

Since $p < 0.05$, we can conclude that the software development technique used by the subjects significantly affected the discussed external code quality indicator (PATP).This test proves only that a difference exists, however, it does not exactly demonstrate where the difference is.

One possible way to identify the differing groups is to study the boxplot diagram in Fig. 5.1. The first thing to note is that the TL groups (TLSP, TLPP) achieved better results, i.e. higher levels of PATP, than the TF groups (TFSP, TFPP). However, this conclusion is subjective. It is advisable to perform the planned contrasts or post hoc tests for specific comparisons mentioned in Sect. 4.2. According to Field [76], non-parametric post hoc procedures are not commonly used, but it is possible to test some specific hypotheses, formulated at the design stage, by means of the Mann–Whitney tests.

Mann–Whitney Tests

Tables 5.6, 5.7, 5.8, 5.9, 5.10 and 5.11 show the test statistics of the Mann–Whitney tests on the set of comparisons between groups.

Table 5.6 Mann–Whitney test statistics (TLSP vs. TFSP)[1]

	PATP
Mann–Whitney U	258.500
Wilcoxon W	664.500
Z	–2.190
Asymp. Sig. (2-tailed)	0.028
Exact Sig. (2-tailed)	0.028
Exact Sig. (1-tailed)	0.014

[1] Grouping Variable: DevTech.

Listing 5.4: Related SPSS syntax

```
NPAR TESTS
  /M-W= PATP BY DevTech(1  2)
  /MISSING ANALYSIS
  /METHOD=EXACT TIMER(5).
```

Table 5.7 Mann–Whitney test statistics (TLPP vs. TFPP)[1]

	PATP
Mann–Whitney U	353.000
Wilcoxon W	983.500
Z	–2.437
Asymp. Sig. (2-tailed)	0.015
Exact Sig. (2-tailed)	0.014
Exact Sig. (1-tailed)	0.007

[1] Grouping Variable: DevTech.

Listing 5.5: Related SPSS syntax

```
NPAR TESTS
  /M-W= PATP BY DevTech(3  4)
  /MISSING ANALYSIS
  /METHOD=EXACT TIMER(5).
```

Table 5.8 Mann–Whitney test statistics (TLSP vs. TLPP)[1]

	PATP
Mann–Whitney U	391.500
Wilcoxon W	797.500
Z	–0.646
Asymp. Sig. (2-tailed)	0.518
Exact Sig. (2-tailed)	0.524
Exact Sig. (1-tailed)	0.262

[1] Grouping Variable: DevTech.

Listing 5.6: Related SPSS syntax

```
NPAR TESTS
  /M-W= PATP BY DevTech(1  3)
  /MISSING ANALYSIS
  /METHOD=EXACT TIMER(5).
```

Table 5.9 Mann–Whitney test statistics (TFSP vs. TFPP)[1]

	PATP
Mann–Whitney U	486.000
Wilcoxon W	1116.000
Z	–0.055
Asymp. Sig. (2-tailed)	0.956
Exact Sig. (2-tailed)	0.959
Exact Sig. (1-tailed)	0.479

[1] Grouping Variable: DevTech.

Listing 5.7: Related SPSS syntax

```
NPAR TESTS
  /M-W= PATP BY DevTech(2  4)
  /MISSING ANALYSIS
  /METHOD=EXACT TIMER(5).
```

When the TLSP and TFSP groups are compared, the observed two-tailed significance value $p = 0.028 < 0.05$ (Table 5.6). Also, when the TLPP and TFPP groups are compared, the observed two-tailed significance value $p = 0.014 < 0.05$ (Table 5.7). However, if we want to control the build-up of Type I errors, we should make some kind of an adjustment to ensure that Type I errors do not build up to more than 0.05 and the easiest method is to use the Bonferroni correction. In its simplest form it means that instead of using 0.05 as the critical value of significance for each test, the critical value of 0.05 divided by the number of conducted tests (i.e. 6) is used $(0.05/6 = 0.0083)$. As a result, the specific hypotheses $H_{0,\text{PATP},TLSP/TFSP}^{A}$ and $H_{0,\text{PATP},TLPP/TFPP}^{A}$ cannot be rejected in spite of the fact that the observed significance levels are < 0.05. The only specific hypothesis that can be rejected is

Table 5.10 Mann–Whitney test statistics (TF vs. TL)[1]

	PATP
Mann–Whitney U	1237.000
Wilcoxon W	3253.000
Z	–3.187
Asymp. Sig. (2-tailed)	0.001
Exact Sig. (2-tailed)	0.001
Exact Sig. (1-tailed)	0.001

[1]   Grouping   Variable: ProgrammingTL0TF1.

Listing 5.8: Related SPSS syntax

```
NPAR TESTS
  /M-W= PATP    BY ProgrammingTL0TF1(0 1)
  /MISSING ANALYSIS
  /METHOD=EXACT TIMER(5).
```

Table 5.11 Mann–Whitney test statistics (PP vs. SP)[1]

	PATP
Mann–Whitney U	1766.000
Wilcoxon W	3362.000
Z	–0.422
Asymp. Sig. (2-tailed)	0.673
Exact Sig. (2-tailed)	0.675
Exact Sig. (1-tailed)	0.338

[1] Grouping Variable: CollaborationSP0PP1.

Listing 5.9: Related SPSS syntax

```
NPAR TESTS
  /M-W= PATP    BY CollaborationSP0PP1(0 1)
  /MISSING ANALYSIS
  /METHOD=EXACT TIMER(5).
```

$H^A_{0,PATP,TFSP\&TFPP/TLSP\&TLPP}$, as it turned out that PATP was significantly lower in the TF (TFSP and TFPP) than in TL (TLSP and TLPP) projects. However, the Bonferroni correction is rather overcautious and one might miss a significant result [219]. More powerful alternatives to the Bonferroni correction, that are designed to deal with the aforementioned problem, are as follows: Holm's sequential Bonferroni correction [104], the Simes–Hochberg correction [102, 228] and Hommel's correction [105]. They are discussed in Box 5.2. Furthermore, some arguments against the Bonferroni correction are given in Box 5.3.

In the case of two-tailed predictions, none of the following specific hypotheses: $H^A_{0,PATP,TLSP/TFSP}$, $H^A_{0,PATP,TLPP/TFPP}$, $H^A_{0,PATP,TLSP/TLPP}$ and $H^A_{0,PATP,TFSP/TFPP}$ can be rejected, regardless of which of the aforementioned correction methods is used. The situation would change if one-tailed predictions were considered (see Box 5.4).

The positive impact of PP on PATP was not confirmed, as the Mann–Whitney tests (see Tables 5.8, 5.9 and 5.11) returned large significance values.

Box 5.2 Multiple tests, the Bonferroni correction and interesting alternatives to the Bonferroni correction

The problem with multiple comparisons is that one would like to control the false positive rate not just for any single test but also for the entire family of closely related tests that makes up an experiment.

The Bonferroni correction is the classic approach for controlling the experiment wise false positive value ($\alpha_{exp-wise}$) by specifying what α value should be used for each individual test. Consequently, we assume a test to be significant if $p \leq \alpha$. The probability of not making any Type I (i.e. false positive) errors in n independent tests is $(1 - \alpha)^n$. The probability of at least one false positive in n independent tests is $\alpha_{exp-wide} = 1 - (1 - \alpha)^n$. Hence, the α value for each test is

$$\alpha = 1 - (1 - \alpha_{exp-wise})^{1/n} \quad \text{(Dunn–Šidák correction)} \quad (5.1)$$

Since $(1 - \alpha)^n \approx 1 - n\alpha$, the Bonferroni corection is often reffered to as

$$\alpha = \alpha_{exp-wise}/n \quad \text{(classic Bonferroni correction)} \quad (5.2)$$

Under the classic Bonferroni correction, only hypotheses with associated $p \leq \alpha_{exp-wide}/n$ are rejected and all the others are accepted. However, there are situations in which some more powerful alternatives to the classic Bonferroni correction may be useful in order to avoid missing a significant result. Such alternatives are Holm's sequential Bonferroni correction [104], the Simes–Hochberg correction [102, 228] and Hommel's correction [105]. All these are uniformly more powerful than the Bonferroni correction. Holm's procedure, derived from the Bonferroni correction, is executed as follows:

- Order the p-values for the n hypotheses being tested from smallest to largest (i.e. $p(1), p(2), \ldots p(n)$) and let the hypothesis $H(i)$ be associated with the $p(i)$
- If $p(1) > \alpha_{exp-wise}/n$, none of the n hypotheses are significant (i.e. accept all the n hypotheses)
- If $p(1) \leq \alpha_{exp-wise}/n$, reject $H(1)$ and consider $H(2)$
- If $p(2) > \alpha_{exp-wise}/(n - 1)$, none of the $H(i)$ (for $i \geq 2$) hypotheses are significant
- If $p(2) \leq \alpha_{exp-wise}/(n - 1)$, reject $H(2)$ and consider $H(3)$
- Proceed with the hypotheses until the first j such that $p(j) > \alpha_{exp-wise}/(n - j + 1)$

Holm's correction is not only uniformly more powerful than the Bonferroni correction but also always controls the family wise error [63]. The Simes–Hochberg correction [102, 228] and Hommel's correction [105] are even more powerful than Holm's correction but do not always control the family wise error. The family wise error is protected if the individual test statistics are independent or positively dependent [218].

Box 5.3 Arguments against the Bonferroni correction

A summary of interesting arguments against the Bonferroni correction is given by Perenger [202]. He presents the "view, widely held by epidemiologists, that the Bonferroni adjustments are, at best, unnecessary and, at worst, deleterious to sound statistical inference". He argues that due to the Bonferroni correction, the interpretation of a finding depends on the number of other tests performed and that the likelihood of Type II errors is also increased, so that truly important differences are considered non-significant. One of the key questions raised by Perenger is "what about tests that were performed, but not published, or tests published in other papers based on the same study?" Finally, he concludes that simply giving the description of what tests of significance have been performed, and why, is generally the best way of dealing with multiple comparisons.

Box 5.4 Two-tailed vs. one-tailed predictions

Interestingly, one of the specific hypotheses concerning differences in PATP between groups could be rejected if formulated as one-tailed prediction. For, example if we use Bonferroni correction in its simplest form we use the critical value of 0.05 divided by the number of conducted tests ($0.05/6 = 0.0083$). It would allow to reject one-tailed specific hypothesis concerning the difference between TLPP and TFPP ($H^A_{0,\text{PATP},TLPP/TFPP}$). As a result, a statistically significant result could be announced.

More sophisticated correction methods (e.g. Holm's sequential Bonferroni correction, the Simes–Hochberg correction and Hommel's correction) are more powerful and in some situations they would allow more hypotheses to be rejected. For example, Holm's sequential Bonferroni correction would reject the second hypothesis if the corresponding $p < 0.01$. Similarly, assuming that the number of tests was limited to only four tests, we would use the critical value of 0.05 divided by the number of conducted tests ($0.05/4 = 0.0125$).

Then it would be possible to reject two one-tailed specific hypotheses concerning the differences between the TLPP and the TFPP group as well as between the TLSP and the TFSP group by means of Holm's sequential Bonferroni correction (as well as the Simes–Hochberg correction and Hommel's correction) but not the classic one. It accounts for the value of more powerful correction methods.

However, doing two-tailed tests keeps us honest [35], especially in the situation in which a one-tailed probability is significant and a two-tailed probability would not be. Therefore, this passage can be seen as an interesting (at least from the statistical point of view) digression, that departs from the main subject, rather than a considered alternative.

Calculating Effect Size

Effect size, in contrast to statistical significance, is much less affected by sample size and, therefore, is a better indicator of practical significance, as mentioned in Sect. 4.7.5. The signs of the reported effect sizes are governed by the rule presented in Box 5.5.

Box 5.5 Effect size sign

By convention, a positive sign is assigned to an effect size when the treatment (i.e. experimental) group performs "better" than the control group and a negative sign – otherwise. Therefore, these signs do not necessarily tally with the arithmetic sign that will result from the calculations [151].

Summarizing a general effect is not as useful as providing the effect sizes for focused comparisons (i.e. the Mann–Whitney tests used to follow up the main analysis). For the first comparison (TLSP vs. TFSP), $Z = -2.190$ (see Table 5.6). An effect size estimate r can be calculated from the Z-score as proposed by Rosenthal [212, p. 19]:

$$r = \sqrt{\frac{Z^2}{N}} = \frac{Z}{\sqrt{N}} \qquad (5.3)$$

where N is the total number of individuals included in the test. As Z was based on the comparison of two groups, each containing 28 observations, there were 56 observations in total. Therefore

$$r_{\text{contrast 1 (TLSP vs. TFSP)}} = \frac{-2.190}{\sqrt{56}} = -0.29 \qquad (5.4)$$

According to the guidelines by Kempenes et al. presented in Table 4.2, this represents a medium effect. Therefore, the effect of TL relative to TF for solo programmers was a fairly substantive effect (TLSP achieved higher PATP than TFSP).

For the second comparison (TLPP vs. TFPP), $Z = -2.437$ (see Table 5.7). The
effect size is calculated from the Z-scores using the same formula:

$$r_{\text{contrast 2 (TLPP vs. TFPP)}} = -0.30 \tag{5.5}$$

According to the guidelines by Kempenes et al. presented in Table 4.2, this represents a medium effect (the effect accounts for 9% of the total variance). Therefore,
the effect of TL in relation to TF for pairs was a fairly substantive effect too (TLPP
achieved higher PATP than TFPP).

For the third comparison (TLSP vs. TLPP), $Z = -0.646$ (see Table 5.8). The
effect size

$$r_{\text{contrast 3 (TLSP vs. TLPP)}} = -0.08 \tag{5.6}$$

According to the guidelines by Kempenes et al. presented in Table 4.2, this represents a small effect (the effect explains below 1% of the total variance). Therefore,
the effect of the PP practice in relation to the SP practice for the TL projects was
rather small, which tells us that there is indeed not much difference between SP and
PP, if the TL practice is used.

For the fourth comparison (TFSP vs. TFPP), $Z = -0.055$ (see Table 5.9). The
effect size is

$$r_{\text{contrast 4 (TFSP vs. TFPP)}} = -0.01 \tag{5.7}$$

According to the guidelines by Kempenes et al. presented in Table 4.2, this represents a small or even tiny effect (as it is close to zero). Therefore, the effect of the
PP practice relative to the SP practice for the TF projects was tiny, which tells us
that there is really no difference between SP and PP, if the TF practice is used.

For the fifth comparison (TF vs. TL), $Z = -3.187$ (see Table 5.9). The effect
size is

$$r_{\text{contrast 5 (TF vs. TL)}} = -0.29 \tag{5.8}$$

According to the guidelines by Kempenes et al. presented in Table 4.2, this repre-
sents a medium effect. Therefore, the effect of TF (TFSP and TFPP) relative to TL
(TLSP and TLPP) was a fairly substantive effect (the TL groups achieved higher
PATP than the TF groups).

For the sixth comparison (PP vs. SP), $Z = -0.422$ (see Table 5.9). The effect
size is

$$r_{\text{contrast 6 (PP vs. SP)}} = -0.04 \tag{5.9}$$

According to the guidelines by Kempenes et al. presented in Table 4.2, this represents a tiny effect. Therefore, the effect of PP (TFPP and TLPP) relative to SP (TFSP and TLSP) was a tiny effect and there is no difference between SP and PP.

Summary

The external code quality indicator PATP was significantly affected by the software development technique (the Kruskal–Wallis test statistics: $H(3) = 10.50$, $p < 0.05$).[1] This means that there is a difference in the percentage of acceptance tests passed (PATP) between the software development teams using the TLSP, TFSP, TLPP and TFPP development techniques.

The Mann–Whitney tests were used to follow up this finding. The Bonferroni correction was applied and so all effects are reported at the 0.0083 level of significance. There was no statistically significant difference in PATP between TLSP and TFSP ($U = 258.50$, $p = 0.028$, $r = -0.29$), TLPP and TFPP ($U = 353.00$, $p = 0.014$, $r = -0.30$), TLSP and TLPP ($U = 391.50$, $p = 0.52$, $r = -0.08$), TFSP and TFPP ($U = 486.00$, $p = 0.96$, $r = -0.01$) and SP (i.e. TLSP&TFSP) and PP (i.e. TLPP&TFPP) ($U = 1766.00$, $p = 0.68$, $r = -0.03$). However, there was a statistically significant difference in PATP between the TL projects (i.e. TLSP&TLPP) and the TF projects (i.e. TFSP&TFPP) ($U = 1237.00$, $p = 0.001$, $r = -0.29$).

We may conclude that, in spite of the doubled effort, the superiority of the PP practice with respect to the percentage of acceptance tests passed was not confirmed. Furthermore, the effect of TF on PATP was negative and statistically significant, even after the Bonferroni correction, if we compare the TL projects (TLSP&TLPP) and the TF projects (TFSP&TFPP).

5.1.1.4 Parametric Analysis

In this section, the hypothesis $H_{0,\text{PATP},TLSP/TLPP/TFSP/TFPP}^{A}$, regarding the difference in PATP between the projects using the TLSP, TLPP, TFSP and TFPP software development techniques, is evaluated using one-way analysis of variance (ANOVA) and covariance (ANCOVA).

Analysis of Variance

SPSS provides two ways of carrying out a one-way, between-subjects ANOVA (see Box 5.6).

---

[1] H is the test statistic function with 3 degrees of freedom, and p is the significance.

Box 5.6 One-way, between-subjects ANOVA in SPSS

SPSS provides two ways of carrying out a one-way, between-subjects ANOVA. The first way employs the **One-Way ANOVA** command via the main dialogue box using the **Analyse⇒Compare Means⇒One-Way ANOVA** menu path, or via SPSS syntax [149] presented in Box 5.10.

The second way uses the **General Linear Model** (GLM) command via the main dialogue box using the **Analyse⇒General Linear Model⇒Univariate** menu path, or via SPSS syntax presented in Box 5.11.

The first command only permits analysis of a one-way ANOVA, but has the advantage of a simpler output. The GLM command has much wider applications (e.g. multi-way ANOVA, repeated measures ANOVA, ANCOVA, MANCOVA).

The ANOVA results are presented using both, the One-Way ANOVA command (see Table 5.12) and the General Linear Model command (see Table 5.13). It is clear from the significance value $p = 0.019$, which is lower than 0.05, that there are differences in PATP between the four groups. Therefore, development technique seems to have a significant effect on PATP. As presented in Table 5.13, the total amount of variance to be explained was 7.64 (Corrected Total), of which experimental manipulation ("DevTech") accounted for 0.62 units, while 7.02 were unexplained. As a result, development technique is able to explain about 8% of the variance in the dependent variable (partial eta-squared $\eta_p^2 = 0.08$, as shown in Table 5.13).

Table 5.12 ANOVA (DV: PATP)

	Sum of Squares	df	Mean Square	F	Significance
Between Groups	0.617	3	0.206	3.456	0.019
Within Groups	7.022	118	0.060		
Total	7.639	121			

Listing 5.10: Related SPSS menu navigation (Analyse⇒Compare Means⇒One-Way ANOVA) and syntax

```
ONEWAY
  PATP BY DevTech
  /CONTRAST= -1 1 0 0   /CONTRAST= 0 0 -1 1   /CONTRAST= -1 0 1 0
  /CONTRAST= 0 -1 0 1   /CONTRAST= -1 1 -1 1   /CONTRAST= -1 -1 1 1
  /STATISTICS DESCRIPTIVES HOMOGENEITY
  /MISSING ANALYSIS
  /POSTHOC = BONFERRONI GABRIEL QREGW GT2 T2 GH ALPHA(.05).
```

Knowing that the overall effect of development technique on PATP was significant ($F(3, 118) = 3.46$, $p < 0.05$, partial eta-squared $\eta_p^2 = 0.08$), the planned comparisons, also called "contrasts" (see Sect. 4.2), can be conducted.

Table 5.13 Test of between-subjects effects (DV: PATP)

Source	Type III Sum of Squares	df	Mean Square	F	Significance	Partial Eta Squared
Corrected Model	0.617[1]	3	0.206	3.456	0.019	0.081
Intercept	20.818	1	20.818	348.805	0.000	0.748
DevTech	0.617	3	0.206	3.456	0.019	0.081
Error	7.022	118	0.060			
Total	28.478	122				
Corrected Total	7.639	121				

[1] R Squared = 0.081.

Listing 5.11: Related SPSS menu navigation (Analyse⇒General Linear Model⇒Univariate) and syntax

```
UNIANOVA
  PATP BY DevTech
  /METHOD = SSTYPE(3)
  /INTERCEPT = INCLUDE
  /PRINT = DESCRIPTIVE ETASQ OPOWER HOMOGENEITY
  /CRITERIA = ALPHA(.05)
  /DESIGN = DevTech .
```

Planned Comparisons

The advantage of planned comparisons over the practice of comparing everything to everything else resides in the possibility of conducting fewer tests and, in consequence, in the lesser Type I error inflation.

If one employs only orthogonal comparisons, then there is no increase in the risk of committing a Type I error [77, 134]. A set of orthogonal comparisons would consist of, for example, TF vs. TL, TFPP vs. TFSP and TLPP vs. TLSP contrasts. However, the planned contrasts, specified before this analysis was undertaken (see Sect. 4.2), are non-orthogonal. Therefore, one of the correction methods mentioned in Box 5.2 will be used.

Table 5.14 shows the results of the planned comparisons (i.e. the statistics for each contrast). The statistics are produced for situations in which the group variances are both equal and unequal.

As Levene's test was not significant, we can use the part of the table labelled *Assume equal variances*. The table presents the values of the contrasts, the standard error of each contrast and a t-statistic (calculated by dividing the contrast value by the SE) and the significance value of the contrast.

Planned comparison (contrast 5) revealed a significant difference in PATP between the TF projects (TFSP and TFPP) and the TL projects (TLSP and TLPP) ($p < 0.008$). For contrast 1 (TLSP vs. TFSP), we can say that TFSP decreased PATP compared to TLSP, however, not significantly, as after Bonferroni's correction, only p-values < 0.008 represent statistically significant differences. For

Table 5.14 Contrast tests

		Contrast	Value of Contrast	Std.Error SE	t	df	Sig.(2-tailed)
PATP	Assume	1(TLSP vs. TFSP)	−0.1306391	0.06519866	−2.004	118	0.047
	equal	2(TLPP vs. TFPP)	−0.1497211	0.06016720	−2.488	118	0.014
	variances	3(TLSP vs. TLPP)	0.0318639	0.06360172	0.501	118	0.617
		4(TFSP vs. TFPP)	0.0127820	0.06185288	0.207	118	0.837
		5(TF vs. TL)	−0.2803602	0.08871842	−3.160	118	0.002
		6(PP vs. SP)	0.0446459	0.08871842	0.503	118	0.616
PATP	Does	1(TLSP vs. TFSP)	−0.1306391	0.06493835	−2.012	50.979	0.050
	not	2(TLPP vs. TFPP)	−0.1497211	0.06079824	−2.463	60.585	0.017
	assume	3(TLSP vs. TLPP)	0.0318639	0.06922718	0.460	55.795	0.647
	equal	4(TFSP vs. TFPP)	0.0127820	0.05586602	0.229	59.862	0.820
	variances	5(TF vs. TL)	0.2803602	0.08895738	−3.152	109.030	0.002
		6(PP vs. SP)	0.0446459	0.08895738	0.502	109.030	0.617

Listing 5.12: Related SPSS syntax

```
ONEWAY
    PATP BY DevTech
    /CONTRAST= −1  1  0  0    /CONTRAST= 0  0 −1  1    /CONTRAST= −1  0  1  0
    /CONTRAST= 0 −1  0  1    /CONTRAST= −1  1 −1  1    /CONTRAST= −1 −1  1  1
    /STATISTICS  DESCRIPTIVES  HOMOGENEITY
    /MISSING  ANALYSIS
    /POSTHOC = BONFERRONI GABRIEL QREGW GT2 T2 GH ALPHA(.05).
```

contrast 2 (TLPP vs. TFPP), we can say that TFPP decreased PATP in comparison with TLPP, nevertheless not significantly due to the Bonferroni correction. It is worth mentioning that it does not matter which correction method we use for our data in the aforementioned cases. Furthermore, other contrasts are not significant either.

Calculating Effect Size

A rough estimate of effect size for ANOVA is available through eta-squared η^2:

$$\eta^2 = \frac{SS_M}{SS_T} \tag{5.10}$$

where SS_M is the between-group effect (i.e. the experimental effect sum of squares) and SS_T is the total sum of squares (i.e. amount of variance in the data). Therefore the effect size can be easily calculated:

$$\eta = \sqrt{\frac{SS_M}{SS_T}} = \sqrt{\frac{0.617}{7.639}} = \sqrt{0.08} = 0.28 \tag{5.11}$$

It is worth mentioning that this simple measure of effect size is flawed for two reasons, as explained in Box 5.7

Partial eta squared (η_p^2) can be calculated on the basis of Eq. (5.14):

$$\eta_p{}^2 = \frac{SS_M}{SS_M + SS_R} = 0.08 \qquad (5.12)$$

Hence, we may conclude that 8% of the variance in PATP can be attributed to the development method. That represents a medium effect, according to the benchmarks for effect sizes presented in Sect. 4.7.5). Therefore, the effect of development technique on PATP represents a fairly substantive finding.

As a general rule, the calculation of the effect size of the overall ANOVA does not reveal any attention-grabbing facts, because it only makes it possible to test the general hypothesis ($H_{0,PATP,TLSP/TLPP/TFSP/TFPP}^A$). Conversely, the effect sizes for contrasts test specific hypotheses (i.e. compare only two groups) and thus, in the end, provide us with the result that is much more meaningful and easier to interpret.

Effect sizes of the planned contrasts are calculated on the basis of the t-test statistic:

$$r = \frac{t}{\sqrt{t^2 + df}} \qquad (5.13)$$

Box 5.7 Problems with eta-squared and partial eta-squared measures of effect size

Eta squared (η^2) measure of effect size is flawed for two reasons.

Firstly, for a particular independent variable, η^2 depends on the number and significance of the other independent variables in the design [240]. Therefore, the alternative called partial eta squared (η_p^2) is sometimes considered and calculated by SPSS:

$$\eta_p{}^2 = \frac{SS_M}{SS_M + SS_R} \qquad (5.14)$$

However, η_p^2s for all significant effects in the design do not sum up to the proportion of systematic variance in the dependent variable [240].

Secondly, η^2 is biased [76, 240], as it is based on the sums of squares from the sample with no adjustment to estimate a population value. To reduce this bias and to measure the effect size in the population, instead of in the sample, a more complex measure, known as omega squared (ω^2), is used:

$$\omega^2 = \frac{SS_M - df_M \times MS_R}{SS_T + MS_R} \qquad (5.15)$$

$MS_M = SS_M/df_M$ is the average amount of variation explained by the model (the systematic variation), and $MS_R = SS_R/df_R$ is the average amount of variation explained by extraneous variables (the unsystematic variation) [77]. Strictly speaking, the presented formula is limited to the between-subjects analysis of variance designs with equal sample sizes [240]. Therefore, when the numbers of subjects in each group are unequal, we cannot calculate ω [77]. It should be mentioned that ω is generally a more accurate measure than η (although the same benchmarks apply for deciding how substantial the effect is).

Rosnow and Rosenthal [214] recommended reducing the df in Eq. (5.13) by the sum of $n_i - 1$ for the excluded groups (i.e. the intent is to exclude those groups for the contrast in question for which there are contrast weights of zero).

Therefore

$$r_{\text{contrast 1 (TLSP vs. TFSP)}} = -0.26 \tag{5.16}$$

$$r_{\text{contrast 2 (TLPP vs. TFPP)}} = -0.30 \tag{5.17}$$

$$r_{\text{contrast 3 (TLSP vs. TLPP)}} = 0.07 \tag{5.18}$$

$$r_{\text{contrast 4 (TFSP vs. TFPP)}} = 0.03 \tag{5.19}$$

$$r_{\text{contrast 5 (TF vs. TL)}} = -0.28 \tag{5.20}$$

$$r_{\text{contrast 6 (PP vs. SP)}} = 0.05 \tag{5.21}$$

The comparison TLSP vs. TFSP, TLPP vs. TFPP, as well as TF (TFSP&TFPP) vs. TL (TLSP&TLPP), represents a medium effect, in accordance with the guidelines by Kempenes et al. The comparison TLSP vs. TLPP, TFSP vs. TFPP, as well as PP vs. SP, represents a small effect based on the same guidelines

Summary

The percentage of acceptance tests passed (PATP) was significantly affected by software development technique (the ANOVA test statistics: $F(3, 118) = 3.46$, $p = 0.02$, partial eta-squared $\eta_p^2 = -0.08$).[2] After the Bonferroni correction, only p-values < 0.008 represent statistically significant differences. As a result, the planned contrasts revealed that there is a significant difference in PATP between the TF projects (TFSP&TFPP) and the TL projects (TLSP&TLPP) ($t(118) = -3.16$,

---

[2] Explanation why the effect size sign do not necessarily tally with the arithmetic sign is given in Box 5.5.

$p = 0.002$, $r = -0.28$). Other contrasts (i.e. differences between groups) are not significant.

General conclusions are similar to those presented in Sect. "Summary" (p. 73): the positive impact of PP on external code quality is not confirmed and the negative impact of TF is statistically significant, even after the Bonferroni correction, if we compare the TL projects (TLSP&TLPP) and the TF projects (TFSP&TFPP).

Analysis of Covariance

In further investigation, it is feasible to take into account pre-existing differences among the subjects by means of covariates, i.e. variables that are not part of the main experimental manipulation, but can influence the outcome, as presented in the conceptual model that guides this research. The so-called pre-test result is often used as a covariate as mentioned in Sect. 4.7.6. Therefore, the pre-test results (i.e. grades obtained by the subjects after the preparation phase of the experiment; see Sect. 3.3.3) are included in the model. A traditional grade system was used: 2.0 (fail), 3.0 (pass), 3.5 (between pass and good), 4.0 (good), 4.5 (between good and very good), 5.0 (very good) along with additional, non-standard 5.5 (the highest grade accepted at WUT). For pairs, the average of the two pre-test results was taken into analysis.

Additional Assumptions of ANCOVA

All the general one-way ANOVA assumptions presented in Sect. 5.1.1.2 apply to ANCOVA. However, additional ANCOVA assumptions should be checked as well. Pre-test grade covariate (*Grade*) introduced in Sect. 3.3.3 is consistent with the conceptual model presented in Sect. 3.2. The assumption that a covariate should be a continuous or discrete variable is satisfied. The assumption that the covariate is measured before the experimental manipulation takes place is also met. The last named assumption is not necessarily considered as the ANCOVA assumption but certainly does affect interpretation. The next assumption is that the covariate is measured without error (as reliably as possible). Unfortunately, grades are (to some extent) subjective rather than objective measures, because they involve human judgement. Hence, reliability of grades poses a threat to validity. Another assumption is that there is a linear relationship between the dependent variable and the covariates for all groups. This was checked by examining the scatterplots for each group. The scatterplots do not show evidence of non-linearity. The final assumption (homogeneity of regression) concerns the relationship between the dependent variable and the covariate for each of the experimental groups. It was checked statistically with the help of the GLM procedure with a customized model offered by SPSS (see Table 5.15). It turned out that there is no statistically significant interaction between the treatment and the covariate ($p = 0.60$ for DevTech $*$ *Grade*), so the considered assumption is satisfied too. It is worth mentioning that the assumption of equality of variance has not been violated, as the significance value in Table 5.16 is greater than 0.05.

Table 5.15 Test of between-subjects effects with covariate and interaction to check homogeneity of regression (DV: PATP)

Source	Type III Sum of Squares	df	Mean Square	F	Sig.
Corrected Model	2.407[1]	7	0.344	7.494	0.000
Intercept	0.862	1	0.862	18.789	0.000
DevTech	0.071	3	0.024	0.514	0.674
Grade	1.711	1	1.711	37.280	0.000
DevTech*Grade	0.087	3	0.029	0.631	0.597
Error	5.232	114	0.046		
Total	28.478	122			
Corrected Total	7.639	121			

[1] R Squared = 0.315.

Listing 5.13: Related SPSS syntax

```
UNIANOVA
    PATP BY DevTech  WITH Grade
    /METHOD = SSTYPE(3)
    /INTERCEPT = INCLUDE
    /CRITERIA = ALPHA(.05)
    /DESIGN = DevTech Grade DevTech*Grade .
```

Table 5.16 Levene's test of equality of error variances[1]

F	df1	df2	Sig.
1.821	3	118	0.147

[1] Dependent Variable: PATP. Design: Intercept+Grade+DevTech.

Adjusting for Pre-Intervention Scores

Once the assumptions have been checked, it is possible to proceed with the ANCOVA analysis to adjust for pre-existing differences between the subjects (based on the pre-intervention *Grade* scores) to remove the variation in PATP due to the differences in *Grades* between the subjects. The main ANCOVA results of between-subjects effects with *Grade* covariate are presented in Table 5.17.

It may be concluded that there is a significant difference in PATP between the groups using different development techniques, after controlling for grades obtained by the subjects at the end of the preparation phase of the experiment ($F(3, 117) = 3.32$, $p = 0.02$, partial eta-squared $\eta_p^2 = 0.08$). That is consistent with the previous results, obtained in Sects. "Analysis of Variance" (p. 73) and 5.1.1.3. Hence, development technique seems to have a significant effect on PATP and about 8% of the variance in the dependent variable ($\eta_p^2 = 0.08$) is explained by the independent variable (DevTech).

Table 5.17 brings to the fore the influence of the covariate (*Grade*), which is another interesting finding. It turned out that there is a significant relationship

Table 5.17 Test of between-subjects effects with covariate (DV: PATP)

Source	Type III Sum of Squares	df	Mean Square	F	Sig.	Partial Eta Squared
Corrected Model	2.321[1]	4	0.580	12.762	0.000	0.304
Intercept	0.808	1	0.808	17.783	0.000	0.132
Grade	1.704	1	1.704	37.473	0.000	0.243
DevTech	0.452	3	0.151	3.315	0.022	0.078
Error	5.319	117	0.045			
Total	28.478	122				
Corrected Total	7.639	121				

[1] R Squared = 0.304.

Listing 5.14: Related SPSS syntax

```
UNIANOVA
    PATP BY DevTech   WITH Grade
    /CONTRAST (DevTech)=SPECIAL(-1  1  0  0
                                 0  0 -1  1
                                -1  0  1  0
                                 0 -1  0  1
                                -1  1 -1  1
                                -1 -1  1  1 )
    /METHOD = SSTYPE(3)
    /INTERCEPT = INCLUDE
    /PRINT = DESCRIPTIVE ETASQ OPOWER HOMOGENEITY
    /CRITERIA = ALPHA(.05)
    /DESIGN = Grade DevTech.
```

---

between the covariate (*Grade*) and the dependent variable (PATP), when the independent variable ($F(1, 117) = 37.47$, $p = 0.00$, partial eta squared $\eta_p^2 = 0.24$) is controlled. The significance value is 0.000 (which actually means less than 0.0005), whereas the covariate explains over 24% of the variance in the dependent variable (PATP). That shows how influential the individual differences between subjects can be.

Planned Comparisons

Since the overall effect of development technique (DevTech) on PATP was significant, it would be suitable to carry out the planned contrasts based on more focused comparisons (mentioned in Sect. 4.2). Unfortunately, there is no option for specifying planned contrasts for ANCOVA in SPSS. In Box 5.8, the author proposes a simple but effective workaround to bypass this misfeature in user interface of SPSS.

Box 5.8 Planned contrasts for ANCOVA in SPSS

There are some limitations concerning planned contrasts in SPSS. The first problem is that although we can ask SPSS to do certain standard contrasts, there is no option for specifying planned contrasts for ANCOVA in SPSS. However, these contrasts can be easily obtained via SPSS syntax, instead of point and click dialogue boxes. A simple example, prepared by the author, specifying six contrasts, is presented in Box 5.14.

The second problem concerns the table "Contrast results (K Matrix)" (e.g. Table 5.18) which contains statistical tests of the contrasts, based on a t-statistic. For some reason SPSS GLM procedure does not include the implied t-value in the table. However, it can be easily obtained as $t = Difference\ (Estimate - Hypothesized)/Standard\ Error$. As soon as t-values are known, the effect sizes (r) for the planned contrasts can be calculated by hand on the basis of Equation 5.13.

The third problem is that SPSS GLM procedure does not include partial eta-squared values for each contrast. Fortunately, partial eta squared can be obtained via SPSS syntax by specifying and running each contrast separately, e.g. /CONTRAST (DevTech) = SPECIAL(-1 1 0 0).

Table 5.18 shows the results of the planned comparisons for ANCOVA. The results of the planned comparisons for ANCOVA are, to a large extent, in line with the previous findings presented in Sects. "Mann-Whitney Tests" (p. 66) and "Planned Comparisons" (p. 75). For example, contrast 5 confirmed the previous finding that there is a significant difference in PATP between the TF (i.e. TFSP and TFPP) and the TL (i.e. TLSP and TLPP) projects. Moreover, the results of contrasts 1, 3, 4 and 6 are consistent with the previous findings and confirm that the differences between groups (TLSP and TFSP, TLSP and TLPP, TFSP and TFPP and PP vs. SP, respectively) are not statistically significant.

An interesting and valuable contribution of ANCOVA is that contrast 2 (TLPP vs. TFPP) revealed a statistically significant difference in PATP between TLPP and TFPP ($p = 0.005 < 0.05/6 = 0.0083$). It is worth mentioning that the previous analyses (i.e. non-parametric as well as parametric analysis but without adjusting for pre-intervention grades) were unable to reject the null hypothesis while controlling the experiment wise false positive rate.

Calculating Effect Size

The effect size in ANCOVA is calculated in a similar way as in ANOVA. However, we are able to calculate the effect of the independent variable(s), as well as the effect of the covariate(s), as both are included in the model. The effect of development technique (DevTech) was calculated by SPSS (see Table 5.17) and may be computed on the basis of Eq. (5.14):

$$\eta_p{}^2 = \frac{SS_M}{SS_M + SS_R} = \frac{0.452}{0.452 + 5.319} = 0.08 \longrightarrow \eta_p = 0.28 \qquad (5.22)$$

Table 5.18 Contrast results (K Matrix)

Contrast		DV: PATP
1(TLSP vs. TFSP)	Difference (Estimate - Hypothesized)	−0.072
	Std. Error SE	0.058
	Sig. (2-tailed)	0.215
	95% Confidence Interval for Difference - Lower Bound	−0.186
	- Upper Bound	0.042
2(TLPP vs. TFPP)	Difference (Estimate - Hypothesized)	−0.151
	Std. Error SE	0.053
	Sig. (2-tailed)	0.005
	95% Confidence Interval for Difference - Lower Bound	−0.255
	- Upper Bound	−0.046
3(TLSP vs. TLPP)	Difference (Estimate - Hypothesized)	0.061
	Std. Error SE	0.056
	Sig. (2-tailed)	0.276
	95% Confidence Interval for Difference - Lower Bound	−0.049
	- Upper Bound	0.172
4(TFSP vs. TFPP)	Difference (Estimate - Hypothesized)	−0.018
	Std. Error SE	0.054
	Sig. (2-tailed)	0.747
	95% Confidence Interval for Difference - Lower Bound	−0.125
	- Upper Bound	0.090
5(TF vs. TL)	Difference (Estimate - Hypothesized)	−0.223
	Std. Error SE	0.078
	Sig. (2-tailed)	0.005
	95% Confidence Interval for Difference - Lower Bound	−0.377
	- Upper Bound	−0.068
6(PP vs. SP)	Difference (Estimate - Hypothesized)	0.044
	Std. Error SE	0.078
	Sig. (2-tailed)	0.576
	95% Confidence Interval for Difference - Lower Bound	−0.110
	- Upper Bound	0.197

> **Related SPSS syntax is presented in Listing 5.14**

We may conclude that 8% of the variance in PATP can be attributed to development technique (as $\eta_p^2 = 0.08$). That represents a medium effect, according to the benchmarks for effect sizes presented in Sect. 4.7.5). Therefore, the effect of development technique on PATP represents a fairly substantive finding.

For the effect of the covariate we get the following:

$$\eta_p{}^2 = \frac{1.704}{1.704 + 5.319} = 0.24 \longrightarrow \eta_p = 0.49 \qquad (5.23)$$

This represents a fairly large effect according to both Cohen's as well as Kempenes et al.'s guidelines (see Table 4.2). Therefore, apart from being statistically significant, this effect is large and, as such, it represents a substantive finding.

The effect size measures (r) for planned contrasts, obtained according to the guidelines presented in Box 5.8 and using Eq. (5.13), are as follows:

$$r_{contrast\ 1\ (TLSP\ vs.\ TFSP)} = -0.17 \qquad (5.24)$$
$$r_{contrast\ 2\ (TLPP\ vs.\ TFPP)} = -0.34 \qquad (5.25)$$
$$r_{contrast\ 3\ (TLSP\ vs.\ TLPP)} = 0.14 \qquad (5.26)$$
$$r_{contrast\ 4\ (TFSP\ vs.\ TFPP)} = -0.04 \qquad (5.27)$$
$$r_{contrast\ 5\ (TF\ vs.\ TL)} = -0.25 \qquad (5.28)$$
$$r_{contrast\ 6\ (PP\ vs.\ SP)} = 0.05 \qquad (5.29)$$

The comparison 2 (TLPP vs. TFPP), as well as 5 (TF(TFSP&TFPP) vs. TL (TLSP&TLPP)) represents a medium effect, while the comparison 1 (TLSP vs. TFSP), 3 (TLSP vs. TLPP), 4 (TFSP vs. TFPP) and 6 (PP vs. SP) represent a small effect.

Summary

This section illustrates how ANCOVA can adjust for pre-existing differences between subjects so that the results reflect, more precisely, the effect of the experimental manipulation. Preliminary checks were conducted to ensure that there was no violation of the ANCOVA assumptions. After adjusting for pre-existing differences between the subjects, there was a significant difference in PATP between the groups $(F(3, 117) = 3.32, p = 0.02$, partial eta-squared $\eta_p^2 = 0.08)$. That is in line with the results obtained in the non-parametric analysis (see Sect. 5.1.1.3) and in the analysis of variance (see Sect. "Analysis of Variance" (p. 73)). Hence, we may conclude that the independent variable DevTech (i.e. development technique) has a significant effect on PATP. DevTech accounts for 8% (according to partial eta squared) of the total variance and represents medium effect size.

An interesting finding is that there is a statistically significant relationship between the covariate $(Grade)$ and the dependent variable (PATP). The covariate was significant $(F(1, 117) = 37.47, p < 0.001$, partial eta-squared $\eta_p^2 = 0.24)$ indicating that pre-existing differences between the subjects (measured by grades) had a significant effect on PATP (the external code quality indicator). Covariate $(Grade)$ explained about 24% (according to partial eta squared) of the total variance in the dependent variable. This represents a large effect size.

We can conclude that initial differences between the subjects are even a more important predictor of their scores on the dependent variable (PATP) than our independent variable DevTech (i.e. development technique). In fact, it is consistent with the expectations of many researchers in the behavioural sciences [178].

The positive impact of PP on PATP is not confirmed. However, planned contrasts revealed that, after adjusting for pre-existing differences in $Grade$ between the subjects, there is a significant difference in PATP between the TL(TLSP&TLPP) and the TF(TFSP&TFPP) group $(t = -2.86, p = 0.005, r = -0.25)$, as well as between the TLPP and the TFPP group ($t = -2.85$, $p = 0.005$, $r = -0.34$). The differences are statistically significant even after the Bonferroni correction. Other differences between the groups are not significant. To establish empirical evidence and to produce a more reliable conclusion concerning the impact of TF on PATP, selective analysis has been conducted in Sect. 5.1.2.

5.1.2 Selective Analysis

Selective analysis, based on the selection criteria presented in Sect. 4.7.7, was motivated by the intention to minimize the threat of process conformance, which is one of the most serious threats in TF experimentation. As a result, the selective analysis of 28 TLSP, 19 TFSP, 31 TLPP and 27 TFPP projects is conducted in this section (i.e. 17 projects have been excluded due to criterion C1 presented in Sect. 4.7.7).

5.1.2.1 Descriptive Statistics

The descriptive statistics of gathered experimental results are summarized in Table 5.19. On the basis of the descriptive statistics, the TF development technique seems to have a negative impact on PATP, as both TF groups (TFSP and TFPP) have lower PATP means, medians and confidence intervals than the TL groups (TLSP and TLPP). Furthermore, a positive effect of PP is not visible, as the TFSP vs. TFPP and the TLSP vs. TLPP results are similar to a large extent.

Table 5.19 Descriptive statistics for the percentage of acceptance tests passed (DV: PATP)

DV	Dev Tech	Mean (M)	Std.Dev. (SD)	Std.Error (SE)	Max	Median (Mdn)	Min	95% CI Lower Bound	Upper Bound
PATP	TLSP	0.469	0.271	0.051	0.974	0.566	0.000	0.364	0.574
	TFSP	0.345	0.203	0.047	0.605	0.421	0.000	0.247	0.443
	TLPP	0.501	0.259	0.047	0.842	0.553	0.000	0.406	0.596
	TFPP	0.335	0.232	0.045	0.842	0.316	0.000	0.243	0.427

Listing 5.16: Related SPSS syntax

```
EXAMINE
    VARIABLES=PATP BY DevTech
    /PLOT BOXPLOT STEMLEAF HISTOGRAM NPPLOT
    /COMPARE GROUP
    /STATISTICS DESCRIPTIVES
    /CINTERVAL 95
    /MISSING LISTWISE
    /NOTOTAL.
```

The accuracy of the mean as a model of data can be assessed by SD which is rather large (compared to the mean) in all cases ($SD > 0.20$). A large SD indicates that the data points are not clustered closely around the mean. Higher SD for the TL groups (TLSP and TLPP) means that there is a greater uncertainty in the TL projects. It should also be noted that the difference in SD between the TL and TF projects is more visible in solo projects (TLSP vs. TFSP) than in pairs (TLPP vs. TFPP). The obtained results are consistent with the results of the preliminary analysis in Sect. 5.1.1.

Visual inspection of Fig. 5.2 suggests that there are differences, with the TL groups (TLSP and TLPP) performing better than the TF (TFSP and TFPP) ones. Moreover, the whiskers on the TLPP and TFPP boxplots coming out of the boxes differ in length. That shows that the distribution is skewed to some extent. Other whiskers on the TLSP and TFSP boxplots coming out of the boxes are more or less equal. Neither extreme points nor outliers can be located in Fig. 5.2.

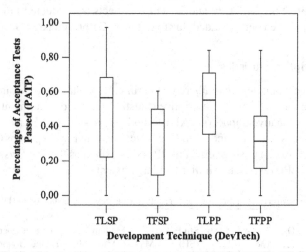

Fig. 5.2 Boxplot for the percentage of acceptance tests passed (DV: PATP) – selective analysis of Experiment ACCOUNTING

Listing 5.17: Related SPSS syntax

```
EXAMINE
   VARIABLES=PATP BY DevTech /PLOT=BOXPLOT/STATISTICS=NONE/NOTOTAL.
```

Summarizing the descriptive statistics in APA format [12], we can conclude that PATP in the TFSP projects ($M = 0.34$, SD $= 0.20$) and the TFPP projects ($M = 0.34$, SD $= 0.23$) are similar. PATP in the TLSP projects ($M = 0.47$, SD $= 0.27$) and the TLPP projects ($M = 0.50$, SD $= 0.26$) are also similar, but somewhat higher levels of PATP are reached in the TL groups (TLSP and TLPP) than in the TF groups (TFSP and TFPP). To answer the question whether the impact of the TF and PP techniques on PATP is significant or not, statistical tests must be performed, preceded by the testing of the underlying assumptions.

5.1.2.2 Assumption Testing

General assumptions of parametric tests are presented in Sect. 4.7.2. The assumption of homogeneity of variance is tested using Levene's test, see Table 5.20. Levene's test is non-significant ($p > 0.05$) so we accept the null hypothesis that the difference between the variances is roughly zero. Consequently, the assumption of homogeneity of variance is not violated.

Table 5.20 Levene's test of equality of error variances[1]

F	df1	df2	Sig.
1.351	3	101	0.262

[1] Dependent Variable: PATP. Design: Intercept+DevTech.

The assumption of normality (i.e. that our data have come from a population that has normal distribution) can be checked by means of the Kolmogorov–Smirnov and the Shapiro–Wilk tests presented in Table 5.21. The significance (Sig.) value is lower than 0.05 for the TLSP group (according to both statistics), as well as for the TFSP and TLPP groups (according to the Shaprio-Wilk statistic). This finding tells us that the data are not normally distributed and the assumption is broken. Therefore, it is required to perform a non-parametric analysis, presented in Sects. 5.1.2.3 and 5.1.2.4.

Table 5.21 Tests of normality

	Kolmogorov–Smirnov[1]			Shapiro–Wilk		
DevTech	Statistic	df[2]	Sig.	Statistic	df[2]	Sig.
TLSP	0.186	28	0.014	0.925	28	0.046
TFSP	0.172	19	0.140	0.900	19	0.049
TLPP	0.120	31	0.200[3]	0.912	31	0.015
TFPP	0.147	27	0.140	0.949	27	0.205

[1] Lilliefors Significance Correction.
[2] Degrees of freedom.
[3] This is a lower bound of the true significance.

The non-parametric analysis presented in Sect. 5.1.2.3 is based on the Kruskal–Wallis and the Mann–Whitney tests. To get a more sensitive measure of our experimental effect, further analysis, presented in Sect. 5.1.2.4, is based on a non-parametric, rank-transformed ANCOVA.

5.1.2.3 Analysis using Kruskal–Wallis and Mann–Whitney Tests

The hypothesis $H^A_{0,\text{PATP,TLSP/TLPP/TFSP/TFPP}}$, regarding the difference in PATP between the projects using the TLSP, TLPP, TFSP and TFPP software development techniques, is evaluated with the help of the Kruskal–Wallis one-way analysis of variance by ranks. The Kruskal–Wallis test is a non-parametric alternative to the parametric ANOVA and can always be used instead of the ANOVA, if it is not sure that the assumptions of ANOVA are met. The Kruskal–Wallis test is employed for testing differences between the four experimental groups (TLSP, TLPP, TFSP and TFPP) when different subjects are used in each group.

Table 5.22 shows a summary of the ranked data and tells us the mean rank in each treatment. The test statistic is a function of these ranks and can be found in Table 5.23. As $p = 0.022 < 0.05$, we can conclude that the software development technique applied by the subjects significantly affected external code quality indicator (PATP). This result, although consistent with the preliminary analysis presented in Sect. 5.1.1, proves only that a difference exists. However, it does not identify exactly where the difference is.

Table 5.22 Ranks

DevTech	N	Mean Rank
TLSP	28	58.50
TFSP	19	43.24
TLPP	31	63.23
TFPP	27	42.43
Total	105	

Table 5.23 Kruskal–Wallis test statistics[1]

	NATP
Chi-Square	9.631
df	3
Asymp. Sig.	0.022

[1] Grouping variable: DevTech (TLSP, TLPP, TFSP, TFPP).

Listing 5.18: Related SPSS syntax

```
NPAR TESTS
  /K-W=PATP    BY DevTech(1  4)
  /MISSING  ANALYSIS.
```

The TL groups (TLSP, TLPP) achieved better results (higher levels of PATP) than the TF groups (TFSP, TFPP), but this conclusion is subjective. We need to perform planned contrasts or post hoc tests for specific comparisons, identified in Sect. 4.2, by means of the Mann–Whitney tests in a similar manner as it was done in Sect. "Mann-Whitney Tests" (p. 66).

Mann–Whitney Tests

Tables 5.24, 5.25, 5.26, 5.27, 5.28 and 5.29 show the test statistics of the Mann–Whitney tests on the set of comparisons between groups.

Table 5.24 Mann–Whitney test statistics (TLSP vs. TFSP)[1]

	PATP
Mann–Whitney U	179.000
Wilcoxon W	369.000
Z	−1.889
Asymp. Sig. (2-tailed)	0.059
Exact Sig. (2-tailed)	0.059
Exact Sig. (1-tailed)	0.030

[1] Grouping Variable: DevTech.

Listing 5.19: Related SPSS syntax

```
NPAR TESTS
  /M-W= PATP BY DevTech(1  2)
  /MISSING ANALYSIS
  /METHOD=EXACT TIMER(5).
```

Table 5.25 Mann–Whitney test statistics (TLPP vs. TFPP)[1]

	PATP
Mann–Whitney U	259.500
Wilcoxon W	637.500
Z	−2.481
Asymp. Sig. (2-tailed)	0.013
Exact Sig. (2-tailed)	0.012
Exact Sig. (1-tailed)	0.006

[1] Grouping Variable: DevTech.

Listing 5.20: Related SPSS syntax

```
NPAR TESTS
  /M-W= PATP BY DevTech(3  4)
  /MISSING ANALYSIS
  /METHOD=EXACT TIMER(5).
```

Two comparisons (TF vs. TL and TLPP vs. TFPP) resulted in the observed two-tailed significance values < 0.05, see Tables 5.25 and 5.28. The other comparisons produce the significance values that are greater than 0.05, so the positive impact of PP on PATP was not confirmed in our selective analysis. However, if we want to control the build-up of Type I errors we should make some kind of adjustment to ensure that Type I errors do not build up to more than 0.05. The easiest method is to use the Bonferroni correction, explained in Sect. "Mann-Whitney Tests" (p. 66) and Box 5.2. As a result, the specific hypotheses $H_{0,\text{PATP,TLPP/TFPP}}^{A}$ cannot be rejected in spite of the fact that the observed significance level is < 0.05. The only specific hypothesis that can be rejected is $H_{0,\text{PATP,TFSP\&TFPP/TLSP\&TLPP}}^{A}$, as PATP was significantly lower in the TF groups (TFSP and TFPP) than in the TL groups (TLSP and TLPP) even after the Bonferroni correction. Using Holm's sequential Bonferroni correction [104] would not change that conclusion. However, it should be recalled that some statisticians argue against the Bonferroni correction, see Box 5.3.

Table 5.26 Mann–Whitney test statistics (TLSP vs. TLPP)[1]

	PATP
Mann–Whitney U	391.500
Wilcoxon W	797.500
Z	−0.646
Asymp. Sig. (2-tailed)	0.518
Exact Sig. (2-tailed)	0.524
Exact Sig. (1-tailed)	0.262

[1] Grouping Variable: DevTech.

Listing 5.21: Related SPSS syntax

```
NPAR TESTS
  /M-W= PATP BY DevTech(1 3)
  /MISSING ANALYSIS
  /METHOD=EXACT TIMER(5).
```

Table 5.27 Mann–Whitney test statistics (TFSP vs. TFPP)[1]

	PATP
Mann–Whitney U	239.500
Wilcoxon W	617.500
Z	−0.380
Asymp. Sig. (2-tailed)	0.704
Exact Sig. (2-tailed)	0.711
Exact Sig. (1-tailed)	0.356

[1] Grouping Variable: DevTech.

Listing 5.22: Related SPSS syntax

```
NPAR TESTS
  /M-W= PATP BY DevTech(2 4)
  /MISSING ANALYSIS
  /METHOD=EXACT TIMER(5).
```

Calculating Effect Size

The effect sizes for focused comparisons, i.e. the Mann–Whitney tests used to follow up the main analysis, are presented in this section. The effect sizes r can be calculated from the Z-scores on the basis of Eq. (5.3):

$$r_{\text{contrast1 (TLSP vs. TFSP)}} = \frac{-1.889}{\sqrt{47}} = -0.28 \tag{5.30}$$

$$r_{\text{contrast2 (TLPP vs. TFPP)}} = -0.33 \tag{5.31}$$

$$r_{\text{contrast3 (TLSP vs. TLPP)}} = -0.08 \tag{5.32}$$

$$r_{\text{contrast4 (TFSP vs. TFPP)}} = -0.06 \tag{5.33}$$

Table 5.28 Mann–Whitney test statistics (TF vs. TL)[1]

	PATP
Mann–Whitney U	886.000
Wilcoxon W	1967.000
Z	−3.044
Asymp. Sig. (2-tailed)	0.002
Exact Sig. (2-tailed)	0.002
Exact Sig. (1-tailed)	0.001

[1] Grouping Variable: ProgrammingTL0TF1.

Listing 5.23: Related SPSS syntax

```
NPAR  TESTS
  /M-W= PATP  BY  ProgrammingTL0TF1(0  1)
  /MISSING  ANALYSIS
  /METHOD=EXACT  TIMER(5).
```

Table 5.29 Mann–Whitney test statistics (PP vs. SP)[1]

	PATP
Mann–Whitney U	1331.500
Wilcoxon W	2459.500
Z	−0.203
Asymp. Sig. (2-tailed)	0.839
Exact Sig. (2-tailed)	0.841
Exact Sig. (1-tailed)	0.420

[1] Grouping Variable: CollaborationSP0PP1.

Listing 5.24: Related SPSS syntax

```
NPAR  TESTS
  /M-W= PATP  BY  CollaborationSP0PP1(0  1)
  /MISSING  ANALYSIS
  /METHOD=EXACT  TIMER(5).
```

$$r_{\text{contrast5 (TFvs.TL)}} = -0.30 \tag{5.34}$$

$$r_{\text{contrast6 (PPvs.SP)}} = -0.02 \tag{5.35}$$

The effect size estimations indicate that the difference in PATP due to the TF practice (used instead of TL) represents a medium effect, while the difference in PATP caused by the PP technique (used instead of SP) represents a small effect.

Summary

The external code quality indicated by PATP was significantly affected by software development technique (the Kruskal–Wallis test statistics: $H(3) = 9.63$, $p = 0.02 < 0.05$). This means that there is a difference in the percentage of acceptance tests passed (PATP) between the software development teams using the TLSP, TFSP, TLPP and TFPP development techniques.

The Mann–Whitney tests were used to follow up this finding. The Bonferroni correction was applied and so all the effects are reported at a 0.0083 level of significance. There was no statistically significant difference in PATP between the TLSP and the TFSP group ($U = 179.50, p = 0.059, r = -0.28$), the TLPP and the TFPP group ($U = 259.50, p = 0.012, r = -0.33$), the TLSP and the TLPP group ($U = 391.50, p = 0.52, r = -0.08$), the TFSP and the TFPP group ($U = 239.50, p = 0.71, r = -0.06$) and the SP (i.e. TLSP&TFSP) and the PP (i.e. TLPP&TFPP) group ($U = 1331.50, p = 0.84, r = -0.02$). However, there was a statistically significant difference in PATP between the TL (i.e. TLSP&TLPP) and the TF (i.e. TFSP&TFPP) group ($U = 886.00, p = 0.002, r = -0.30$).

After selective analysis we may conclude that, in spite of doubled effort due to the PP practice, the positive impact of PP on external code quality was not confirmed. Furthermore, the effect of TF on PATP is negative and statistically significant, even after the Bonferroni correction, if we compare the TL groups (TLSP&TLPP) and the TF groups (TFSP&TFPP). It is worth mentioning that the aforesaid results are consistent with the previous findings coming from the preliminary analysis.

5.1.2.4 Rank-Transformed Analysis of Covariance

To get a more sensitive measure of the experimental effect, we take into account the pre-test results to control, to some extent, pre-existing differences among the subjects. As our data are not normally distributed, the analysis performed in this section is based on a non-parametric ANCOVA using the rank transformation. Formal justification of rank-transformed analysis is discussed in Sect. 4.7.6.1. It should also be noted that SPSS provides support for ranking data (see Box 5.9).

Box 5.9 Ranking data in SPSS

SPSS provides support for ranking data via the main dialogue box using the **Transform⇒Rank Cases...** menu path or via SPSS syntax, e.g.:

```
RANK
   VARIABLES=PATP   (A)  /RANK  /PRINT=YES
   /TIES=MEAN .
```

Rank-Transformed Analysis of Variance

One-Way ANOVA results are presented using both One-Way ANOVA command (see Table 5.30) and General Linear Model command (see Table 5.31). It is clear from the significance value $p = 0.02$, which is lower than 0.05, that there are differences in PATP between the four groups. Therefore, development technique (DevTech) seems to have a significant effect on PATP which is consistent with previous findings. As presented in Table 5.31, the total amount of variance to be explained was 96304.00 (Corrected Total), of which experimental manipulation accounted for 8918.55 units, while 87385.46 were unexplained. As a result, development technique (DevTech) is able to explain about 9% of the variance in the dependent variable PATP (partial eta-squared $\eta_p{}^2 = 0.09$, see Table 5.31).

Table 5.30 ANOVA

	Sum of Squares	df	Mean Square	F	Significance
Between Groups	8918.545	3	2972.848	3.436	0.020
Within Groups	87385.455	101	865.203		
Total	96304.000	104			

Listing 5.25: Related SPSS menu navigation and syntax
Analyse⇒Compare Means⇒One-Way ANOVA

```
ONEWAY
  PATPRanked BY DevTech
  /CONTRAST= −1  1  0  0    /CONTRAST= 0  0  −1  1    /CONTRAST= −1  0  1  0
  /CONTRAST= 0−1  0  1    /CONTRAST= −1  1  −1  1    /CONTRAST= −1  −1  1  1
  /STATISTICS  DESCRIPTIVES  HOMOGENEITY
  /MISSING  ANALYSIS
  /POSTHOC = BONFERRONI  GABRIEL  QREGW  GT2  T2  GH  ALPHA(.05).
```

Table 5.31 Test of between-subjects effects

Source	Type III Sum of Squares	df	Mean Square	F	Significance	Partial Eta Squared
Corrected Model	8918.545[1]	3	2972.848	3.436	0.020	0.093
Intercept	272835.303	1	272835.303	315.343	0.000	0.757
DevTech	8918.545	3	2972.848	3.436	0.020	0.093
Error	87385.455	101	865.203			
Total	391249.000	105				
Corrected Total	96304.000	104				

[1] R Squared = 0.093.

Listing 5.26: Related SPSS menu navigation and syntax
Analyse⇒General Linear Model⇒Univariate

```
UNIANOVA
  PATPRanked  BY DevTech
  /METHOD = SSTYPE(3)
  /INTERCEPT = INCLUDE
  /PRINT = DESCRIPTIVE  ETASQ  OPOWER  HOMOGENEITY
  /CRITERIA = ALPHA(.05)
  /DESIGN = DevTech .
```

Keeping in mind that the overall effect of development technique on PATP was significant ($F(3, 101) = 3.44$, $p < 0.05$, partial eta-squared $\eta_p{}^2 = 0.09$), the planned contrasts, based on the specific comparisons formulated earlier, can be conducted.

Planned Comparisons

Since the overall effect of development technique was significant, the six planned comparisons (presented in Sect. 4.2) are performed. Table 5.32 shows the results of the planned comparisons, i.e. the statistics for each contrast. As Levene's test was not significant, we can use the part of the table labelled *Assume equal variances*.

Table 5.32 Contrast tests

		Contrast	Value of Contrast	Std.Error SE	t	df	Sig.(2-tailed)
PATP	Assume equal variances	1(TLSP vs. TFSP)	−15.26316	8.7428294	−1.746	101	0.084
		2(TLPP vs. TFPP)	−20.79988	7.7430160	−2.686	101	0.008
		3 (TLSP vs. TLPP)	4.725806	7.6687580	0.616	101	0.539
		4(TFSP vs. TFPP)	−0.810916	8.8080369	−0.092	101	0.927
		5(TF vs. TL)	−36.06304	11.6786713	−3.088	101	0.003
		6(PP vs. SP)	3.914890	11.6786713	0.335	101	0.738
PATP	Does not assume equal variances	1(TLSP vs. TFSP)	−15.26316	8.0686052	−1.892	44.616	0.065
		2 (TLPP vs. TFPP)	−20.79988	7.7985840	−2.667	55.997	0.010
		3 (TLSP vs. TLPP)	4.725806	8.3011621	0.569	56.429	0.571
		4 (TFSP vs. TFPP)	−0.810916	7.5505636	−0.107	42.266	0.915
		5 (TF vs. TL)	−36.06304	11.2214216	−3.214	98.453	0.002
		6(PP vs. SP)	3.914890	11.2214216	0.349	98.453	0.728

Listing 5.27: Related SPSS syntax

```
ONEWAY
  PATPRanked BY DevTech
  /CONTRAST= −1 1 0 0   /CONTRAST= 0 0 −1 1   /CONTRAST= −1 0 1 0
  /CONTRAST= 0 −1 0 1   /CONTRAST= −1 1 −1 1   /CONTRAST= −1 −1 1 1
  /STATISTICS DESCRIPTIVES HOMOGENEITY
  /MISSING ANALYSIS
  /POSTHOC = BONFERRONI GABRIEL QREGW GT2 T2 GH ALPHA(.05).
```

Contrast 5 revealed a significant difference in PATP between the TF projects (TFSP and TFPP) and the TL projects (TLSP and TLPP) ($p = 0.003$). The difference is statistically significant even after the Bonferroni correction. Also, contrast 2 revealed a difference in PATP between the TLPP and TFPP projects ($p = 0.008$ is close to α value after the Bonferroni correction). Other contrasts are not significant.

Calculating Effect Size

A rough estimate of effect size for ANOVA is available through r^2, usually called eta-squared η^2, based on Eq. (5.10):

$$\eta = \sqrt{\frac{SS_M}{SS_T}} = \sqrt{\frac{8918.545}{96304.000}} = \sqrt{0.09} = 0.30 \qquad (5.36)$$

Furthermore, partial eta square was calculated by SPSS (see Table 5.34) and can be easily calculated on the basis of Eq. (5.14):

$$\eta_p^{\,2} = \frac{SS_M}{SS_M + SS_R} = \frac{8918.545}{8918.545 + 87385.455} = 0.09 \qquad (5.37)$$

$$\eta_p = 0.30 \qquad (5.38)$$

We may conclude that 9% of the variance in PATP can be attributed to the development method ($\eta^2 = 0.09$, $\eta_p^2 = 0.09$). In line with the benchmark for effect sizes (see Table 4.2) that represents a medium effect size. Therefore, the effect of development technique on PATP represents a fairly substantive finding.

In fact, it is more interesting to calculate effect sizes for the contrasts (because they are testing specific hypotheses, i.e. compare only two groups and so the effect size is much easier to interpret) than the effect size for the overall ANOVA. The effect sizes of the planned contrasts can be estimated on the basis of Eq. (5.13) with the t-statistics presented in Table 5.32.

Consequently

$$r_{\text{contrast1 (TLSPvs.TFSP)}} = -0.25 \qquad (5.39)$$

$$r_{\text{contrast2 (TLPPvs.TFPP)}} = -0.34 \qquad (5.40)$$

$$r_{\text{contrast3 (TLSPvs.TLPP)}} = 0.08 \qquad (5.41)$$

$$r_{\text{contrast4 (TFSPvs.TFPP)}} = -0.01 \qquad (5.42)$$

$$r_{\text{contrast5 (TFvs.TL)}} = -0.29 \qquad (5.43)$$

$$r_{\text{contrast6 (PPvs.SP)}} = 0.03 \qquad (5.44)$$

It appeared that the PP practice had very little effect on PATP compared to the SP practice ($r \leq 0.08$). However, the TF practice had medium effect on PATP.

Summary

The external code quality indicated by PATP was significantly affected by software development technique (the ANOVA test statistics: $F(3, 101) = 3.44$, $p = 0.02$, partial eta-squared $\eta_p^{\,2} = -0.09$).

Planned contrasts revealed that there is a significant difference in PATP between the TF projects (TFSP&TFPP) and the TL projects (TLSP&TLPP) ($t = -3.09$, $p = 0.003$, $r = -0.29$). Also, there is a difference in PATP between TFPP and TLPP ($t = -2.69$, $p = 0.008$, $r = -0.34$). The former is statistically significant even after the Bonferroni correction. The latter is on the threshold. Other differences between the groups are not statistically significant.

Adjusting for Pre-Intervention Scores

In further investigation, it is feasible to take into account the pre-test results of the subjects. As a result, the so-called pre-test results (grades obtained by the subjects after the preparation phase of the experiment – see Sect. 4.4.7) are included in the model.

Additional Assumptions of ANCOVA

Pre-test grade covariate (*Grade*) introduced in Sect. 3.3.3 is consistent with the conceptual model presented in Sect. 3.2. The assumption that a covariate should be a continuous or discrete variable is satisfied. The assumption that the covariate is measured before the experimental manipulation takes place is met too. Another assumption is that there is a linear relationship between the dependent variable and the covariates for all the groups. It was checked by examining the scatterplots for each group. The scatterplots do not show evidence of non-linearity. The final assumption (homogeneity of regression slopes) concerns the relationship between the dependent variable and the covariate for each of the experimental groups. It was checked statistically with the help of the GLM procedure with a customized model offered by SPSS (see Table 5.33). It appeared that there is no statistically significant interaction between the treatment and the covariate ($p = 0.69$ for DevTech*$Grade$), so this assumption is satisfied too.

Table 5.33 Test of between-subjects effects with covariate and interaction to check homogeneity of regression

Source	Type III Sum of Squares	df	Mean Square	F	Sig.
Corrected Model	31216.159[1]	7	4459.451	6.646	0.000
Intercept	10955.181	1	10955.181	16.326	0.000
DevTech	759.390	3	253.130	0.377	0.770
Grade	21809.437	1	21809.437	32.502	0.000
DevTech*Grade	988.043	3	329.348	0.491	0.689
Error	65087.841	97	671.009		
Total	391249.000	105			
Corrected Total	96304.000	104			

[1] R Squared $= 0.324$.

```
Listing 5.28: Related SPSS syntax

UNIANOVA
    PATPRanked  BY DevTech   WITH Grade
    /METHOD = SSTYPE(3)
    /INTERCEPT = INCLUDE
    /PRINT = DESCRIPTIVE ETASQ OPOWER PARAMETER TEST(LMATRIX) HOMOGENEITY
    /PLOT = SPREADLEVEL RESIDUALS
    /CRITERIA = ALPHA(.05)
    /DESIGN = DevTech Grade DevTech*Grade .
```

Covariate Included in Analysis

The main ANCOVA results of between-subjects effects with *Grade* covariate are presented in Table 5.34. It appeared that there is a significant difference in PATP between the groups, after controlling for grades obtained by the subjects after the preparation phase of the experiment ($F(3, 100) = 3.79$, $p = 0.013$, partial eta-squared $\eta_p^2 = 0.10$). Hence, development technique (DevTech) seems to have a significant effect on the dependent variable. It is consistent with the previously obtained results. Moreover, about 10% of the variance in the dependent variable ($\eta_p^2 = 0.10$) is explained by the independent variable (DevTech).

Table 5.34 Test of between-subjects effects with covariate

Source	Type III Sum of Squares	df	Mean Square	F	Sig.	Partial Eta Squared
Corrected Model	30228.117[1]	4	7557.029	11.473	0.000	0.314
Intercept	10385.752	1	10385.752	15.718	0.000	0.136
Grade	21309.572	1	21309.572	32.250	0.000	0.244
DevTech	7502.332	3	2500.777	3.785	0.013	0.102
Error	66075.883	100	660.759			
Total	391249.000	105				
Corrected Total	96304.000	104				

[1] R Squared = 0.314.

```
Listing 5.29: Related SPSS syntax

UNIANOVA
  PATPRanked  BY DevTech   WITH Grade
  /CONTRAST (DevTech)=SPECIAL(-1   1   0   0
                              0   0  -1   1
                             -1   0   1   0
                              0  -1   0   1
                             -1   1  -1   1
                             -1  -1   1   1 )
  /METHOD = SSTYPE(3)
  /INTERCEPT = INCLUDE
  /PRINT = DESCRIPTIVE ETASQ OPOWER HOMOGENEITY
  /CRITERIA = ALPHA(.05)
  /DESIGN = Grade DevTech.
```

Table 5.34 exhibits some other attention-grabbing facts concerning the influence of the covariate *Grade*. It turned out that there is a significant relationship between the covariate (*Grade*) and the dependent variable (PATP) ($F(1, 117) = 32.25$, $p = 0.00$, partial eta-squared $\eta_p^2 = 0.24$). The significance value is 0.000 (i.e. less than 0.0005). Moreover, on the basis of eta-squared value, the covariate explained over 24% of the variance in the dependent variable. That accounts for the potentially great influence of individual differences in SE experiments.

Planned Contrasts

Keeping in mind that the overall effect of DevTech on PATP was significant, it would be suitable to carry out the planned contrasts. Unfortunately, there is no option for specifying planned contrasts for ANCOVA in SPSS. In Box 5.8, the author proposes a simple workaround to bypass this misfeature. Based on the proposed solution, the results of the planned comparisons for ANCOVA are presented in Table 5.35.

Table 5.35 Contrast results (K Matrix)

Contrast		DV: PATP*Ranked*
1(TLSP vs. TFSP)	Difference (Estimate - Hypothesized)	−10.011
	Std. Error SE	7.696
	Sig. (2-tailed)	0.196
	95% Confidence Interval for Difference - Lower Bound	−25.280
	- Upper Bound	5.258
2(TLPP vs. TFPP)	Difference (Estimate - Hypothesized)	−20.663
	Std. Error SE	6.767
	Sig. (2-tailed)	0.003
	95% Confidence Interval for Difference - Lower Bound	−34.088
	- Upper Bound	−7.239
3(TLSP vs. TLPP)	Difference (Estimate - Hypothesized)	8.471
	Std. Error SE	6.734
	Sig. (2-tailed)	0.211
	95% Confidence Interval for Difference - Lower Bound	−4.889
	- Upper Bound	21.832
4(TFSP vs. TFPP)	Difference (Estimate - Hypothesized)	−2.181
	Std. Error SE	7.701
	Sig. (2-tailed)	0.778
	95% Confidence Interval for Difference - Lower Bound	−17.460
	- Upper Bound	13.098
5(TF vs. TL)	Difference (Estimate - Hypothesized)	−30.674
	Std. Error SE	10.250
	Sig. (2-tailed)	0.003
	95% Confidence Interval for Difference - Lower Bound	−51.010
	- Upper Bound	−10.338
6(PP vs. SP)	Difference (Estimate - Hypothesized)	6.290
	Std. Error SE	10.215
	Sig. (2-tailed)	0.539
	95% Confidence Interval for Difference - Lower Bound	−13.975
	- Upper Bound	26.556

Related SPSS syntax is presented in Listing 5.29

Results of planned comparisons for ANCOVA are, to a large extent, consistent with the previous findings presented in Sects. "Mann-Whitney Tests" (p. 88) and "Planned Comparisons" (p. 94). For example contrast 2 (TLPP vs. TFPP) and contrast 5 (TL vs. TF, where TF means the TFSP and TFPP projects combined together, while TF means the TLSP and TLPP projects combined together) are statistically significant, even after the Bonferroni correction. Hence, both contrasts confirm the previous findings. Moreover, the results of contrasts 1, 3, 4 and 6 are consistent with the previous findings and confirm that the differences between groups (TLSP and TFSP, TLSP and TLPP, TFSP and TFPP and PP and SP, respectively) are not statistically significant.

Calculating Effect Size

We are able to calculate the effect of the independent variable as well as the effect of the covariate, as both are included in the model. The effect of development technique (DevTech) was computed by SPSS (see Table 5.34) but can be calculated by hand on the basis of Eq. 5.14:

$$\eta_p^2 = \frac{SS_M}{SS_M + SS_R} = \frac{7502.332}{7502.332 + 66075.883} = 0.10 \tag{5.45}$$

$$\eta_p = 0.32 \tag{5.46}$$

That represents a medium effect, according to the benchmarks for effect sizes presented in Sect. 4.7.5).

For the effect of the covariate we get the following:

$$\eta_p^2 = \frac{SS_M}{SS_M + SS_R} = \frac{21309.572}{21309.572 + 66075.883} = 0.24 \tag{5.47}$$

$$\eta_p = 0.49 \tag{5.48}$$

That is consistent with the result presented in Table 5.34 and represents a fairly large effect according to Cohen's as well as Kempenes et al.'s guidelines. Therefore, apart from being statistically significant, this effect is large and, as such, it represents a substantive finding.

Effect size measures (r) for planned contrasts, obtained in accordance with the guidelines presented in Box 5.8 and using Eq. (5.13), are as follows:

$$r_{contrast1 \ (TLSPvs.TFSP)} = -0.19 \ (< 0.193) \tag{5.49}$$
$$r_{contrast2 \ (TLPPvs.TFPP)} = -0.38 \tag{5.50}$$
$$r_{contrast3 \ (TLSPvs.TLPP)} = 0.16 \tag{5.51}$$
$$r_{contrast4 \ (TFSPvs.TFPP)} = -0.04 \tag{5.52}$$
$$r_{contrast5 \ (TFvs.TL)} = -0.29 \tag{5.53}$$
$$r_{contrast6 \ (PPvs.SP)} = 0.06 \tag{5.54}$$

These effect sizes are the same or a little bit higher than those obtained in the preliminary analysis in Sect. "Calculating Effect Size" (p. 82). Comparison 2 (TLPP vs. TFPP), as well as 5 (TF(TFSP&TFPP) vs. TL(TLSP&TLPP)), represents a medium effect, while the comparison 1 (TLSP vs. TFSP), 3 (TLSP vs. TLPP), 4 (TFSP vs. TFPP) and 6 (PP vs. SP) represent a small effect according to the guidelines by Kempenes et al. [133] presented in Sect. 4.7.5, in Box 4.2.

Summary

This section illustrates how the rank-transformed ANCOVA can adjust for pre-existing differences between subjects so that the results reflect, more precisely, the effect of the experimental manipulation. A statistically significant result is not always of practical significance. That is why not only statistical significance, but also effect size measures were reported, as suggested by APA [12].

After adjusting for grades obtained by the subjects once the preparation phase of the experiment had been completed, there was a statistically significant difference in PATP between the groups ($F(3, 117) = 3.32$, $p = 0.02$, partial eta-squared $\eta_p{}^2 = -0.10$). It is consistent with the results obtained by means of the Kruskal–Wallis and the Mann–Whitney tests (see Sect. 5.1.2.3), the analysis of variance (see Sect. "Summary" (p. 95)), as well as preliminary analysis (see Sect. "Summary" (p. 84)).

Hence, we may conclude that the independent variable DevTech (i.e. development technique) has a significant effect on PATP. After adjusting for pre-intervention scores, the effect of development technique accounts for 10% (according to partial eta squared) of the total variance and represents medium effect size in keeping with the guidelines for the effect size magnitude by Kempenes et al.

A statistically significant relationship between the covariate (*Grade*) and the dependent variable (PATP), while controlling for the independent variable (development technique DevTech), is a noteworthy finding. The covariate was significant ($F(1, 100) = 32.25$, $p < 0.001$, partial eta-squared $\eta_p{}^2 = 0.24$), which indicates that pre-existing differences between the subjects (measured by grades) had a statistically significant effect on PATP. Grades explained about 24% (according to partial eta squared) of the total variance in the dependent variable. This represents a large effect size and represents a substantive finding.

In conclusion, initial differences between the subjects are even a more important predictor of their scores on the dependent variable (PATP) than our independent variable DevTech (i.e. development technique). In fact, it is in line with the expectations of many researchers in behavioural sciences [178]. Interestingly, in spite of the doubled effort due to the PP practice, the positive impact of PP on PATP was not confirmed. It is also interesting that, after adjusting for the pre-existing differences in *Grade* between the subjects, there is a significant difference in PATP between the TL (TLSP&TLPP) and the TF (TFSP&TFPP) group ($t = -2.99$, $p = 0.003$, $r = -0.29$), as well as the TLPP and the TFPP group ($t = -3.05$, $p = 0.003$, $r = -0.38$), even after the Bonferroni correction. It would suggest that TF might have a negative impact on PATP. Other contrasts are not significant. For example, the difference between the TFSP and the TLSP group is not statistically significant ($t = 1.30$, $p = 0.196$, $r = -0.19$).

The results of Experiment ACCOUNTING influenced the decision to focus further empirical investigations (see Experiments SUBMISSION and SMELLS&LIBRARY) solely on the impact of the TF practice on PATP, since the effect of the PP practice appeared to be weak. Further experiments have been conducted to establish empirical evidence and to produce a more reliable conclusion concerning the impact of the TF practice on PATP.

5.2 Analysis of Experiment Submission

The hypothesis $H_{0,PATP,TLSP/TFSP}^{SUBMISSION}$ regarding the difference in PATP between the projects using the TLSP and TFSP software development techniques in Experiment SUBMISSION is evaluated in this section. The preliminary analysis of all 24 projects (11 TLSP and 13 TFSP) is conducted in Sect. 5.2.1, while further, selective analysis of 20 projects (selected on the basis of selection criteria presented in Sect. 4.7.7) is presented in Sect. 5.2.2. A preliminary analysis is included in this chapter to show the difference in the results that occurred due to the exclusion of some of the projects. The experiment data are analysed with descriptive analysis and statistical tests.

5.2.1 Preliminary Analysis

A descriptive analysis is presented in Sect. 5.2.1.1. Since there are only two groups (TLSP and TFSP), we may use the t-test (see Sect. 5.2.1.3) if assumptions of parametric tests are satisfied. Assumption testing was conducted beforehand in Sect. 5.2.1.2. The analysis of variance without adjusting for pre-existing differences between subjects is presented in Sect. 5.2.1.4, while the analysis of covariance, i.e. with adjusting for initial differences between subjects, is presented in Sect. 5.2.1.5.

5.2.1.1 Descriptive Statistics

The descriptive statistics of gathered experimental results are summarized in Table 5.36.

The first impression is that the TF practice has a negative impact on PATP, as the TFSP group has a lower mean, median and maximum than the TLSP group. On the other hand, TFSP has a higher minimum as well as lower SD and SE.[3] The accuracy of the mean as a model of data can be assessed by SD which is rather large in TLSP. The higher SD in TLSP means that there is a greater uncertainty concerning PATP in the TL projects. As a result, the descriptive statistics are, to a large extent, consistent with the results of the previously reported Experiment ACCOUNTING.

---

[3] Standard abbreviations for statistical values are presented in Box 5.1.

Table 5.36 Descriptive statistics for the percentage of acceptance tests passed (DV: PATP)

DV	Dev Tech	Mean (M)	Std.Dev. (SD)	Std.Err. (SE)	Max	Median (Mdn)	Min	95% CI Lower Bound	95% CI Upper Bound
PATP	TLSP	0.638	0.320	0.096	1.000	0.717	0.083	0.423	0.853
	TFSP	0.444	0.229	0.064	0.800	0.517	0.100	0.305	0.582

Listing 5.31: Related SPSS syntax

```
EXAMINE
  VARIABLES=PATP BY DevTech
  /PLOT BOXPLOT STEMLEAF HISTOGRAM NPPLOT
  /COMPARE GROUP
  /STATISTICS DESCRIPTIVES
  /CINTERVAL 95
  /MISSING LISTWISE
  /NOTOTAL.
```

A boxplot seemed a useful way to exhibit the results of the experiment and to learn more about the shape of the result distribution. It is shown in Fig. 5.3. Even a cursory reading of that boxplot reveals that the TLSP group performed better than the TFSP group. Moreover, the whiskers on the TLSP boxplot coming out of the box differ in length and show that the distribution is skewed to some extent. Fortunately, neither extreme points nor outliers can be located in Fig. 5.3.

Summarizing the descriptive statistics in APA format [12], it may be concluded that PATP in the TLSP projects ($M = 0.64$, $SD = 0.32$) and TFSP projects ($M = 0.44$, $SD = 0.23$) are different. To answer the question whether the impact of the TF practice on PATP is significant or not, statistical tests must be performed, preceded by the testing of the underlying assumptions.

5.2.1.2 Assumption Testing

An exploratory analysis will make it possible to check if the collected data follow the assumptions of parametric tests listed in Sect. 4.7.2. The assumption that the dependent variable (i.e. PATP) is measured at the interval or ratio level, as well as the assumption that the observations are independent of one another, is satisfied. The assumption of homogeneity of variance is tested using Levene's test (see Table 5.37). Levene's test is non-significant ($p > 0.05$) so we accept the null hypothesis that the variances in the experimental groups are roughly equal (i.e. not significantly different). It means that the assumption of homogeneity of variance is not violated. The assumption of normality is that our data have come from a population that has normal distribution. Objective tests of the distribution are the Kolmogorov–Smirnov and the Shapiro–Wilk tests presented in Table 5.38. The significance ($Sig.$) values are higher than the criterion of 0.05 (according to both the Kolmogorov–Smirnov and the Shapiro–Wilk test statistics; see Table 5.38) so the final assumption for parametric tests is satisfied.

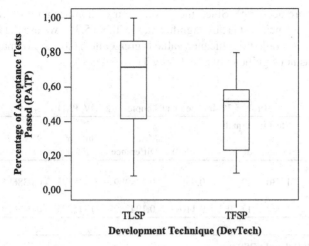

Fig. 5.3 Boxplot for the percentage of acceptance tests passed (DV: PATP) – preliminary analysis of Experiment SUBMISSION

Listing 5.32: Related SPSS syntax

```
EXAMINE
   VARIABLES=PATP BY DevTech /PLOT=BOXPLOT/STATISTICS=NONE/NOTOTAL.
```

Table 5.37 Levene's test of equality of error variances[1]

F	df1	df2	Sig.
1.382	1	22	0.252

[1] Dependent Variable: PATP. Design: Intercept+DevTech.

Table 5.38 Tests of normality

DevTech	Kolmogorov–Smirnov[1]			Shapiro–Wilk		
	Statistic	df[2]	Sig.	Statistic	df[2]	Sig.
TLSP	0.213	11	0.173	0.907	11	0.227
TFSP	0.164	13	0.200[3]	0.936	13	0.405

[1] Lilliefors Significance Correction.
[2] Degrees of freedom.
[3] This is a lower bound of the true significance.

5.2.1.3 Independent *t*-Test

Table 5.39 shows the results of the main statistics of the *t*-test. There are two rows in Table 5.39: one is used when there are equal variances, and the other is used when the variances differ (and some adjustments have to be made to the test statistic to make it more accurate). Since the assumption of homogeneity of variances is satisfied (i.e. Levene's test is non-significant, see Table 5.37), we use the first row of the table. The two-tailed significance value is greater than 0.05, so we may conclude that PATP was not significantly affected by TF.

Table 5.39 Independent samples test (DV: PATP)

	t	df	Sig. (2-tailed)	Mean Difference	Std.Err. Dif.(SE)	95% CI Lower	Upper
Equal variances assumed	1.730	22	0.098	0.194289	0.112338	−0.038685	0.427263
Equal variances not assumed	1.682	17.79	0.110	0.194289	0.115525	−0.048623	0.437202

t-test for Equality of Means

Listing 5.33: Related SPSS syntax

```
T–TEST
   GROUPS = DevTech(1  2)
   /MISSING = ANALYSIS
   /VARIABLES = PATP
   /CRITERIA = CI(.95)  .
```

The 95% confidence interval (95% CI) points to the fact that the boundaries within which 95 of 100 mean differences between TFSP and TLSP results lie are −0.04 and 0.43. Unless that interval contained zero, we might be confident that our samples were taken from different populations induced by our experimental manipulation (i.e. TF). However, that is not the case.

Calculating Effect Size

It is possible to convert a t-value into an effect size r-value on the basis of Eq. (5.13).[4] The necessary values of t and df are taken from Table 5.39:

$$r = \sqrt{\frac{t^2}{t^2 + df}} = \sqrt{\frac{1.73^2}{1.73^2 + 22}} = -0.35 \qquad (5.55)$$

The Effect Size Calculator by Wilson, the co-author of [151], returned a similar result ($r = 0.33$ and $d = 0.71$ calculated on the basis of $t = 1.730$, $n_{treatment} = 13$, $n_{comparison} = 11$). According to the guidelines by Kempenes et al. presented in Table 4.2, this can be considered a medium effect.

---

[4] By convention, a negative sign is assigned to the effect size when the treatment (i.e. experimental) group performs "worse" than the control group (see Box 5.5).

Summary

Reported PATP in the TFSP and TLSP groups were not significantly different ($t(22) = 1.73$, $p > 0.05$, $r = -0.35$) but the effect size, which represents a fairly large effect, indicates that the reason is a small sample size rather than lack of the effect of the experimental manipulation.

5.2.1.4 Analysis of Variance

Table 5.40 shows the main results of ANOVA. It becomes clear from the significance value $p = 0.098$, which is higher than 0.05, that there is no statistically significant difference in PATP between the TFSP and the TLSP group ($F(1, 22) = 2.99$, $p > 0.05$, partial eta-squared $\eta_p^2 = 0.12$). As presented in Table 5.40, the total amount of variance to be explained was 1.88 (Corrected Total), of which experimental manipulation accounted for 0.23 units, while 1.65 were unexplained. As a result, development technique (DevTech) is able to explain about 12% of the variance in the dependent variable (according to partial eta-squared $\eta_p^2 = 0.12$).

Table 5.40 Test of between-subjects effects (DV: PATP)

Source	Type III Sum of Squares	df	Mean Square	F	Significance	Partial Eta Squared
Corrected Model	0.225[1]	1	0.225	2.991	0.098	0.120
Intercept	6.969	1	6.969	92.678	0.000	0.808
DevTech	0.225	1	0.225	2.991	0.098	0.120
Error	1.654	22	0.075			
Total	8.688	24				
Corrected Total	1.879	23				

[1] R Squared = 0.120.

Listing 5.34: Related SPSS syntax (2 variants)

```
UNIANOVA
    PATP  BY DevTech
    /METHOD = SSTYPE(3)
    /INTERCEPT = INCLUDE
    /PRINT = DESCRIPTIVE ETASQ OPOWER HOMOGENEITY
    /CRITERIA = ALPHA(.05)
    /DESIGN = DevTech .

ONEWAY
    PATP  BY DevTech
    /STATISTICS DESCRIPTIVES EFFECTS HOMOGENEITY
    /MISSING ANALYSIS .
```

Calculating Effect Size

Rough estimations of effect size for ANOVA can be calculated on the basis of Eqs. (5.10) and (5.14):[5]

$$\eta = \sqrt{\frac{SS_M}{SS_T}} = \sqrt{\frac{0.225}{1.879}} = \sqrt{0.12} = -0.35 \qquad (5.56)$$

$$\eta_p{}^2 = \frac{SS_M}{SS_M + SS_R} = \frac{0.225}{1.879} = 0.12 \qquad (5.57)$$

Actually, the effect size measure r can also be calculated when ANOVA has been used and there is only 1 degree of freedom for the effect (two groups are being compared) [212]:

$$r = \sqrt{\frac{F(1, -)}{F(1, -) + df_R}} = \sqrt{\frac{2.991}{2.991 + 22}} = \sqrt{0.12} = -0.35 \qquad (5.58)$$

where $F(1, -)$ is the F for the effect with 1 degree of freedom, while df_R is degrees of freedom for the error term. The Effect Size Calculator by Wilson [151] returned a similar effect size ($r = 0.33$ and $d = 0.71$ calculated on the basis of $F = 2.991$, $n_{treatment} = 13$, $n_{comparison} = 11$). The obtained result is consistent with the result reported previously in Sect. "Calculating Effect Size" (p. 104).

We may conclude that 12% of the variance in PATP can be attributed to the independent variable. That represents a medium effect, according to the benchmarks for effect sizes presented in Sect. 4.7.5). Therefore, the effect of development technique on PATP is fairly substantial.

Summary

PATP, which is an external code quality indicator, was not significantly affected by the TF software development technique (the ANOVA test statistics: $F(1, 22) = 2.99$, $p = 0.10$, partial eta-squared $\eta_p{}^2 = 0.12$, $r = -0.35$). However, the effect size estimate indicates that there is a medium effect to be detected. Hence, it is worth considering if we might have not detected that effect because our sample was relatively small.

5.2.1.5 Analysis of Covariance

In further investigation, it is feasible to take into account the pre-test results of the subjects (i.e. grades obtained by the subjects after the preparation phase of the experiment, see Sect. 4.4.7). The grades were based on the quality of the delivered

---

[5] By convention, a negative sign is assigned to the effect size when the treatment (i.e. experimental) group performs "worse" than the control group, see Box 5.5.

software solutions as well as on whether the subjects delivered the software on time.
A traditional 2 to 5 grade system was used: 2.0 (fail), 3.0 (pass) and 3.5, 4.0, 4.5 and
5.0 (very good).

Additional Assumptions of ANCOVA

All the general one-way ANOVA assumptions presented in Sect. 5.2.1.2 apply to
ANCOVA. Moreover, additional ANCOVA assumptions are checked in this section.
Pre-test grade covariate (*Grade*), introduced in Sect. 3.3.3, is consistent with the
conceptual model presented in Sect. 3.2. The assumption that a covariate should
be a continuous or discrete variable is satisfied. The discussion concerning dummy
coding of categorical covariates is presented in Sect. 3.3.3. The assumption that the
covariate is measured before the experimental manipulation takes place is satisfied
as well. The next assumption is that the covariate is measured without error (as
reliably as possible). One threat to the validity of this assumption relates to the fact
that it is a subjective rather than objective measure (i.e. involves human judgement).
Another assumption is that there is a linear relationship between the dependent variable and the covariates for all groups. It was checked by examining the scatterplots
for each group and the scatterplots do not show evidence of non-linearity. The final
assumption (homogeneity of regression slopes) regards the relationship between the
dependent variable and the covariate for each of experimental groups. Homogeneity
of regression slopes was checked statistically with the help of the GLM procedure
with a customized model offered by SPSS (see Table 5.41). It appeared that there
is no statistically significant interaction between the treatment and the covariate
(DevTech*Grade), so this assumption is satisfied too. It is worth mentioning that
the assumption of equality of variance has not been violated, as the significance
value (Sig.) in Table 5.42 is greater than 0.05.

ANCOVA Results

After checking the ANCOVA assumptions, it is possible to perform the ANCOVA
test to explore the differences between our experimental groups.

The main ANCOVA results of between-subjects effects with *Grade* covariate are
presented in Table 5.43. We may conclude that there is no significant difference
in PATP between groups, after adjusting for grades obtained by subjects after the
preparation phase of the experiment ($F(1, 21) = 3.09$, $p = 0.09$, partial eta-squared
$\eta_p^2 = 0.13$). Hence, TF seems not to have a significant effect on PATP. Moreover,
according to partial eta-squared $\eta_p^2 = 0.13$, about 13% of the variance in the
dependent variable was explained by the independent variable (DevTech).

In Table 5.43, it is the covariate (*Grade*) that draws particular attention. It
turned out that there is a significant relationship between the covariate (*Grade*)
and the dependent variable (PATP) ($F(1, 21) = 5.08$, $p = 0.04$, partial eta-
squared $\eta_p^2 = 0.20$). Furthermore, according to partial eta-squared $\eta_p^2 = 0.20$, the
covariate explained about 20% of the variance in the dependent variable (PATP).

Table 5.41 Test of between-subjects effects with covariate and interaction to check homogeneity of regression (DV: PATP)

Source	Type III Sum of Squares	df	Mean Square	F	Sig.
Corrected Model	0.637[1]	3	0.212	3.416	0.037
Intercept	0.095	1	0.095	1.533	0.230
DevTech	0.059	1	0.059	0.943	0.343
Grade	0.411	1	0.411	6.612	0.018
DevTech*Grade	0.090	1	0.090	1.442	0.244
Error	1.242	20	0.062		
Total	8.688	24			
Corrected Total	1.879	23			

[1] R Squared = 0.339.

Listing 5.35: Related SPSS syntax

```
UNIANOVA
   PATP  BY DevTech  WITH Grade
   /METHOD = SSTYPE(3)
   /INTERCEPT = INCLUDE
   /CRITERIA = ALPHA(.05)
   /DESIGN = DevTech Grade DevTech*Grade .
```

Table 5.42 Levene's test of equality of error variances[1]

F	df1	df2	Sig.
0.499	1	22	0.487

[1] Dependent Variable: PATP. Design: Intercept+Grade+DevTech.

That highlights the potentially great influence of the initial differences between the subjects.

Calculating Effect Size

In ANCOVA we are able to calculate the effect of the independent variable (or variables in general) as well as the effect of the covariate(s). The effect size of the TF practice, as indicated by the corresponding partial eta-squared ($\eta_p{}^2$) value presented in Table 5.43, is 0.13. We may conclude that 13% of the variance in PATP can be attributed to the development method (as $\eta_p^2 = 0.13$). That represents a medium effect, keeping in line with the benchmarks for effect sizes introduced in Sect. 4.7.5). Therefore, the effect of development technique on PATP represents a fairly substantive finding.

For the effect of the covariate, we get partial eta-squared $\eta_p{}^2 = 0.195$, see Table 5.43. That represents a medium (but close to large) effect, according to

Table 5.43 Test of between-subjects effects with covariate (DV: PATP)

Source	Type III Sum of Squares	df	Mean Square	F	Sig.	Partial Eta Squared
Corrected Model	0.547[1]	2	0.274	4.313	0.027	0.291
Intercept	0.033	1	0.033	0.516	0.480	0.024
Grade	0.322	1	0.322	5.079	0.035	0.195
DevTech	0.196	1	0.196	3.086	0.094	0.128
Error	1.322	21	0.063			
Total	8.688	24				
Corrected Total	1.879	23				

[1] R Squared = 0.291.

Listing 5.36: Related SPSS syntax

```
UNIANOVA
    PATP  BY DevTech  WITH Grade
    /METHOD = SSTYPE(3)
    /INTERCEPT = INCLUDE
    /PRINT = DESCRIPTIVE ETASQ OPOWER HOMOGENEITY
    /CRITERIA = ALPHA(.05)
    /DESIGN = Grade DevTech .
```

---

benchmarks for effect sizes presented in Sect. 4.7.5). Therefore, as well as being statistically significant, this effect represents a fairly substantive finding.

We can calculate r^2 (usually called η^2) based on Eq. (5.10):[6]

$$r^2 = \frac{SS_M}{SS_T} = \frac{.196}{1.879} = 0.104 \longrightarrow r = -0.32 \tag{5.59}$$

Hence, taking into account the guidelines summarized in Table 4.2, that represents a medium effect.

It is worth mentioning that the Effect Size Calculator by Wilson [151] also returned $r = -0.32$ and $d = -0.68$ (calculated on the basis of treatment group mean = 0.4436, comparison group mean = 0.6379, $MS_R = 0.063$, $df_R = 21$ and the correlation between the covariate and the dependent variable $r_{CV*DV} = 0.432$).

Summary

Adjusting for pre-existing differences between the subjects provides a purer measure of the effect of TF and, therefore, the results reflect more precisely the effect

---

[6] By convention, a negative sign is assigned to the effect size when the treatment (i.e. experimental) group performs "worse" than the control group, see Box 5.5.

of the experimental manipulation. Preliminary checks were conducted as usual to ensure that there was no violation of the ANCOVA assumptions. After adjusting for the initial differences in grades between the subjects, there was no significant difference in PATP between the TFSP and the TLSP group ($F(1, 21) = 3.09$, $p = 0.09$, partial eta-squared $\eta_p{}^2 = 0.13$). It is consistent with the results obtained by means of ANOVA (see Sect. 5.2.1.4). Hence, we may conclude that PATP was not significantly affected by the TF practice.

There is a statistically significant relationship between the covariate (*Grade*) and the dependent variable (PATP). The covariate was statistically significant ($F(1, 21) = 5.08$, $p = 0.04$, partial eta-squared $\eta_p{}^2 = 0.20$), which indicates that pre-existing differences between the subjects (measured by pre-intervention grades) had a significant effect on PATP. According to partial eta squared, pre-intervention grades explained almost 20% of the total variance in the dependent variable. This represents a medium (but close to large) effect size.

The obtained results reinforce the previous finding from Experiment ACCOUNTING that the initial differences between subjects are even a more important predictor of their scores on the dependent variable (PATP) than development technique (DevTech). As mentioned before, that is consistent with the expectations of many researchers in the behavioural sciences [178]. The aforementioned differences between subjects should be taken into account by researchers as, even with randomization, there are usually some differences between groups. In Experiment SMELLS&LIBRARY each subject serves as his own control reducing the variance due to individual differences between the subjects.

5.2.2 Selective Analysis

Selective analysis, based on the selection criteria presented in Sect. 4.7.7, has the aim to minimize the threat of process conformance and relative difficulty of the TF practice (see Box 4.7.7). As a result, a selective analysis of 20 projects (11 TLSP and 9 TFSP) is conducted in this section. The experiment data are analysed with descriptive analysis and statistical tests.

5.2.2.1 Descriptive Statistics

The decision to remove the subjects who deviated obviously from the TF rules resulted in some changes in descriptive statistics, presented in Table 5.44 and Fig. 5.4.

Summarizing the descriptive statistics in APA format [12], it may be concluded that PATP in the TLSP projects ($M = 0.64$, SD = 0.32) and TFSP projects ($M = 0.48$, SD = 0.23) are different (see Table 5.44).

To answer the question whether the impact of the TF practice on PATP is significant or not, statistical tests must be performed.

Table 5.44 Descriptive statistics for the percentage of acceptance tests passed (DV: PATP) – selective analysis

DV	Dev. Tech.	Mean (M)	Std.Dev. (SD)	Std.Err. (SE)	Max	Median (Mdn)	Min	95% CI Lower Bound	Upper Bound
PATP	TLSP	0.638	0.320	0.096	1.000	0.717	0.083	0.423	0.853
	TFSP	0.480	0.226	0.075	0.800	0.517	0.150	0.306	0.653

Listing 5.37: Related SPSS syntax

```
EXAMINE
  VARIABLES=PATP BY DevTech
  /PLOT BOXPLOT STEMLEAF HISTOGRAM NPPLOT
  /COMPARE GROUP
  /STATISTICS DESCRIPTIVES
  /CINTERVAL 95
  /MISSING LISTWISE
  /NOTOTAL.
```

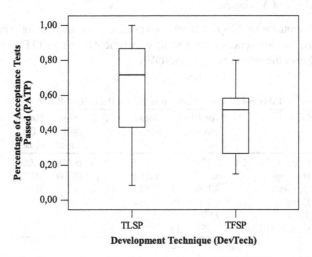

Fig. 5.4 Boxplot for the percentage of acceptance tests passed (DV: PATP) – selective analysis of Experiment SUBMISSION

Listing 5.38: Related SPSS syntax

```
EXAMINE
  VARIABLES=PATP BY DevTech /PLOT=BOXPLOT/STATISTICS=NONE/NOTOTAL.
```

5.2.2.2 Assumption Testing

Assumption testing was conducted beforehand with no serious violations noted. Table 5.45 shows the results of Levene's test, while Table 5.46 shows the results of normality tests. Both are non-significant ($p > 0.05$). Hence, the assumptions have not been broken.

Table 5.45 Levene's test of equality of error variances[1] – selective analysis

F	df1	df2	Sig.
1.427	1	18	0.248

[1] Dependent Variable: PATP. Design: Intercept+DevTech.

Table 5.46 Tests of normality – selective analysis

DevTech	Kolmogorov–Smirnov[1]			Shapiro–Wilk		
	Statistic	df[2]	Sig.	Statistic	df[2]	Sig.
TL	0.213	11	0.173	0.907	11	0.227
TF	0.232	9	0.178	0.924	9	0.430

[1] Lilliefors Significance Correction.
[2] Degrees of freedom.

5.2.2.3 Analysis of Variance

Once the assumptions of ANOVA have been checked, we may perform the ANOVA test to explore the differences between the experimental groups (TFSP and TLSP). Table 5.47 shows the main results of ANOVA.

Table 5.47 Test of between-subjects effects (DV: PATP)

Source	Type III Sum of Squares	df	Mean Square	F	Significance	Partial Eta Squared
Corrected Model	0.124[1]	1	.124	1.560	0.228	0.080
Intercept	6.182	1	6.182	77.785	0.000	0.812
DevTech	0.124	1	0.124	1.560	0.228	0.080
Error	1.430	18	0.079			
Total	7.977	20				
Corrected Total	1.554	19				

[1] R Squared = 0.080.

Listing 5.39: Related SPSS syntax

```
UNIANOVA
  PATP  BY DevTech
  /METHOD = SSTYPE(3)
  /INTERCEPT = INCLUDE
  /PRINT = DESCRIPTIVE ETASQ OPOWER HOMOGENEITY
  /CRITERIA = ALPHA(.05)
  /DESIGN = DevTech .
```

The significance value $p = 0.23$ is higher than 0.05 so there is no statistically significant difference in PATP between the TFSP and the TLSP group ($F(1, 18) = 1.56$, $p > 0.05$, partial eta-squared $\eta_p^2 = 0.08$).

Calculating Effect Size

Partial eta-squared ($\eta_p^2 = 0.08$), presented in Table 5.47, is a rough estimation of effect size. It means that about 8% of the variance in the dependent variable (PATP) can be attributed to the development method. That represents a medium effect, according to the benchmarks for effect sizes presented in Sect. 4.7.5.

We can calculate r^2, usually called η^2, on the basis of Eq. (5.10):[7]

$$r^2 = \frac{SS_M}{SS_T} = \frac{.124}{1.554} = 0.08 \longrightarrow r = -0.28 \qquad (5.60)$$

That represents a medium effect, in accordance with the guidelines summarized in Table 4.2.

The Effect Size Calculation Program by Wilson [151] returned a similar effect size ($r = 0.27$ and $d = 0.56$ based on $F = 1.560$, $n_{treatment} = 9$, $n_{comparison} = 11$).

Summary

The external code quality indicated by PATP was not significantly affected by the TF software development practice (the ANOVA test statistics: $F(1, 18) = 1.56$, $p = 0.23$, partial eta-squared $\eta_p^2 = 0.08$, $r = -0.28$). The effect size estimate indicates that there is a medium effect to be detected. It seems that the effect size was slightly reduced (in comparison to the preliminary analysis of all the projects performed in Sect. 5.2.1.4) due to the removal of the subjects who made serious deviations from the TF practice.

5.2.2.4 Analysis of Covariance

In further investigation, it is feasible to take into account the pre-test results that can influence our dependent variable as mentioned in Sect. 5.2.1.5. Assumption testing was conducted beforehand in Sect. "Additional Assumptions of ANCOVA" (p. 113).

Additional Assumptions of ANCOVA

All the general assumptions presented in Section 4.7.2 apply to ANCOVA. However, additional ANCOVA assumptions should be checked as well. The pre-test grade covariate (*Grade*) introduced in Sect. 3.3.3 is consistent with the conceptual model presented in Sect. 3.2. The assumption that a covariate should be a continuous or discrete variable is satisfied. The assumption that the covariate is measured before the experimental manipulation takes place is met too. The next assumption is that the covariate is measured without error (as reliably as possible). However, as mentioned before, it is difficult to ensure reliability of the covariate, since grades involve

---

[7] By convention, a negative sign is assigned to the effect size when the treatment (i.e. experimental) group performs "worse" than the control group (see Box 5.5).

Table 5.48 Test of between-subjects effects with covariate and interaction to check homogeneity of regression (DV: PATP)

Source	Type III Sum of Squares	df	Mean Square	F	Sig.
Corrected Model	0.496[1]	3	0.165	2.496	0.097
Intercept	0.073	1	0.073	1.106	0.309
DevTech	0.073	1	0.073	1.110	0.308
Grade	0.369	1	0.369	5.580	0.031
DevTech*Grade	0.097	1	0.097	1.459	0.245
Error	1.059	16	0.066		
Total	7.977	20			
Corrected Total	1.554	19			

[1] R Squared $= 0.319$.

Listing 5.40: Related SPSS syntax

```
UNIANOVA
    PATP  BY DevTech   WITH Grade
    /METHOD = SSTYPE(3)
    /INTERCEPT = INCLUDE
    /CRITERIA = ALPHA(.05)
    /DESIGN = DevTech Grade DevTech*Grade  .
```

Table 5.49 Levene's test of equality of error variances[1]

F	df1	df2	Sig.
0.837	1	18	0.372

[1] Dependent Variable: PATP. Design: Intercept+Grade+DevTech.

human judgement. That can be seen as a threat to validity. Another assumption is that there is a linear relationship between the dependent variable and the covariates for all groups. This was checked by examining the scatterplots for each group. The final assumption (homogeneity of regression) concerns the relationship between the dependent variable and the covariate for each of experimental groups. It was checked statistically with the help of the GLM procedure with a customized model offered by SPSS (see Table 5.48). It appeared that there is no statistically significant interaction between the treatment and the covariate (DevTech $*$ $Grade$), so this assumption is satisfied too. It is worth mentioning that the assumption of the equality of error variances has not been violated, as the significance value ($Sig.$) in Table 5.49 is greater than 0.05.

ANCOVA Results

Once the ANCOVA assumptions have been checked, it is possible to perform the ANCOVA test to explore the differences between the experimental groups, as shown in Table 5.50.

Table 5.50 Test of between-subjects effects with covariate (DV: PATP) – selective analysis

Source	Type III Sum of Squares	df	Mean Square	F	Sig.	Partial Eta Squared
Corrected Model	0.399[1]	2	0.200	2.935	0.080	0.257
Intercept	0.021	1	0.021	0.311	0.584	0.018
Grade	0.275	1	0.275	4.047	0.060	0.192
DevTech	0.074	1	0.074	1.092	0.311	0.060
Error	1.155	17	0.068			
Total	7.977	20				
Corrected Total	1.554	19				

[1] R Squared = 0.257.

Listing 5.41: Related SPSS syntax

```
UNIANOVA
   PATP  BY DevTech  WITH Grade
   /METHOD = SSTYPE(3)
   /INTERCEPT = INCLUDE
   /PRINT = DESCRIPTIVE ETASQ OPOWER HOMOGENEITY
   /CRITERIA = ALPHA(.05)
   /DESIGN = Grade DevTech .
```

We may conclude that there is no significant difference in PATP between the groups (TFSP and TLSP), after adjusting for grades obtained by the subjects after the preparation phase of the experiment, as well as after excluding the subjects who violated the TF criteria mentioned in Section 4.7.7 ($F(1, 18) = 1.09$, $p = 0.31$, partial eta-squared $\eta_p^2 = 0.06$).

Calculating Effect Size

The effect size of the TF practice, as indicated by the corresponding partial eta-squared (η_p^2) value presented in Table 5.50, is 0.06. Hence, we may conclude that about 6% of the variance in PATP can be attributed to DevTech (i.e. development method). That represents a medium effect, according to the benchmarks for effect sizes presented in Sect. 4.7.5.

We can calculate r^2 on the basis of Eq. (5.10):[8]

$$r^2 = \frac{SS_M}{SS_T} = \frac{.074}{1.554} = 0.05 \longrightarrow r = -0.22 \tag{5.61}$$

Hence, relying on the guidelines summarized in Table 4.2, that represents a medium effect.

---

[8] By convention, a negative sign is assigned to the effect size when the treatment (i.e. experimental) group performs "worse" than the control group (see Box 5.5).

The Effect Size Calculator by Wilson returned a similar effect size ($r = -0.25$ and $d = -0.52$ calculated on the basis of treatment group mean = 0.4796, comparison group mean = 0.6379, $MS_R = 0.068$, $df_R = 17$ and the correlation between the covariate and the dependent variable $r_{CV*DV} = 0.457$).

For the effect of the covariate, we have obtained partial eta-squared $\eta_p^2 = 0.192$ (see Table 5.43). That represents a medium (but close to large) effect, according to the benchmarks for effect sizes presented in Sect. 4.7.5. Therefore, although not statistically significant, this effect represents a fairly substantive finding.

Summary

Adjusting for pre-existing differences between the subjects, as well as the excluding of the subjects who made serious deviations from the TF practice, gives us a purer measure of the effect of TF. Hence, the results reflect more precisely the effect of the experimental manipulation. Preliminary checks were conducted as usual to ensure whether there was no violation of the ANCOVA assumptions. The main effect of TF remained non-significant ($F(1, 17) = 1.09$, $p = 0.31$, partial eta-squared $\eta_p^2 = 0.06$) after adjusting for the pre-test results and when subjects who made serious deviations from the TF rules were removed. The covariate (*Grade*) became non-significant ($F(1, 17) = 4.05$, $p = 0.06$, partial eta-squared $\eta_p^2 = 0.19$) but the effect size of the covariate still is substantial.

It is intriguing, however, that the effect size of TF became smaller in comparison to the preliminary analysis of all the projects performed in Sect. 5.2.1.4. This observation shows that the process conformance threat can be a serious threat to the validity of the findings.

5.3 Analysis of Experiment SMELLS&LIBRARY

The same hypothesis $H_{0,\text{PATP,TLSP/TFSP}}^{\text{SMELLS\&LIBRARY}}$, regarding the difference in PATP between the projects using the TLSP and TFSP software development techniques, is evaluated in Experiment SMELLS&LIBRARY. A preliminary analysis of all 27 projects is conducted in Sect. 5.3.1, while a selective analysis of 22 projects (selected on the basis of the selection criteria explained in Sect. 4.7.7) is presented in Sect. 5.3.2. The experiment data are analysed with descriptive analysis and statistical tests.

In Experiment SMELLS&LIBRARY, since the subjects are their own control, the experimental group (TFSP) is perfectly matched with the control group (TLSP). The advantages and disadvantages of repeated measures experimental design, used in Experiment SMELLS&LIBRARY, are reported in Sect. 1.2.2.4. As a result, covariates (mentioned in the conceptual model in Sect. 3.2) are not additionally included in the analysis of Experiment SMELLS&LIBRARY, as each subject serves as his own control due to the aforesaid experimental design.

5.3.1 Preliminary Analysis

The descriptive statistics, presented in Sect. 5.3.1.1, is followed by assumption testing in Sect. 5.3.1.2 and statistical analysis in Sect. 5.3.1.3.

5.3.1.1 Descriptive Statistics

The descriptive statistics of gathered experimental results are summarized in Table 5.51. The TF development practice seems to have little impact on PATP, because similar means, medians and 95% confidence intervals were obtained in both projects (P3 and P4), also when the TLSP and TFSP results were combined across projects.

Table 5.51 Descriptive statistics for the percentage of acceptance tests passed (DV: PATP)

DV	Dev. Tech.	Mean (M)	Std. Dev. (SD)	Std. Error (SE)	Max	Median (Mdn)	Min	95% CI Lower Bound	95% CI Upper Bound
PATP in P3	TLSP	0.616	0.231	0.062	0.882	0.657	0.275	0.483	0.750
	TFSP	0.646	0.155	0.043	0.863	0.647	0.275	0.552	0.739
PATP in P4	TLSP	0.484	0.274	0.076	0.907	0.537	0.093	0.319	0.650
	TFSP	0.524	0.266	0.071	0.926	0.417	0.222	0.370	0.678
PATP combined	TLSP	0.553	0.257	0.049	0.907	0.556	0.093	0.451	0.654
	TFSP	0.582	0.224	0.043	0.926	0.608	0.222	0.494	0.671

Listing 5.42: Related SPSS syntax

```
EXAMINE
   VARIABLES=P3PATP P4PATP BY DevTech
   /PLOT BOXPLOT STEMLEAF HISTOGRAM NPPLOT
   /COMPARE GROUP
   /STATISTICS DESCRIPTIVES
   /CINTERVAL 95
   /MISSING LISTWISE
   /NOTOTAL.
```

Boxplots in Figs. 5.5 and 5.6 present the results of the experiment and the shape of the distribution. In course of the visual inspection of the figures, minimal differences come to the fore.

Summarizing descriptive statistics for project P3 in APA format [12], it may be concluded that PATP in the TLSP projects ($M = 0.62$, $SD = 0.23$) and TFSP projects ($M = 0.65$, $SD = 0.16$) are similar with only slight differences. PATP in the TLSP projects ($M = 0.52$, $SD = 0.27$) and TFSP projects ($M = 0.48$, $SD = 0.27$) are similar as well. Hence, it is no wonder that the combined TLSP results ($M = 0.55$, $SD = 0.26$, $SE = 0.05$, 95% CI between 0.45 and 0.65) and TFSP results ($M = 0.58$, $SD = 0.22$, $SE = 0.04$, 95% CI between 0.49 and 0.67) across the projects P3 and P4 are similar too. In order to answer the question whether the impact of the TF practice on PATP is significant or not, statistical tests are performed

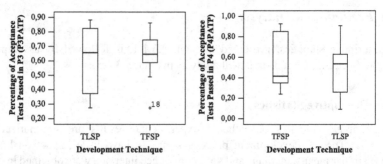

Fig. 5.5 Boxplots for the percentage of acceptance tests passed (PATP) in projects P3 and P4 – preliminary analysis of Experiment SMELLS&LIBRARY

Listing 5.43: Related SPSS syntax

```
EXAMINE
  VARIABLES=P3PATP BY DevTech
  /PLOT=BOXPLOT
  /STATISTICS=NONE/NOTOTAL.
```

Listing 5.44: Related SPSS syntax

```
EXAMINE
  VARIABLES=P4PATP BY DevTech
  /PLOT=BOXPLOT
  /STATISTICS=NONE/NOTOTAL.
```

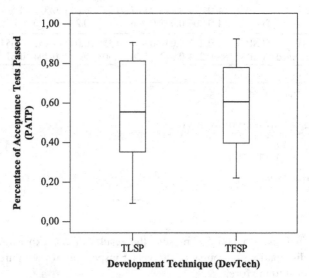

Fig. 5.6 Boxplots for the percentage of acceptance tests passed (PATP) in TLSP and TFSP (combined across projects P3 and P4) – preliminary analysis of Experiment SMELLS&LIBRARY

Listing 5.45: Related SPSS syntax

```
EXAMINE
  VARIABLES=PATPinTL PATPinTF /COMPARE VARIABLE/PLOT=BOXPLOT/STATISTICS=NONE
  /NOTOTAL
  /MISSING=LISTWISE.
```

in Sect. 5.3.1.3, preceded by the testing of the underlying assumptions, which might have been broken, carried out in Sect. 5.3.1.2. Furthermore, the issues related to the effect of carry-over are discussed in Sect. 4.7.3.

5.3.1.2 Assumption Testing

The assumption testing starts with the exploratory analysis of the collected data in order to check whether they follow the assumptions of parametric tests listed in Sect. 4.7.2.

The assumption of normality is tested by means of the Kolmogorov–Smirnov and the Shapiro–Wilk tests. The significance values are higher than the criterion of 0.05 according to the Kolmogorov–Smirnov test statistics but equal to the aforementioned criterion according to the Shapiro–Wilk test statistics (see Table 5.52).

Table 5.52 Tests of normality

| DevTech | Kolmogorov–Smirnov[1] | | | Shapiro–Wilk | | |
	Statistic	df[2]	Sig.	Statistic	df[2]	Sig.
TL	0.150	27	0.124	0.924	27	0.050
TF	0.099	27	0.200[3]	0.936	27	0.097

[1] Lilliefors Significance Correction.
[2] Degrees of freedom.
[3] This is a lower bound of the true significance.

The Shapiro–Wilk test is one of the best currently available procedures for testing normality [180, 241]. It is also worth mentioning that the t-test is robust, to some extent, against violations of certain assumptions (e.g. the normality assumption). However, to err on the safe side, a non-parametric analysis is conducted in Sect. 5.3.1.3.

5.3.1.3 Wilcoxon Signed-Rank Test

The non-parametric Wilcoxon signed-rank test is used instead of its parametric counterpart, i.e. the dependent t-test (see Table 5.53). The subjects have two scores (each obtained under one of the two experimental treatments). A difference is computed for each subject by subtracting the subject's score in one treatment from his score in another treatment. To control the order effects, the assignment of the treatments is random.

We report only one of the test statistics presented in Table 5.53, i.e. the one that has the lowest value ($T^- = 182.00$). On the basis of the Wilcoxon signed-rank test, we may conclude that there was no significant difference between the TLSP (Mdn = 0.56) and TFSP (Mdn = 0.61) experimental groups ($T = 182.00$, $p = 0.873$).

Table 5.53 Wilcoxon signed-rank test (ranks and test statistics)

Ranks PATPinTF – PATPinTL	N	Mean Rank	Sum of Ranks
Negative Ranks	17[1]	11.53	196.00
Positive Ranks	10[2]	18.20	182.00
Ties	0[3]		
Total	27		

[1] PATPinTF < PATPinTL.
[2] PATPinTF > PATPinTL.
[3] PATPinTF = PATPinTL.

Test Statistics	PATPinTF – PATPinTL
Z	−0.168[1]
Asymp. Sig. (2-tailed)	0.866
Exact Sig. (2-tailed)	0.873
Exact Sig. (1-tailed)	0.437

[1] Based on positive ranks.

Listing 5.46: Related SPSS syntax

```
NPAR TEST
   /WILCOXON=PATPinTL WITH PATPinTF (PAIRED)
   /SIGN= PATPinTL WITH PATPinTF (PAIRED)
   /MH= PATPinTL WITH PATPinTF (PAIRED)
   /STATISTICS DESCRIPTIVES
   /MISSING ANALYSIS
   /METHOD=EXACT TIMER(5).
```

Calculating Effect Size

According to Field [76], the effect size for the Wilcoxon singed-rank test can be calculated in a similar manner as for the Mann–Whitney test (see Eq. (5.3) on p. 71).

$$r = \sqrt{\frac{Z^2}{N}} = \sqrt{\frac{(-0.168)^2}{54}} = 0.02 \qquad (5.62)$$

However, it is worth mentioning that N is the number of observations, not the number of subjects.

As a double-check, i.e. to assure accuracy of the above calculation of effect size estimation, an alternative $r_{equivalent}$ approach, by Rosenthal and Rubin [213], is used. On the basis of the $r_{equivalent}$ approach, one-tailed $p = 0.437$ and $N = 54$ can be used to find $t(52) = 0.1594$ (T Calculator from http://www.stat.tamu.edu/west/applets/tdemo.html can be helpful) and $r_{equivalent}$ can be calculated from the following equation [213]:

$$r_{\text{equivalent}} = \sqrt{\frac{t^2}{t^2 + (N - 2)}} = 0.02 \qquad (5.63)$$

In conclusion, this effect is consistent with the earlier result and represents a very small effect.

Summary

The percentage of acceptance tests passed (PATP) measured in the TLSP (Mdn = 0.56) and TFSP experimental group (Mdn = 0.61) was not significantly different (the Wilcoxon test statistics: $T = 182.00$, $p > 0.05$, $r = 0.02$). Moreover, the effect size estimate ($r = 0.02$) indicates that there is a tiny, i.e. not substantive, effect of TF on PATP. It is noteworthy that the findings are true on condition that the carry-over effect has not altered them seriously [222] (see Sect. 4.7.3).

5.3.2 Selective Analysis

Thanks to the SmartSensor Eclipse plugin (which is an improved ActivitySensor plugin used in Experiment SUBMISSION) it was possible to exclude from the analysis, performed in this section, 5 subjects (4 subjects due to criterion C1 and 1 subject due to criterion C2 described in Sect. 4.7.7) who made serious deviations from the TF rules.

5.3.2.1 Descriptive Statistics

The decision to remove subjects who deviated seriously from the TF rules resulted in some changes in descriptive statistics (see Table 5.54). Boxplots presented in Figs. 5.7 and 5.8 display the results of the experiment, as well as the shape of the distribution.

PATP in the TLSP projects ($M = 0.58$, SD = 0.25, SE = 0.05, 95% CI is between 0.47 and 0.69) and the TFSP projects ($M = 0.63$, SD = 0.21, SE = 0.05, 95% CI is between 0.54 and 0.72) are similar with slightly higher results of the TF projects. To answer the question whether the impact of the TF practice on PATP is significant or not, statistical tests are performed, preceded by the testing of the underlying assumptions.

5.3.2.2 Assumption Testing

In order to check whether the collected data follow the assumptions of parametric tests listed in Sect. 4.7.2, an exploratory analysis has to be performed.

The assumption of normality is tested by means of the Kolmogorov–Smirnov and the Shapiro–Wilk tests. In spite of different results of the Kolmogorov–Smirnov and the Shapiro–Wilk test statistics presented in Table 5.55, we may conclude that the normality assumption is not satisfied as the Shapiro–Wilk test, which is the

Table 5.54 Descriptive statistics for the percentage of acceptance tests passed (DV: PATP)

DV	Dev. Tech.	Mean (M)	Std. Dev. (SD)	Std. Error (SE)	Max	Median (Mdn)	Min	95% CI Lower Bound	Upper Bound
PATP in P3	TLSP	0.655	0.238	0.075	0.882	0.765	0.275	0.484	0.825
	TFSP	0.650	0.161	0.046	0.863	0.657	0.275	0.548	0.752
PATP in P4	TLSP	0.517	0.259	0.075	0.907	0.546	0.185	0.353	0.681
	TFSP	0.607	0.264	0.084	0.926	0.611	0.241	0.418	0.797
PATP combined	TLSP	0.580	0.254	0.054	0.907	0.565	0.185	0.467	0.692
	TFSP	0.631	0.210	0.045	0.926	0.657	0.241	0.538	0.724

Listing 5.47: Related SPSS syntax

```
EXAMINE
  VARIABLES=P3PATP P4PATP BY DevTech
  /PLOT BOXPLOT STEMLEAF HISTOGRAM NPPLOT
  /COMPARE GROUP
  /STATISTICS DESCRIPTIVES
  /CINTERVAL 95
  /MISSING LISTWISE
  /NOTOTAL.
```

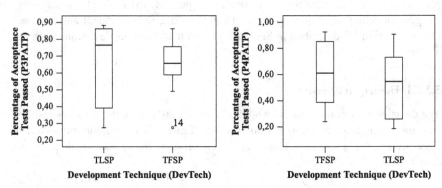

Fig. 5.7 Boxplots for the percentage of acceptance tests passed (PATP) in projects P3 and P4 – selective analysis of Experiment SMELLS&LIBRARY

Listing 5.48: Related SPSS syntax

```
EXAMINE
  VARIABLES=P3PATP BY DevTech
  /PLOT=BOXPLOT
  /STATISTICS=NONE/NOTOTAL.
```

Listing 5.49: Related SPSS syntax

```
EXAMINE
  VARIABLES=P4PATP BY DevTech
  /PLOT=BOXPLOT
  /STATISTICS=NONE/NOTOTAL.
```

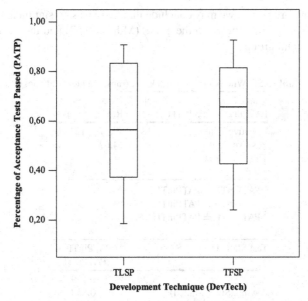

Fig. 5.8 Boxplots for the percentage of acceptance tests passed (PATP) in TLSP and TFSP (combined across projects P3 and P4) – selective analysis of Experiment SMELLS&LIBRARY

Listing 5.50: Related SPSS syntax

```
EXAMINE
   VARIABLES=PATPinTL PATPinTF  /COMPARE VARIABLE/PLOT=BOXPLOT/STATISTICS=NONE
   /NOTOTAL
   /MISSING=LISTWISE .
```

Table 5.55 Tests of normality

DevTech	Kolmogorov–Smirnov[1]			Shapiro–Wilk		
	Statistic	df[2]	Sig.	Statistic	df[2]	Sig.
TL	0.175	22	0.077	0.899	22	0.029
TF	0.116	22	0.200[3]	0.935	22	0.157

[1] Lilliefors Significance Correction.
[2] Degrees of freedom.
[3] This is a lower bound of the true significance.

preferred test of normality because of its good power properties [180, 241], is statistically significant ($p < 0.05$). Since the normality assumption is not satisfied, a non-parametric analysis is performed in Sect. 5.3.2.3.

5.3.2.3 Wilcoxon Signed-Rank Test

The use of the non-parametric Wilcoxon signed-rank test (see Table 5.56) is justified by the fact that the normality assumption has not been satisfied. On the basis of the

Wilcoxon signed-rank test, we may conclude that there was no significant difference ($T = 121.00$, $p = 0.874$) between the TLSP (Mdn = 0.57) and the TFSP (Mdn = 0.66) experimental groups.

Table 5.56 Wilcoxon signed-rank test (ranks and test statistics)

Ranks PATPinTF – PATPinTL	N	Mean Rank	Sum of Ranks
Negative Ranks	13[1]	9.31	121.00
Positive Ranks	9[2]	14.67	132.00
Ties	0[3]		
Total	22		

[1] PATPinTF < PATPinTL.
[2] PATPinTF > PATPinTL.
[3] PATPinTF = PATPinTL.

Test Statistics	PATPinTF – PATPinTL
Z	−0.179[1]
Asymp. Sig. (2-tailed)	0.858
Exact Sig. (2-tailed)	0.874
Exact Sig. (1-tailed)	0.437

[1] Based on negative ranks.

Listing 5.51: Related SPSS syntax

```
NPAR TEST
    /WILCOXON=PATPinTL   WITH PATPinTF (PAIRED)
    /SIGN= PATPinTL   WITH PATPinTF (PAIRED)
    /MH= PATPinTL   WITH PATPinTF (PAIRED)
    /STATISTICS DESCRIPTIVES
    /MISSING ANALYSIS
    /METHOD=EXACT TIMER(5).
```

Calculating Effect Size

Statistical significance tells us nothing about whether the effect is of practical importance, i.e. substantive. As suggested by Field [76], to discover whether the effect is substantive, we calculated the effect size for the Wilcoxon singed-rank test based on Eq. (5.3):

$$r = \sqrt{\frac{Z^2}{N}} = \sqrt{\frac{(-0.179)^2}{44}} = 0.027 \tag{5.64}$$

where N is the number of observations, not the number of subjects. This effect is very small and, as such, it represents a trivial finding.

As a double-check, an alternative $r_{\text{equivalent}}$ approach, by Rosenthal and Rubin [213], to effect size estimation is used. Following this approach, one-tailed $p = 0.437$ and $N = 44$ can be used to find $t(42) = 0.1596$ and $r_{\text{equivalent}}$ can be calculated from the following equation [213]:

$$r_{\text{equivalent}} = \sqrt{\frac{t^2}{t^2 + (N - 2)}} = 0.025 \qquad (5.65)$$

This effect is very small and, as such, it represents a trivial finding.

Summary

The percentage of acceptance tests passed (PATP) measured in the TLSP (Mdn = 0.57) and TFSP experimental group (Mdn = 0.66) was not significantly different (the Wilcoxon test statistics: $T = 121.00$, $p > 0.05$, $r = 0.03$). Moreover, the effect size estimate ($r = 0.03$) indicates that there is a tiny, that is not substantive, effect of TF on PATP. It is noteworthy that the findings are true assuming that the carry-over effect has not altered them seriously [222] (see Sect. 4.7.3).

5.4 Instead of Summary

It is crucial to give a single, reliable and unbiased conclusion whether the effect of TF on PATP has both the statistical, as well as practical, importance. However, this can be difficult as the results of the analysed empirical studies differ. Moreover, any subjective review or narrative summary of the obtained results may be biased. Therefore, a statistical technique called meta-analysis, based on effect sizes (which indicate practical significance [237, 243]) and p-values (which reflect statistical significance), is used in Chap. 9 to draw the final conclusion.

Chapter 6
Effect on the Number of Acceptance Tests Passed per Hour

If it's worth building, it's worth testing.
If it's not worth testing, why are you
wasting your time working on it?

Scott W. Ambler [11]

In Experiment ACCOUNTING, the programming time was fixed for all the subjects, while in Experiments SUBMISSION and SMELLS&LIBRARY, the development time was measured by means of Eclipse plugin. One serious threat to the analysis performed in Chap. 5 is that the subjects in Experiments SUBMISSION and SMELLS&LIBRARY might have spent different times developing software in spite of the same deadlines. Therefore, an additional analysis of the impact of TF on the number of acceptance tests passed per hour (NATPPH), carried out in this section, is justified.

The number of acceptance tests passed (NATP) was used as an indicator of external code quality by several researchers, e.g. George and Williams [87, 88], Pančur et al. [201], Madeyski [157], Gupta and Jalote [94]. Moreover, as pointed out in Sect. 1.3.3, NATP per unit of effort can be considered an indicator of software development productivity. In contrast to LOC per unit of effort (which is a common productivity measure) NATP per unit of effort (e.g. the aforementioned NATPPH) takes into account the functionality and quality of software products developed in a given time frame.

As mentioned in Sect. 4.7.7, to keep the book concise and, simultaneously, present the most essential results, this chapter presents only the results of the final (i.e. selective) analysis, while the preliminary analysis of all the projects is not included.

6.1 Analysis of Experiment Accounting

For Experiment ACCOUNTING, where development time was equal for all subjects, the impact of development techniques on NATPPH will be exactly the same as on PATP (see Sect. 5.1). Therefore, only descriptive statistics, final statistical significance values and effect sizes are presented.

L. Madeyski, *Test-Driven Development*,
DOI 10.1007/978-3-642-04288-1_6, © Springer-Verlag Berlin Heidelberg 2010

6.1.1 Descriptive Statistics

The descriptive statistics of the experimental results are summarized in Table 6.1.

Table 6.1 Descriptive statistics for the number of acceptance tests passed per hour (DV: NATPPH)

DV	Dev Tech	Mean (*M*)	Std. Dev. (SD)	Std. Error (SE)	Median Max	(Mdn)	Min	95% CI Lower bound	Upper bound
NATPPH	TLSP	1.485	0.858	0.162	3.083	1.792	0.000	1.152	1.818
	TFSP	1.092	0.644	0.148	1.917	1.333	0.000	0.782	1.403
	TLPP	1.586	0.821	0.148	2.667	1.750	0.000	1.285	1.887
	TFPP	1.062	0.735	0.141	2.667	1.000	0.000	0.770	1.353

Listing 6.1: Related SPSS syntax

```
EXAMINE
   VARIABLES=NATPPH BY DevTech
   /PLOT BOXPLOT STEMLEAF HISTOGRAM NPPLOT
   /COMPARE GROUP
   /STATISTICS DESCRIPTIVES
   /CINTERVAL 95
   /MISSING LISTWISE
   /NOTOTAL.
```

On the basis of the descriptive statistics, the TF development technique seems to have a negative impact on NATPPH as the TF groups (TFSP and TFPP) have lower NATPPH means, medians and confidence intervals than the TL groups (TLSP and TLPP). A positive effect of PP is not visible as the TFSP vs. TFPP and TLSP vs. TLPP results do not differ much. Higher SD values for the TL groups (TLSP and TLPP) mean that there is greater uncertainty in the TL projects. The difference in SD between the TL and the TF projects is more visible in solo projects (TLSP vs. TFSP) than in pairs (TLPP vs. TFPP).

Figure 6.1 presents the boxplot of the distributions of NATPPH for the four experimental groups and suggests that there are differences, with the TL groups (TLSP and TLPP) performing better than the TF groups (TFSP and TFPP). It shows also that the distribution is skewed to some extent, as the whiskers on the TLPP and TFPP boxplots coming out of the boxes differ in length. Neither the extreme points nor the outliers can be located in Fig. 6.1.

Summarizing the descriptive statistics in APA format, it may by concluded that NATPPH in the TFSP projects ($M = 1.09$, SD $= 0.64$) and TFPP projects ($M = 1.06$, SD $= 0.74$) are similar to each other but lower than in the TLSP projects ($M = 1.49$, SD $= 0.86$) and TLPP projects ($M = 1.59$, SD $= 0.82$).

6.1.2 Non-Parametric Analysis

There is no need to repeat the analysis of Experiment ACCOUNTING, as the results will be exactly the same as presented in Sect. 5.1.2.3 and 5.1.2.4. Hence, we only

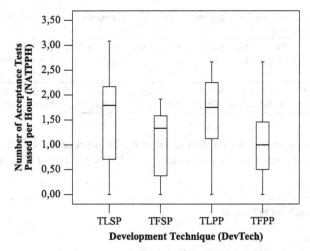

Fig. 6.1 Boxplot for the number of acceptance tests passed per hour (DV: NATPPH)—selective analysis of Experiment ACCOUNTING

Listing 6.2: Related SPSS syntax

```
EXAMINE
    VARIABLES=NATPPH BY DevTech /PLOT=BOXPLOT/STATISTICS=NONE/NOTOTAL.
```

---

conclude (on the basis of the rank-transformed analysis of covariance) that the difference between TFSP and TLSP is not statistically significant ($t(45) = 1.30$, $p = 0.196$), while the effect size estimation is $r_{contrast1 \text{ (TLSP vs. TFSP)}} = -0.19$.

6.2 Analysis of Experiment SUBMISSION

Selective analysis of 20 projects (11 TLSP and 9 TFSP) has been performed in this section on the basis of the selection criteria presented in Sect. 4.7.7.

6.2.1 Descriptive Statistics

The descriptive statistics of the collected experimental results are presented in Table 6.2 and Fig. 6.2. Summarizing the descriptive statistics in APA format [12], we can conclude that NATPPH in the TLSP group ($M = 0.50$, SD $= 0.29$) and the TFSP experimental group ($M = 0.37$, SD $= 0.09$) are different. The TFSP group has a higher minimum and lower mean, median, SD as well as SE than the TLSP group. A much higher SD in the TLSP group than in the TFSP group means that there is greater uncertainty concerning NATPPH in the TLSP projects.

Table 6.2 Descriptive statistics for the number of acceptance tests passed per hour (DV: NATPPH)—selective analysis

DV	Dev. Tech.	Mean (*M*)	Std.Dev. (SD)	Std. Error (SE)	Max	Median (Mdn)	Min	95% *CI* Lower bound	Upper bound
NATPPH	TLSP	0.503	0.294	0.089	0.998	0.503	0.126	0.306	0.701
	TFSP	0.367	0.091	0.030	0.552	0.346	0.262	0.298	0.437

To answer the question whether the impact of the TF practice on NATPPH is significant or not, statistical tests are performed, preceded by the testing of the underlying assumptions.

Listing 6.3: Related SPSS syntax

```
EXAMINE
    VARIABLES=NATPPH BY DevTech
    /PLOT BOXPLOT STEMLEAF HISTOGRAM NPPLOT
    /COMPARE GROUP
    /STATISTICS DESCRIPTIVES
    /CINTERVAL 95
    /MISSING LISTWISE
    /NOTOTAL.
```

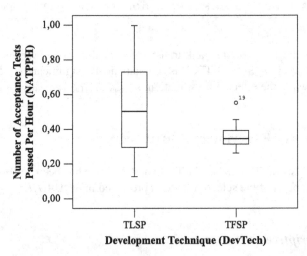

Fig. 6.2 Boxplot for the number of acceptance tests passed per hour (DV: NATPPH)—selective analysis of Experiment SUBMISSION

Listing 6.4: Related SPSS syntax

```
EXAMINE
    VARIABLES=NATPPH BY DevTech  /PLOT=BOXPLOT/STATISTICS=NONE/NOTOTAL.
```

6.2.2 Assumption Testing

Exploratory analysis of the collected data, necessary to check if the assumptions of parametric tests (listed in Sect. 4.7.2) are satisfied, starts with Levene's test of homogeneity of variance (see Table 6.3). Levene's test is significant ($p < 0.05$), so we reject the null hypothesis that the variances in the experimental groups are roughly equal. This finding alerts us that the assumption has been broken and, therefore, a non-parametric analysis is performed in Sect. 6.2.3.

Table 6.3 Levene's test of equality of error variances[1]

F	df1	df2	Sig.
11.445	1	18	0.003

[1] Dependent variable: NATPPH. Design: Intercept+DevTech.

6.2.3 Non-Parametric Analysis

A non-parametric analysis presented in this section is based on the Mann–Whitney test (Sect. 6.2.3.1) and the rank-transformed analysis of covariance (Sect. 6.2.3.2).

6.2.3.1 Mann–Whitney Test

The Mann–Whitney test makes it possible to find the differences in ranked scores between the TFSP and the TLSP group. Table 6.4 tells us the average and total ranks in each treatment.

Table 6.4 Ranks

DevTech	N	Mean rank	Sum of ranks
TLSP	11	11.45	126.00
TFSP	9	9.33	84.00
Total	20		

Table 6.5 shows the test statistics of the Mann–Whitney test. The comparison (TLSP vs. TFSP) resulted in the observed two-tailed significance value $p = 0.456 > 0.05$.

Calculating Effect Size

The effect size r can be calculated from the Z-score on the basis of Eq. (5.3):

$$r_{\text{contrast1 (TLSP vs. TFSP)}} = \frac{-0.798}{\sqrt{20}} = -0.18 \tag{6.1}$$

Table 6.5 Mann–Whitney test statistics (TLSP vs. TFSP)[1]

	NATPPH
Mann–Whitney U	39.000
Wilcoxon W	84.000
Z	−0.798
Asymp. Sig. (two-tailed)	0.425
Exact Sig. (two-tailed)	0.456
Exact Sig. (one-tailed)	0.228

[1] Grouping variable: DevTech.

Listing 6.5: Related SPSS syntax

```
NPAR TESTS
    /M-W= NATPPH    BY DevTech(1  2)
    /MISSING ANALYSIS
    /METHOD=EXACT TIMER(5).
```

This effect size estimation indicates that the difference in NATPPH created by the TF practice followed instead of TL by solo programmers represents a small (but close to medium) effect (see Table 4.2).

Summary

The TLSP (Mdn = 0.50) and TFSP (Mdn = 0.35) groups did not significantly differ in NATPPH ($U = 39.0$, $p > 0.05$, $r = -0.18$).

6.2.3.2 Rank-Transformed Analysis of Covariance

In order to get a more sensitive measure of the experimental effect, pre-existing differences among the subjects should be taken into account. Since our data do not satisfy the assumption of homogeneity of variance, the analysis preformed in this section is based on a non-parametric ANCOVA using the rank transformation. Formal justification of a rank-transformed analysis is presented in Sect. 4.7.6.1. It is worth recalling that SPSS provides support for ranking data (see Box 5.9).

Rank-Transformed Analysis of Variance

The one-way ANOVA results are presented in Table 6.6. It is clear from the significance value $p = 0.44$, which is higher than 0.05, that there is not a statistical significant difference in NATPPH between the TLSP and the TFSP experimental groups. Moreover, development technique (DevTech) is able to explain about 3% of the variance in the dependent variable (partial eta squared $\eta_p^2 = 0.03$; see Table 6.6).

Table 6.6 Test of between-subjects effects

Source	Type III sum of squares	df	Mean square	F	Significance	Partial eta squared
Corrected model	22.273[1]	1	22.273	0.624	0.440	0.033
Intercept	2139.073	1	2139.073	59.906	0.000	0.769
DevTech	22.273	1	22.273	0.624	0.440	0.033
Error	642.727	18	35.707			
Total	2870.000	20				
Corrected total	665.000	19				

[1] R squared $= 0.033$.

Listing 6.6: Related SPSS menu navigation (Analyse $\Rightarrow$ General Linear Model $\Rightarrow$ Univariate) and syntax

```
UNIANOVA
  NATPPHRanked  BY DevTech
  /METHOD = SSTYPE(3)
  /INTERCEPT = INCLUDE
  /PRINT = DESCRIPTIVE ETASQ OPOWER HOMOGENEITY
  /CRITERIA = ALPHA(.05)
  /DESIGN = DevTech.
```

Calculating Effect Size

A rough estimate of the effect size for ANOVA is available through r^2, usually called eta squared η^2, on the basis of Eq. (5.10):

$$\eta = \sqrt{\frac{SS_M}{SS_T}} = \sqrt{\frac{22.273}{665.000}} = \sqrt{0.033} = -0.18 \tag{6.2}$$

Partial eta square was calculated by SPSS (see Table 6.6) but can be easily calculated by hand on the basis of Eq. (5.14):

$$\eta_p^2 = \frac{SS_M}{SS_M + SS_R} = \frac{22.273}{22.273 + 642.727} = 0.03 \tag{6.3}$$

$$\eta_p = -0.18 \tag{6.4}$$

We may conclude that 3% of the variance in NATPPH can be attributed to the development method. Hence, relying on the guidelines summarized in Table 4.2 that represents a small (but close to medium) effect size.

Summary

Levene's test was significant ($F(1, 18) = 11.45$, $p < 0.05$), which indicates that the assumption of homogeneity of variance had been broken. Hence, a non-parametric analysis by means of the rank-transformed analysis of variance was performed. The effect of TFSP, although not significant ($F(1, 18) = 0.62$, $p > 0.05$, $r = -0.18$), represents a medium effect size.

Adjusting for Pre-intervention Scores

In further investigation, it is feasible to take into account the pre-test results of the subjects. Therefore, grades obtained by subjects after the preparation phase of the experiment are included in the model.

Additional Assumptions of ANCOVA

The assumption that a covariate should be a continuous or discrete variable is satisfied. The assumption that the covariate is measured before the experimental manipulation takes place is met, too. Another assumption that there is a linear relationship between the dependent variable and the covariates for all the groups was checked by examining the scatterplots for each group. The scatterplots do not show evidence of non-linearity. The final assumption (the homogeneity of regression slopes) concerns the relationship between the dependent variable and the covariate for each of the groups (TFSP and TLSP). It was checked statistically with the help of the GLM procedure with a customized model offered by SPSS (see Table 6.7). It turned out that there is no statistically significant interaction ($p = 0.77$) between the treatment and the covariate ($DevTech*Grade$), so that assumption is satisfied, too.

Table 6.7 Test of between-subjects effects with covariate and interaction to check homogeneity of regression

Source	Type III sum of squares	df	Mean square	F	Sig.
Corrected model	117.875[1]	3	39.292	1.149	0.360
Intercept	9.482	1	9.482	0.277	0.606
DevTech	1.628	1	1.628	0.048	0.830
Grade	88.414	1	88.414	2.586	0.127
DevTech*Grade	3.009	1	3.009	0.088	0.771
Error	547.125	16	34.195		
Total	2870.000	20			
Corrected total	665.000	19			

[1] R squared = 0.177.

Listing 6.7: Related SPSS syntax

```
UNIANOVA
  NATPPHRanked  BY DevTech  WITH Grade
  /METHOD = SSTYPE(3)
  /INTERCEPT = INCLUDE
  /PRINT = DESCRIPTIVE ETASQ OPOWER PARAMETER TEST(LMATRIX) HOMOGENEITY
  /PLOT = SPREADLEVEL RESIDUALS
  /CRITERIA = ALPHA(.05)
  /DESIGN = DevTech Grade DevTech*Grade.
```

Covariance Included in Analysis

The main ANCOVA results of between-subjects effects with *Grade* covariate are presented in Table 6.8.

Table 6.8 Test of between-subjects effects with covariate

Source	Type III sum of squares	df	Mean square	F	Sig.	Partial eta squared
Corrected model	114.866[1]	2	57.433	1.775	0.200	0.173
Intercept	6.615	1	6.615	0.204	0.657	0.012
Grade	92.593	1	92.593	2.861	0.109	0.144
DevTech	10.731	1	10.731	0.332	0.572	0.019
Error	550.134	17	32.361			
Total	2870.000	20				
Corrected total	665.000	19				

[1] R squared $= 0.173$.

```
Listing 6.8: Related SPSS syntax
UNIANOVA
  NATPPHRanked  BY DevTech   WITH Grade
  /METHOD = SSTYPE(3)
  /INTERCEPT = INCLUDE
  /PRINT = DESCRIPTIVE ETASQ OPOWER HOMOGENEITY
  /CRITERIA = ALPHA(.05)
  /DESIGN = Grade DevTech.
```

The main effect of the TFSP development technique on NATPPH was non-significant ($F(1, 17) = 0.33$, $p > 0.05$, partial eta squared $\eta_p^2 = 0.02$) while controlling for grades obtained by subjects after the preparation phase of the experiment. It means that about 2% of the variance in NATPPH ($\eta_p^2 = 0.02$) can be explained by the independent variable (DevTech).

It turned out that the relationship between the covariate (*Grade*) and the dependent variable (NATPPH) ($F(1, 17) = 2.86$, $p > 0.05$, partial eta squared $\eta_p^2 = 0.14$) is not significant. The covariate explained about 14% of the variance in the dependent variable. It shows that individual differences between subjects can be quite influential.

Calculating Effect Size

We are able to calculate the effect of the independent variable, as well as the effect of the covariate, as both are included in the model.

The effect of the TFSP development technique was calculated by SPSS as partial eta squared (see Table 6.8). However, estimations of the effect size for ANOVA can be calculated by hand on the basis of Eqs. (5.10) and (5.14):

$$\eta_p{}^2 = \frac{SS_M}{SS_M + SS_R} = \frac{10.731}{10.731 + 550.134} = 0.02 \longrightarrow \eta_p = -0.14 \qquad (6.5)$$

$$r = \sqrt{\frac{SS_M}{SS_T}} = \sqrt{\frac{10.731}{665.000}} = -0.13 \qquad (6.6)$$

For the effect of the covariate we get the following:

$$\eta_p{}^2 = \frac{SS_M}{SS_M + SS_R} = \frac{92.593}{92.593 + 550.134} = 0.14 \longrightarrow \eta_p = -0.38 \qquad (6.7)$$

$$r = \sqrt{\frac{SS_M}{SS_T}} = \sqrt{\frac{92.593}{665.000}} = -0.37 \qquad (6.8)$$

Relying on the guidelines summarized in Table 4.2, the main effect of the TFSP development technique represents a medium effect size and a fairly substantive finding. About 14% of the variance in NATPPH can be attributed to DevTech. Moreover, the effect of the covariate is small.

Summary

Levene's test was significant ($F(1, 18) = 11.45$, $p < 0.05$), which indicates that the assumption of homogeneity of variance had been broken. Hence, a non-parametric analysis by means of the rank-transformed analysis of covariance was performed. The effect of TFSP, although non-significant ($F(1, 17) = 0.33$, $p > 0.05$, $r = -0.13$), represents a medium effect size. The covariate was also non-significant ($F(1, 17) = 2.86$, $p > 0.05$, $\eta_p{}^2 = 0.14$).

6.3 Analysis of Experiment SMELLS&LIBRARY

A selective analysis of 22 projects (using the TLSP and TFSP techniques, randomly assigned) has been performed in this section. It is worth recalling that five projects were excluded from the selective analysis on the basis of the selection criteria presented in Sect. 4.7.7.

6.3.1 Descriptive Statistics

The descriptive statistics of collected experimental results are presented in Table 6.9 and Figure 6.3.

Table 6.9 Descriptive statistics for the number of acceptance tests passed per hour (DV: NATPPH)—selective analysis

DV	Dev. Tech.	Mean (M)	Std.Dev. (SD)	Std. Error (SE)	Max	Median (Mdn)	Min	95% CI Lower bound	Upper bound
NATPPH	TLSP	1.404	1.450	0.309	5.415	0.798	0.277	0.761	2.046
Combined	TFSP	1.666	1.866	0.398	9.005	1.185	0.362	0.839	2.494

Listing 6.9: Related SPSS syntax

```
EXAMINE
   VARIABLES=NATPPH BY DevTech
   /PLOT BOXPLOT STEMLEAF HISTOGRAM NPPLOT
   /COMPARE GROUP
   /STATISTICS DESCRIPTIVES
   /CINTERVAL 95
   /MISSING LISTWISE
   /NOTOTAL.
```

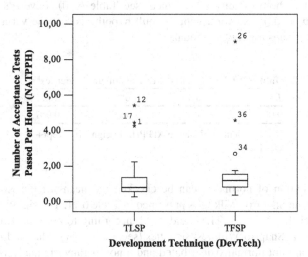

Fig. 6.3 Boxplot for the number of acceptance tests passed per hour (DV: NATPPH)—selective analysis of Experiment SMELLS&LIBRARY

Listing 6.10: Related SPSS syntax

```
EXAMINE
   VARIABLES=NATPPH BY DevTech /PLOT=BOXPLOT/STATISTICS=NONE/NOTOTAL.
```

The TFSP group has a higher mean, median, minimum, maximum, standard deviation and standard error than the TLSP group. Extreme points (that extend more than three box-lengths from the edge of the box) as well as outliers (that extend more than 1.5 box-lengths) can be located in Fig. 6.3. These outliers suggest abnormal behaviour requiring further investigation. However, the scores of the outliers appeared genuine, not just errors (e.g. the highest score was achieved by the subject not only with the longest recent industrial experience in programming, but also with the longest recent industrial experience in programming in Java).

Summarizing the descriptive statistics in APA format [12], we can conclude that the NATPPH values in the TLSP projects ($M = 1.40$, $SD = 1.45$) and TFSP projects ($M = 1.67$, $SD = 1.87$) are slightly different. In order to answer the question whether the impact of the TF practice on NATPPH is significant or not, statistical tests are performed, preceded by testing of the underlying assumptions.

6.3.2 Assumption Testing

The exploratory analysis of the collected data, undertaken in order to check whether the assumptions of parametric tests (listed in Sect. 4.7.2) are satisfied, starts with Levene's test of homogeneity of variance (see Table 6.10). Levene's test is not significant ($p < 0.05$) so we accept the null hypothesis that the variances in the experimental groups are roughly equal.

Table 6.10 Levene's test of equality of error variances[1]

F	df1	df2	Sig.
0.002	1	42	0.967

[1] Dependent variable: NATPPH. Design: Intercept+ DevTech.

The assumption of normality can be checked by means of the Kolmogorov–Smirnov and the Shapiro–Wilk tests presented in Table 6.11. The significance (Sig.) value is lower than 0.05 for TLSP and TFSP according to both the Kolmogorov–Smirnov and the Shaprio-Wilk test statistics (see Table 6.11). This finding alerts us that the data are not normally distributed and a non-parametric analysis should be performed.

Table 6.11 Tests of normality

DevTech	Kolmogorov–Smirnov[1]			Shapiro–Wilk		
	statistic	df[2]	Sig.	statistic	df[2]	Sig.
TLSP	0.296	22	0.000	0.700	22	0.000
TFSP	0.347	22	0.000	0.572	22	0.000

[1] Lilliefors significance correction.
[2] Degrees of freedom.

6.3.3 Non-Parametric Analysis

A non-parametric analysis presented in this section is based on the Wilcoxon signed-rank test (see Sect. 6.3.3.1).

6.3.3.1 Wilcoxon Signed-Rank Test

The Wilcoxon signed-rank test, being a non-parametric equivalent of the dependent t-test, is used for testing the differences between the groups (TLSP and TFSP) when the same subjects have been used in both treatments. Table 6.12 tells us the average and total ranks in each treatment. We report only one of the test statistics presented in Table 6.12, i.e. the one that has the lowest value ($T^- = 103.00$). On the basis of the Wilcoxon signed-rank test we may conclude that there was no significant difference between the TLSP (Mdn $= 0.80$) and the TFSP (Mdn $= 1.19$) group ($T = 103.00$, $p = 0.463$).

Table 6.12 Wilcoxon signed rank test

Ranks NATPPHinTF− NATPPHinTL	N	Mean rank	Sum of ranks
Negative Ranks	8^1	12.88	103.00
Positive Ranks	14^2	10.71	150.00
Ties	0^3		
Total	22		

[1] NATPPHinTF < NATPPHinTL.
[2] NATPPHinTF > NATPPHinTL.
[3] NATPPHinTF = NATPPHinTL.

Test statistics	NATPPHinTF− NATPPHinTL
Z	-0.763^1
Asymp. Sig. (two-tailed)	0.445
Exact Sig. (two-tailed)	0.463
Exact Sig. (one-tailed)	0.231

[1] Based on negative ranks.

Listing 6.11: Related SPSS syntax

```
NPAR TEST
    /WILCOXON=NATPPHinTL  WITH NATPPHinTF (PAIRED)
    /STATISTICS DESCRIPTIVES
    /MISSING ANALYSIS
    /METHOD=EXACT TIMER(5).
```

Calculating Effect Size

The effect size r can be calculated from the Z-score on the basis of Eq. (5.3):

$$r_{\text{contrast1 (TLSP vs. TFSP)}} = 0.12 \tag{6.9}$$

This effect size estimation indicates that the difference in NATPPH, due to the TF practice followed instead of TL by solo programmers, represents a small effect (relying on the guidelines in Table 4.2).

Summary

The TLSP (Mdn $= 0.80$) and TFSP (Mdn $= 1.19$) groups did not differ significantly in the number of acceptance tests passed per development hour (NATPPH), ($T = 103.00$, $p > 0.05$, $r = 0.12$).

6.4 Instead of Summary

On the basis of the conducted experiments, it is difficult to arrive at a single, reliable and unbiased conclusion whether the effect of the TF practice on NATPPH is significant or not. Since the results of the analysed empirical studies vary, no subjective review or narrative summary of the results will close this chapter. Instead, the already mentioned Chapter 9 provides a meta-analysis of the effect sizes (which address the issue of practical significance [237, 243]) and p-values (which reflect the statistical significance).

Chapter 7
Effect on Internal Quality Indicators

> *Anything you need to quantify can be measured in some way*
> *that is superior to not measuring at all.*
> Tom DeMarco and Timothy Lister [61]

According to Bansiya [18], internal quality indicators influence external quality attributes and, therefore, evaluating a product's internal characteristics is reasonable. As a result, some useful conclusions can be drawn about the product's external quality attributes on the basis of its internal characteristics [18]. Relying on Briand et al. [31], measures of structural design properties are considered to be indicators of external system quality attributes, such as reliability or maintainability. Bøegh [30] mentioned class-level metrics proposed by Chidamber and Kemerer (CK metrics) [43] as typical examples of internal measures. This chapter concentrates on the CBO, WMC and RFC metrics (from the CK metrics suite) as their suitability for assessing fault proneness and fault content has already been empirically confirmed (see Sect. 3.3.2.2). The question is whether those metrics, often called design complexity metrics [238], are influenced by the TF practice.

It is important to note that average values of class-level code metrics (i.e. CBO_{Mean}, WMC_{Mean}, RFC_{Mean}) have been calculated for each project and analysed in this section. Another approach would be a class level analysis violating the assumption of independent observations. Furthermore, to keep the book concise and, simultaneously, present the most essential results for the meta-analysis conducted in Chap. 9, this chapter is focused on the TLSP vs. TFSP selective analysis (see Sect. 4.7.7). It is also worth mentioning that none of the collected pre-test results seemed to be a good candidate to include in the model as a covariate because none of them was related to internal code quality concepts like, for example, coupling.

7.1 Confounding Effect of Class Size on the Validity of Object-Oriented Metrics

El Emam et al. [70] proposed that size should be taken into account as a confounding variable when validating object-oriented metrics. However, a confounding variable is considered to occur causally prior to a treatment [71]. Moreover, a confounding

L. Madeyski, *Test-Driven Development*,
DOI 10.1007/978-3-642-04288-1_7, © Springer-Verlag Berlin Heidelberg 2010

variable is characterized as one which correlates with both the treatment and the outcome. Evanco [73] showed that we could hardly claim that class size (usually measured by lines of code LOC metric), as a causal factor, precedes many OO metrics proposed by different researchers (e.g. WMC, CBO, RFC). Therefore, including size as a confounding variable in a model would result in a misspecified model [73].

7.2 Analysis of Experiment Accounting

The experiment data are analysed by means of descriptive analysis and statistical tests.

7.2.1 Descriptive Statistics

The descriptive statistics of experimental results are summarized in Table 7.1.

Table 7.1 Descriptive statistics for code metrics (DV: CBO_{Mean}, WMC_{Mean} and RFC_{Mean})

DV	DevTech	Mean (M)	Std. Dev. (SD)	Std. error (SE)	Median Max	(Mdn)	Min	95% CI Lower bound	Upper bound
CBO_{Mean}	TLSP	1.461	0.404	0.076	2.29	1.423	0.75	1.304	1.618
	TFSP	1.130	0.407	0.093	2.42	1.000	0.67	0.933	1.326
	TLPP	1.393	0.443	0.080	2.42	1.375	0.60	1.230	1.555
	TFPP	1.100	0.455	0.088	2.55	1.100	0.50	0.920	1.280
WMC_{Mean}	TLSP	6.291	2.035	0.385	10.00	5.811	3.40	5.502	7.080
	TFSP	5.756	1.496	0.343	8.00	5.500	3.58	5.034	6.477
	TLPP	6.627	1.738	0.312	10.80	6.889	3.33	5.990	7.265
	TFPP	6.506	1.722	0.331	11.18	6.300	3.73	5.825	7.187
RFC_{Mean}	TLSP	7.965	3.149	0.595	13.83	7.444	1.92	6.744	9.186
	TFSP	6.007	2.170	0.498	12.05	5.500	2.15	4.961	7.053
	TLPP	8.283	2.818	0.506	15.80	8.333	3.33	7.250	9.317
	TFPP	6.831	2.957	0.569	16.64	6.455	2.55	5.661	8.000

Listing 7.1: Related SPSS syntax

```
EXAMINE
  VARIABLES=CBO_Mean WMC_Mean RFC_Mean BY DevTech
  /PLOT BOXPLOT STEMLEAF HISTOGRAM NPPLOT SPREADLEVEL(1)
  /COMPARE GROUP
  /STATISTICS DESCRIPTIVES
  /CINTERVAL 95
  /MISSING LISTWISE
  /NOTOTAL.
```

The TF development technique seems to have a positive impact on CBO_{Mean}, WMC_{Mean} and RFC_{Mean} as the TFSP experimental group has lower means, medians and confidence intervals than the TLSP group. Furthermore, a positive effect of PP is not visible. The results in the groups working in pairs (TLPP and TFPP) seem to be similar (CBO_{Mean}) or a bit worse (WMC_{Mean}, RFC_{Mean}) than the results in the groups working solo (TLSP and TFSP). Further empirical investigation is focused on the TFSP and TLSP experimental groups.

Figures 7.1, 7.2 and 7.3 present the boxplots comparing the CBO_{Mean}, WMC_{Mean} and RFC_{Mean} results between the two experimental groups (TLSP and TFSP).

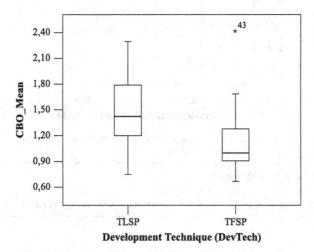

Fig. 7.1 Boxplot for CBO_{Mean} – selective analysis of Experiment ACCOUNTING

Listing 7.2: Related SPSS syntax

```
EXAMINE
    VARIABLES=CBO_Mean BY DevTech  /PLOT=BOXPLOT/STATISTICS=NONE/NOTOTAL.
```

Figures 7.1 and 7.3 suggest that there are differences in CBO_{Mean} and RFC_{Mean}, with the TFSP group performing better (i.e. having lower scores) than the TLSP group. Moreover, one extreme point can be located in Fig. 7.1 and one outlier in Fig. 7.3. The extreme point and outlier come from the same developer. Since the scores of the aforementioned developer proved correct, and not erroneous, they were not excluded from further analysis.

Summarizing the descriptive statistics in APA format [12], it may be concluded that CBO_{Mean} in the TFSP group ($M = 1.13$, SD $= 0.41$) is lower than in the TLSP one ($M = 1.46$, SD $= 0.40$). WMC_{Mean} in the TFSP group ($M = 5.76$, SD $= 1.50$) is slightly lower than in the TLSP one ($M = 6.29$, SD $= 2.04$). RFC_{Mean} in the TFSP group ($M = 6.01$, SD $= 2.17$) is lower than in the TLSP one ($M = 7.97$, SD $= 3.15$). However, to answer the question whether the impact of TF on the dependent variables is significant, or not, statistical tests must be performed, preceded by the testing of the underlying assumptions.

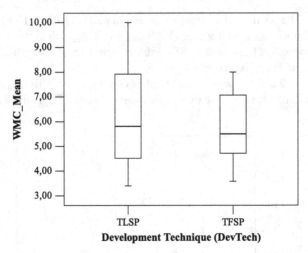

Fig. 7.2 Boxplot for WMC$_{\text{Mean}}$ – selective analysis of Experiment ACCOUNTING

Listing 7.3: Related SPSS syntax

```
EXAMINE
    VARIABLES=WMC_Mean BY DevTech  /PLOT=BOXPLOT/STATISTICS=NONE/NOTOTAL.
```

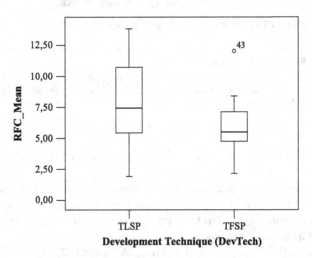

Fig. 7.3 Boxplot for RFC$_{\text{Mean}}$ – selective analysis of Experiment ACCOUNTING

Listing 7.4: Related SPSS syntax

```
EXAMINE
    VARIABLES=RFC_Mean BY DevTech  /PLOT=BOXPLOT/STATISTICS=NONE/NOTOTAL.
```

7.2.2 Assumption Testing

The general assumptions of parametric tests are presented in Sect. 4.7.2. The assumption of normality was checked by means of the Kolmogorov–Smirnov and the Shapiro–Wilk tests presented in Table 7.2. It appeared that for the CBO_{Mean} data, from the TFSP experimental group, the significance (Sig.) value was lower than 0.05, according to both statistics (see Table 7.2). This finding alerts us that the assumption of normality is broken and the CBO_{Mean} data are not normally distributed.

Table 7.2 Tests of normality

DV	DevTech	Kolmogorov–Smirnov[1]			Shapiro–Wilk		
		statistic	df[2]	Sig.	statistic	df[2]	Sig.
CBO_{Mean}	TLSP	0.104	28	0.200^3	0.969	28	0.565
	TFSP	0.204	19	0.037	0.831	19	0.003
WMC_{Mean}	TLSP	0.114	28	0.200^3	0.941	28	0.115
	TFSP	0.147	19	0.200^3	0.921	19	0.119
RFC_{Mean}	TLSP	0.165	28	0.050	0.956	28	0.282
	TFSP	0.126	19	0.200^3	0.938	19	0.240

[1] Lilliefors significance correction.
[2] Degrees of freedom.
[3] This is a lower bound of the true significance.

The assumption of homogeneity of variance is tested using Levene's test (see Table 7.3). Levene's test is statistically significant ($p < 0.05$) for RFC_{Mean} so we reject the null hypothesis that the difference between the variances is roughly 0. Consequently, the assumption of homogeneity of variance is violated for RFC_{Mean}.

Table 7.3 Levene's test of equality of error variances

DV	F	df1	df2	Sig.
CBO_{Mean}	.319	1	45	.575
WMC_{Mean}	2.754	1	45	.104
RFC_{Mean}	6.890	1	45	.012

As the aforesaid assumptions of parametric tests are violated, a non-parametric analysis is performed in Sect. 7.2.3.

7.2.3 Mann–Whitney Tests

Table 7.4 shows the test statistics of the Mann–Whitney tests for the three dependent variables.

The Mann–Whitney tests have been conducted to compare the CBO_{Mean}, WMC_{Mean} and RFC_{Mean} data between the TLSP and the TFSP group. Two tests (for CBO_{Mean} and RFC_{Mean} but not WMC_{Mean}) produce the two-tailed significance (Sig.) values that are smaller than 0.05. As a result the specific hypothesis $H^A_{0,WMC_{Mean},TLSP/TFSP}$

Table 7.4 Mann–Whitney test statistics (TLSP vs. TFSP)[1](DV: CBO_{Mean}, WMC_{Mean}, RFC_{Mean})

	CBO_{Mean}	WMC_{Mean}	RFC_{Mean}
Mann–Whitney U	125.000	230.000	168.500
Wilcoxon W	315.000	420.000	358.500
Z	−3.062	−0.781	−2.114
Asymp. Sig. (two-tailed)	0.002	0.435	0.035
Exact Sig. (two-tailed)	0.002	0.442	0.034
Exact Sig. (one-tailed)	0.001	0.221	0.017

[1] Grouping Variable: DevTech.

Listing 7.5: Related SPSS syntax

```
NPAR TESTS
    /M-W= CBO_Mean WMC_Mean RFC_Mean    BY DevTech(1 2)
    /STATISTICS= DESCRIPTIVES
    /MISSING ANALYSIS
    /METHOD=EXACT TIMER(5).
```

---

cannot be rejected. However, if we want to control Type I errors we should make some kind of adjustment to ensure that Type I errors do not build up to more than 0.05. As mentioned before, the classic method is to use the Bonferroni correction explained in Sect. "Mann–Whitney Tests" (p. 66) and Box 5.2. As a result the specific hypothesis $H^{A}_{0,RFC_{Mean},TLSP/TFSP}$ cannot be rejected in spite of the fact that the observed significance level is < 0.05. The only hypothesis that can be rejected (on the basis of Experiment ACCOUNTING) is $H^{A}_{0,CBO_{Mean},TFSP\&TFPP/TLSP\&TLPP}$ as CBO_{Mean} is significantly lower in the TFSP than in the TLSP group even after the Bonferroni correction. It should also be mentioned that some arguments against the Bonferroni correction are sometimes heard (see Box 5.3).

7.2.3.1 Calculating Effect Size

The effect sizes for the three dependent variables are calculated in this section from the Z-scores on the basis of Eq. (5.3):

$$r_{CBO_{Mean}} = \sqrt{\frac{-3.062^2}{47}} = 0.45 \qquad (7.1)$$

That represents a medium effect (in fact, it is close to 0.456, which means a large effect according to Kempenes et al.'s [133] benchmark presented in Table 4.2) which tells us that the result of using or not the TF practice by the solo programmers was a substantive effect.

$$r_{WMC_{Mean}} = \sqrt{\frac{-0.781^2}{47}} = 0.11 \qquad (7.2)$$

That represents a small effect, which demonstrates that there is not much difference between TFSP and TLSP with respect to WMC_{Mean}.

$$r_{RFC_{Mean}} = \sqrt{\frac{-2.114^2}{47}} = 0.31 \tag{7.3}$$

This represents a medium effect and, therefore, a substantive finding.

7.2.3.2 Summary

CBO_{Mean} was significantly lower in the TFSP (Mdn $= 1.00$) than in the TLSP (Mdn $= 1.42$) group ($U = 125.00$, $p = 0.002$, $r = 0.45$) even after the Bonferroni correction. The TLSP (Mdn $= 7.44$) and TFSP (Mdn $= 5.50$) groups did not significantly differ in RFC_{Mean} ($U = 168.50$, $p = 0.034$, $r = 0.31$) after the Bonferroni correction. The TLSP (Mdn $= 5.81$) and TFSP (Mdn $= 5.50$) groups did not significantly differ in WMC_{Mean} ($U = 230.00$, $p > 0.05$, $r = 0.11$).

7.3 Analysis of Experiment SUBMISSION

The selective analysis of 20 projects (11 TLSP and 9 TFSP ones) has been performed in this section on the basis of the selection criteria presented in Sect. 4.7.7.

7.3.1 Descriptive Statistics

On the basis of the descriptive statistics of experimental results (presented in Table 7.5.), the TF practice seems to have a positive impact on CBO_{Mean}, WMC_{Mean} and RFC_{Mean}, since the TFSP experimental group has lower means and confidence intervals than the TLSP one.

Figures 7.4, 7.5 and 7.6 present the boxplots comparing the CBO_{Mean}, WMC_{Mean} and RFC_{Mean} results between the two experimental groups (TLSP and TFSP). Figures 7.4 and 7.6 suggest that there are large differences in CBO_{Mean} and RFC_{Mean}, with the TFSP group performing better (i.e. having lower scores) than the TLSP

Table 7.5 Descriptive statistics for code metrics (DV: CBO_{Mean}, WMC_{Mean} and RFC_{Mean})

DV	DevTech	Mean (M)	Std. Dev. (SD)	Std. Error (SE)	Max	Median (Mdn)	Min	95% CI Lower bound	Upper bound
CBO_{Mean}	TLSP	2.734	0.427	0.129	3.55	2.652	2.125	2.447	3.021
	TFSP	1.953	0.480	0.160	2.80	2.022	1.161	1.584	2.322
WMC_{Mean}	TLSP	7.469	1.580	0.476	10.97	7.327	5.06	6.408	8.530
	TFSP	7.056	1.626	0.542	9.25	7.559	4.88	5.806	8.306
RFC_{Mean}	TLSP	14.022	3.467	1.045	21.06	13.469	8.11	11.693	16.352
	TFSP	11.913	3.573	1.191	19.43	11.846	8.34	9.167	14.659

Listing 7.6: Related SPSS syntax

```
EXAMINE
    VARIABLES=CBO_Mean WMC_Mean RFC_Mean BY DevTech
    /PLOT BOXPLOT STEMLEAF HISTOGRAM NPPLOT SPREADLEVEL(1)
    /COMPARE GROUP
    /STATISTICS DESCRIPTIVES
    /CINTERVAL 95
    /MISSING LISTWISE
    /NOTOTAL.
```

---

group. Moreover, outliers can be located in Figs. 7.4, 7.5 and 7.6. The outliers in Fig. 7.4 do not influence the mean considerably, owing to the fact that one increases the mean while the other decreases it. The outlier (1) in Figs. 7.5 and 7.6 comes from the same developer with a different software development style. As all the outliers turned out to be valid, and not erroneous, they were not excluded from further analysis.

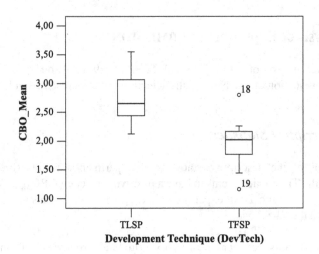

Fig. 7.4 Boxplot for CBO_{Mean} – selective analysis of Experiment SUBMISSION

Listing 7.7: Related SPSS syntax

```
EXAMINE
    VARIABLES=CBO_Mean BY DevTech /PLOT=BOXPLOT/STATISTICS=NONE/NOTOTAL.
```

Summarizing the descriptive statistics in APA format [12], we can conclude that CBO_{Mean} in the TFSP experimental group ($M = 1.95$, SD $= 0.48$) is lower than in the TLSP one ($M = 2.73$, SD $= 0.43$). WMC_{Mean} in the TFSP ($M = 7.06$, SD $= 1.63$) and TLSP ($M = 7.47$, SD $= 1.58$) experimental groups are similar. RFC_{Mean} in the TFSP experimental group ($M = 11.91$, SD $= 3.57$) is lower than in

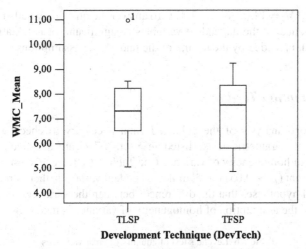

Fig. 7.5 Boxplot for WMC$_{Mean}$ – selective analysis of Experiment SUBMISSION

Listing 7.8: Related SPSS syntax

```
EXAMINE
   VARIABLES=WMC_Mean BY DevTech /PLOT=BOXPLOT/STATISTICS=NONE/NOTOTAL.
```

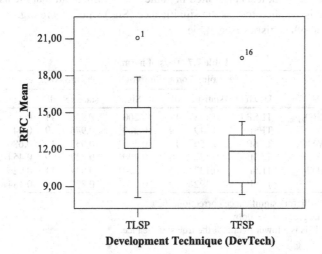

Fig. 7.6 Boxplot for RFC$_{Mean}$ – selective analysis of Experiment SUBMISSION

Listing 7.9: Related SPSS syntax

```
EXAMINE
   VARIABLES=RFC_Mean BY DevTech /PLOT=BOXPLOT/STATISTICS=NONE/NOTOTAL.
```

the TLSP one ($M = 14.02$, SD $= 3.47$). To answer the question whether the impact of the TF practice on the dependent variables is significant, or not, statistical tests are performed, preceded by the testing of the underlying assumptions.

7.3.2 Assumption Testing

The exploratory analysis of the collected data, necessary to check whether the assumptions of parametric tests (listed in Sect. 4.7.2) are satisfied, starts with Levene's test of homogeneity of variance (see Table 7.6). Levene's test is not statistically significant ($p > 0.05$) for all of the dependent variables, therefore, we cannot reject the null hypotheses that the differences between the variances are roughly 0. Consequently, the assumption of homogeneity of variance is met.

Table 7.6 Levene's test of equality of error variances

DV	F	df1	df2	Sig.
CBO_{Mean}	0.033	1	18	0.857
WMC_{Mean}	0.413	1	18	0.528
RFC_{Mean}	0.032	1	18	0.859

The assumption of normality was checked by means of the Kolmogorov–Smirnov and the Shapiro–Wilk tests presented in Table 7.7. It turned out that the assumption of normality is satisfied too, as the significance (Sig.) values were higher than 0.05 according to both statistics (see Table 7.7).

Table 7.7 Tests of normality

DV	DevTech	Kolmogorov–Smirnov[1]			Shapiro–Wilk		
		statistic	df[2]	Sig.	statistic	df[2]	Sig.
CBO_{Mean}	TLSP	0.168	11	0.200[3]	0.956	11	0.725
	TFSP	0.149	9	0.200[3]	0.976	9	0.942
WMC_{Mean}	TLSP	0.159	11	0.200[3]	0.953	11	0.680
	TFSP	0.177	9	0.200[3]	0.927	9	0.454
RFC_{Mean}	TLSP	0.127	11	0.200[3]	0.974	11	0.926
	TFSP	0.192	9	0.200[3]	0.887	9	0.184

[1] Lilliefors significance correction.
[2] Degrees of freedom.
[3] This is a lower bound of the true significance.

7.3.3 Independent t-Test

The parametric analysis presented in this section is based on a t-test that makes it possible to reveal the statistically significant differences in scores between the TFSP and the TLSP group. Table 7.8 shows the t-test statistics. The two-tailed significance values for WMC_{Mean} and RFC_{Mean} are greater than 0.05 so we may conclude that both were not significantly affected by TF. However, the two-tailed significance value for CBO_{Mean} is much lower than 0.05 ($p = 0.001$), which points to the fact that CBO_{Mean} was significantly affected by TF even after the Bonferroni correction. By means of the 95% confidence interval (95% CI) it is possible to ascertain that 95 of 100 mean differences between the TFSP and the TLSP results lie between the boundaries of 0.35 and 1.21. Since this interval does not contain 0, it is undeniable that the samples come from different populations induced by our experimental manipulation (i.e. TF).

Table 7.8 Independent samples t-test (DV: WMC_{Mean}, CBO_{Mean}, RFC_{Mean})[1]

| | | | | | | 95% CI | |
DV	t	df	Sig.(two-tailed)	Mean Diff.	Std.Err. Dif.(SE)	Lower	Upper
CBO_{Mean}	3.849	18	0.001	0.7808455	0.2028560	0.3546608	1.2070301
WMC_{Mean}	0.573	18	0.574	0.4123889	0.7193166	−1.09884	1.9236170
RFC_{Mean}	1.335	18	0.198	2.1094636	1.5796370	−1.20923	5.4281579

[1] Equal variances assumed.

Listing 7.10: Related SPSS syntax

```
T-TEST
   GROUPS = DevTech(1 2)
   /MISSING = ANALYSIS
   /VARIABLES = WMC_Mean CBO_Mean RFC_Mean
   /CRITERIA = CI(.95).
```

7.3.3.1 Calculating Effect Size

The effect size r can be calculated from the t-statistic on the basis of Eq. (5.13):

$$r_{CBO_{Mean}} = \frac{t}{\sqrt{t^2 + df}} = \frac{3.849}{\sqrt{3.849^2 + 18}} = 0.67 \qquad (7.4)$$

This effect size estimation indicates that the difference in CBO_{Mean} created by the TF, used instead of TL, practice by the solo programmers represents a large effect (see Table 4.2) and, as such, it signifies a substantive finding.

$$r_{WMC_{Mean}} = \frac{0.573}{\sqrt{0.573^2 + 18}} = 0.13 \qquad (7.5)$$

$$r_{RFC_{Mean}} = \frac{1.335}{\sqrt{1.335^2 + 18}} = 0.30 \qquad (7.6)$$

The difference in RFC_{Mean} created by TF represents a medium effect, while the difference in WMC_{Mean} represents a small effect.

7.3.3.2 Summary

The mean value of coupling between objects (CBO_{Mean}) was significantly lower in the TFSP than in the TLSP group ($t(18) = 3.85$, $p < 0.05$, $r = 0.67$). The effect size estimate indicates that the difference in CBO_{Mean} created by the TF development practice represents a large, and therefore substantive, effect. TLSP and TFSP did not significantly differ in WMC_{Mean} ($t(18) = 0.57$, $p > 0.05$, $r = 0.13$) as well as RFC_{Mean} ($t(18) = 1.34$, $p > 0.05$, $r = 0.30$).

7.4 Analysis of Experiment SMELLS&LIBRARY

A selective analysis of 22 projects has been performed in this section. It is worth recalling that five projects were excluded from the selective analysis on the basis of the selection criteria presented in Sect. 4.7.7.

7.4.1 Descriptive Statistics

The descriptive statistics of the collected experimental results (presented in Table 7.9) show that the TFSP experimental group has a lower CBO_{Mean} but similar WMC_{Mean} and RFC_{Mean} measures of central tendency (mean and median).

Table 7.9 Descriptive statistics for code metrics (DV: CBO_{Mean}, WMC_{Mean}, RFC_{Mean})

| | | | Std. | Std. | | | | 95% CI | |
| | | Mean | Dev. | Error | | Median | | Lower | Upper |
DV	DevTech	(M)	(SD)	(SE)	Max	(Mdn)	Min	bound	bound
CBO_{Mean}	TLSP	1.653	0.457	0.097	2.66	1.633	1.00	1.450	1.855
	TFSP	1.479	0.428	0.091	2.37	1.405	0.75	1.289	1.688
WMC_{Mean}	TLSP	5.226	1.249	0.266	7.91	5.200	3.22	4.672	5.779
	TFSP	5.446	1.465	0.312	9.07	5.101	2.88	4.797	6.096
RFC_{Mean}	TLSP	8.786	2.251	0.480	13.36	8.833	5.06	7.788	9.784
	TFSP	8.860	2.525	0.538	13.20	8.740	3.63	7.741	9.979

Listing 7.11: Related SPSS syntax

```
EXAMINE
    VARIABLES=CBO_Mean WMC_Mean RFC_Mean BY DevTech
    /PLOT BOXPLOT STEMLEAF HISTOGRAM NPPLOT SPREADLEVEL(1)
    /COMPARE GROUP
    /STATISTICS DESCRIPTIVES
    /CINTERVAL 95
    /MISSING LISTWISE
    /NOTOTAL.
```

Figures 7.7, 7.8 and 7.9 suggest that there are some differences in CBO_{Mean} (with the TFSP group performing slightly better than the TLSP one), but not in WMC_{Mean}

and RFC$_{Mean}$. One outlier can be located in Fig. 7.8. The outlier turned out to be valid, not erroneous, and was not excluded from further analysis.

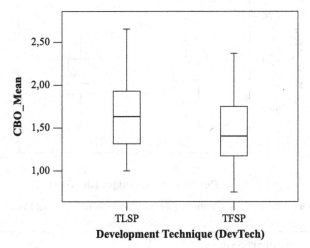

Fig. 7.7 Boxplot for CBO$_{Mean}$ – selective analysis of Experiment SMELLS&LIBRARY

Listing 7.12: Related SPSS syntax

```
EXAMINE
    VARIABLES=CBO_Mean BY DevTech  /PLOT=BOXPLOT/STATISTICS=NONE/NOTOTAL.
```

Summarizing the descriptive statistics in APA format [12], we can conclude that CBO$_{Mean}$ in the TFSP experimental group ($M = 1.48$, SD $= 0.43$) is somewhat lower than in the TLSP one ($M = 1.65$, SD $= 0.46$). WMC$_{Mean}$ in the TFSP ($M = 5.45$, SD $= 1.47$) and TLSP group ($M = 5.23$, SD $= 1.25$) are similar. RFC$_{Mean}$ in the TFSP ($M = 8.86$, SD $= 2.53$) and TLSP group ($M = 8.79$, SD $= 2.25$) are similar as well. To answer the question whether the impact of the TF practice on the dependent variables is significant, or not, statistical tests are performed, preceded by the testing of the underlying assumptions.

7.4.2 Assumption Testing

The exploratory analysis of the collected data, necessary to check whether the assumptions of parametric tests (listed in Sect. 4.7.2) are satisfied, consists of Levene's test of homogeneity of variance, presented in Table 7.10, and normality tests (i.e. the Kolmogorov–Smirnov and the Shapiro–Wilk tests), presented in Table 7.11.

The assumption of homogeneity of variance is met, as Levene's test is not statistically significant ($p > 0.05$) for all of the dependent variables.

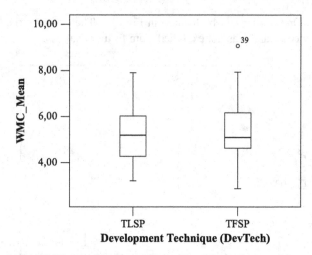

Fig. 7.8 Boxplot for WMC$_{\text{Mean}}$ – selective analysis of Experiment SMELLS&LIBRARY

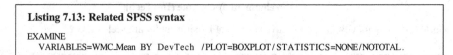

Listing 7.13: Related SPSS syntax

```
EXAMINE
  VARIABLES=WMC_Mean BY DevTech  /PLOT=BOXPLOT/STATISTICS=NONE/NOTOTAL.
```

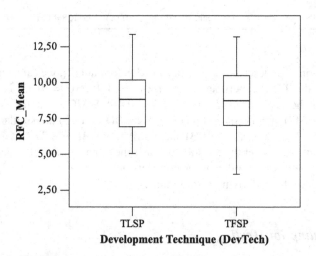

Fig. 7.9 Boxplot for RFC$_{\text{Mean}}$ – selective analysis of Experiment SMELLS&LIBRARY

Listing 7.14: Related SPSS syntax

```
EXAMINE
  VARIABLES=RFC_Mean BY DevTech  /PLOT=BOXPLOT/STATISTICS=NONE/NOTOTAL.
```

Table 7.10 Levene's test of equality of error variances

DV	F	df1	df2	Sig.
CBO_{Mean}	0.188	1	42	0.667
WMC_{Mean}	0.384	1	42	0.539
RFC_{Mean}	0.201	1	42	0.656

The assumption of normality is satisfied, too, as the significance (Sig.) values are higher than 0.05 according to both the Kolmogorov–Smirnov and the Shapiro–Wilk test statistics (see Table 7.11).

Table 7.11 Tests of normality

DV	DevTech	Kolmogorov–Smirnov[1]			Shapiro–Wilk		
		Statistic	df[2]	Sig.	Statistic	df[2]	Sig.
CBO_{Mean}	TLSP	0.119	22	0.200[3]	0.963	22	0.542
	TFSP	0.153	22	0.198	0.964	22	0.572
WMC_{Mean}	TLSP	0.081	22	0.200[3]	0.975	22	0.830
	TFSP	0.126	22	0.200[3]	0.960	22	0.487
RFC_{Mean}	TLSP	0.120	22	0.200[3]	0.966	22	0.626
	TFSP	0.097	22	0.200[3]	0.973	22	0.780

[1] Lilliefors significance correction.
[2] Degrees of freedom.
[3] This is a lower bound of the true significance.

7.4.3 Dependent t-Test

The statistic analysis, included in this section, consists in a dependent t-test used to identify the differences in scores between the subjects using the TFSP and TLSP techniques.

Table 7.12 shows paired samples Pearson correlations between the two treatment conditions. Those correlations will be used in effect size calculations in Sect. 7.4.3.1.

Table 7.12 Paired samples correlations

	N	Correlation	Sig.
CBO_{Mean} in TFSP & CBO_{Mean} in TLSP	22	0.066	0.772
WMC_{Mean} in TFSP & WMC_{Mean} in TLSP	22	0.224	0.317
RFC_{Mean} in TFSP & RFC_{Mean} in TLSP	22	0.178	0.427

Table 7.13 shows the main test statistics of the dependent t-test. The two-tailed significance values are greater than 0.05, therefore, we may conclude that CBO_{Mean}, WMC_{Mean} and RFC_{Mean} were not significantly affected by TF.

Table 7.13 Dependent (paired) samples t-test (DV: CBO_{Mean}, WMC_{Mean}, RFC_{Mean})

| | | Std. Dev. | Std. Err. | 95% CI | | | | Sig.(two- |
	Mean	(SD)	(SE)	Lower	Upper	t	df	tailed)
CBO_{Mean} in TFSP – CBO_{Mean} in TLSP	−0.1744	0.6049	0.1290	−0.4426	0.0938	−1.352	21	0.191
WMC_{Mean} in TFSP – WMC_{Mean} in TLSP	0.2207	1.6994	0.3623	−0.5327	0.9742	0.609	21	0.549
RFC_{Mean} in TFSP – RFC_{Mean} in TLSP	0.0737	3.0680	0.6541	−1.2866	1.4339	0.113	21	0.911

Listing 7.15: Related SPSS syntax

```
T-TEST
  PAIRS = CBO_MeanInTF WMC_MeanInTF RFC_MeanInTF  WITH CBO_MeanInTL
  WMC_MeanInTL RFC_MeanInTL (PAIRED)
  /CRITERIA = CI(.95)
  /MISSING = ANALYSIS.
```

7.4.3.1 Calculating Effect Size

Calculating the effect size estimations in this case is somewhat tricky, as Eq. (5.13) should not be used for a dependent t-test. It was explained by Dunlap et al. [64] that if an effect size is computed from the test statistic without taking the correlation between the measures into account, effect size will be overestimated. According to Dunlap et al. [64], some sources ignore the difference between experimental designs completely [99] or provide incorrect suggestions [212] concerning effect size calculation. Moreover, some effect size calculations presented in [76, 77] are not consistent with the guidelines by Dunlap et al. and, therefore, are considered incorrect as well. Hence, keeping in line with the guidelines by Dunlap et al. [64], the appropriate procedure for computing effect size from the repeated measures design (when a dependent t-test is used) is presented in Box 7.1.

Box 7.1 Effect size d and r calculation based on dependent t-statistic

The formula for computing d from the repeated measures experimental design, when the dependent t-test statistics are available, is as follows [64]:

$$d = t_r \times \sqrt{\frac{2 \times (1 - r_r)}{n}} \qquad (7.7)$$

where r_r is the value of Pearson's correlation coefficient between the experimental and the control scores in the repeated measures design (i.e. correlation across pairs of measures), t_r is the repeated measures t-statistic, while n is the sample size per group. On the basis of Eq. (4.1) from Box 4.7.6,

$$r = \frac{d}{\sqrt{(d^2 + 4)}} = \sqrt{\frac{d^2}{d^2 + 4}} = \sqrt{1 - \frac{4}{d^2 + 4}} \qquad (7.8)$$

Hence, the effect size r can be calculated from the repeated measures experimental design, when the dependent t-test statistics are available:

$$r = \sqrt{1 - \frac{4}{d^2 + 4}} = \sqrt{1 - \frac{4}{t_r^2 \times \frac{2\times(1-r_r)}{n} + 4}} \qquad (7.9)$$

On the basis of the procedure presented in Box 7.1:

$$r_{CBO_{Mean}} = \sqrt{1 - \frac{4}{t_r^2 \times \frac{2\times(1-r_r)}{n} + 4}} = \sqrt{1 - \frac{4}{(-1.352)^2 \times \frac{2\times(1-0.066)}{22} + 4}} = 0.19$$
$$(7.10)$$

This effect size estimation indicates that the difference in CBO_{Mean} created by the TF, used instead of the TL, practice by the solo programmers represents a small to medium effect (see Table 4.2).

$$r_{WMC_{Mean}} = \sqrt{1 - \frac{4}{0.609^2 \times \frac{2\times(1-0.224)}{22} + 4}} = -0.08 \qquad (7.11)$$

This effect size estimation[1] indicates that the difference in WMC_{Mean} created by the TF practice represents a small effect.

$$r_{RFC_{Mean}} = \sqrt{1 - \frac{4}{0.113^2 \times \frac{2\times(1-0.178)}{22} + 4}} = -0.02 \qquad (7.12)$$

This effect size estimation[1] indicates that the difference in RFC_{Mean} created by the TF practice represents a tiny effect (as it is close to 0) which means that both groups do not differ much.

7.4.3.2 Summary

CBO_{Mean} ($t(21) = -1.35$, $p > 0.05$, $r = 0.19$), WMC_{Mean} ($t(21) = 0.61$, $p > 0.05$, $r = -0.08$) and RFC_{Mean} ($t(21) = 0.11$, $p > 0.05$, $r = -0.02$)

---

[1] By convention, a positive sign is assigned to the effect size when the treatment (i.e. experimental) group performs "better" than the control group (see Box 5.5).

were not affected by the TF development practice. The effect size estimate indicates that the difference in CBO_{Mean} created by the TF development practice represents a medium to small effect, while the effects on WMC_{Mean} and RFC_{Mean} are small or even tiny.

7.5 Instead of Summary

The results of the empirical studies presented above differ from one another and thus obscure the conclusion whether or not the TF practice has a significant effect on the conducted experiments. In order to find a single, reliable and unbiased answer to that question, it is indispensable to apply a statistical technique called meta-analysis. Instead of drawing conclusions based on a subjective review of the results presented in this chapter, a more objective technique has been chosen and presented in Chap. 9: an analysis of analyses, that means meta-analysis, of the effect sizes and p-values which address the issue of practical significance [237, 243] and statistical significance across the conducted experiments.

Chapter 8
Effects on Unit Tests – Preliminary Analysis

> *Count what is countable, measure what is measurable and*
> *what is not measurable, make measurable*
>
> Galileo Galilei

With the rising acceptance of XP, and agile methodologies in general, a growing
number of software projects develop and maintain large test suites. Tests are considered a kind of a live documentation for the production code, because tests are
always kept in sync with the code as opposed to typical text-based documentation
which may not be in sync with the code. However, the first and foremost tests are
used to execute a program with the intent of finding errors [191]. Hence, not only the
thoroughness of developed tests (which is often taken into consideration by means of
code coverage measures) but also the fault detection effectiveness of developed tests
play the key part in software development. As explained in Sect. 3.3.2.4, code coverage measures can be useful as indicators of the thoroughness of unit test suites [170],
while mutation score is a more powerful and more effective measure of the fault
finding effectiveness of test suites than statement and branch coverage [250], and
data-flow [82, 197]. Unfortunately, the empirical evidence on the impact of the TF
practice on unit test suite characteristics is limited to code coverage. Therefore, preliminary results, presented in this section, extend the body of knowledge in software
engineering by means of the analysis of the impact of the TF practice on mutation
score indicator (an indicator of the fault detection effectiveness of developed unit
tests).

It is worth mentioning that the first evaluation of the impact of the PP practice on
the fault detection effectiveness based on mutation score indicator was performed
by Madeyski [160, 161] with the help of a new mutation testing tool, called Judy
[163], introduced in Sect. 4.3.3.

TF is regarded as one of the software development practices that can enforce
more rigorous, thorough, and effective unit testing. Astels [15] suggests that TF
leads to improved test coverage. Ambler argues that TF "does not replace traditional
testing, instead it defines a proven way to ensure effective unit testing" [11]. Mattu
and Shankar [173] come to the same conclusion. Furthermore, the quality of tests
can be an indicator of the quality of the related production code [201], as writing
tests is part of the development method. According to the TF development practice,
tests should be written for any piece of the production code that could possibly break

L. Madeyski, *Test-Driven Development*, 159
DOI 10.1007/978-3-642-04288-1_8, © Springer-Verlag Berlin Heidelberg 2010

[129]. Therefore, TF may have a positive impact on unit tests (e.g. their fault detection effectiveness and thoroughness). However, the question is whether the effect of TF on mutation score indicator (MSI) and branch coverage (BC) is significant or not. Therefore, the aim of this chapter is to present the preliminary empirical evidence to answer this question and to test the null hypothesis that there is no difference in MSI and BC between the TLSP and TFSP projects.

In contrast to the previous Chaps. (5, 6 and 7), concerning the effects of the TF practice, this chapter reports preliminary results which come from one experiment. Those results are clearly insufficient to be included in the meta-analysis performed in Chapter 9; they deserve, however, a brief presentation, since they are brand new research findings.

It is also worth mentioning that non of the collected pre-test results were included in the model as a covariate. In fact, *JSPExp* (programming experience in Java Server Pages technology collected by means of a pre-test questionnaire) meets formal assumptions to be included in the model (e.g. *JSPExp* is measured before the experimental manipulation takes place, and correlates with the dependent variables). Even though the aforesaid formal requirements are fulfilled, it cannot be taken for granted that there is a reliable relationship between *JSPExp* and the dependent variables.

8.1 Analysis of Experiment SUBMISSION

The selective analysis of 19 projects (10 TLSP and 9 TFSP ones) of Experiment SUBMISSION[1] has been performed in this section on the basis of the selection criteria presented in Sect. 4.7.7.

8.1.1 Descriptive Statistics

The descriptive statistics of the results are presented in Table 8.1.

The TF development practice seems to have no impact on MSI but a positive impact on BC, as in the latter case, the TFSP experimental group has a higher mean, median and 95% confidence interval than the TLSP group.

Figures 8.1 and 8.2 present the boxplots comparing the MSI and BC results between the two experimental groups (TLSP and TFSP).

There is one extreme point and one outlier in Figs. 8.1 and 8.2, respectively. However, there was no reason to exclude them from further analysis.

Summarizing the descriptive statistics in APA format [12], it may be concluded that MSI in the TFSP ($M = 0.17$, SD $= 0.13$) and TLSP ($M = 0.17$, SD $= 0.10$) groups are similar. However, BC in the TFSP experimental group ($M = 0.64$,

---

[1] Metrics calculation was not possible in one of the projects. Hence, the number of analysed projects was reduced to 19.

Table 8.1 Descriptive statistics for mutation score indicator and branch coverage (DV: MSI, BC)

DV	Dev Tech	Mean (M)	Std. Dev. (SD)	Std. Error (SE)	Max	Median (Mdn)	Min	95% CI Lower Bound	Upper Bound
MSI	TLSP	0.167	0.100	0.032	0.330	0.160	0.030	0.095	0.239
	TFSP	0.168	0.125	0.042	0.470	0.150	0.060	0.072	0.264
BC	TLSP	0.565	0.140	0.044	0.721	0.569	0.294	0.465	0.664
	TFSP	0.641	0.175	0.058	0.857	0.683	0.304	0.507	0.776

```
Listing 8.1: Related SPSS syntax

EXAMINE
   VARIABLES=MSI BC BY DevTech
   /PLOT BOXPLOT STEMLEAF HISTOGRAM NPPLOT SPREADLEVEL(1)
   /COMPARE GROUP
   /STATISTICS DESCRIPTIVES
   /CINTERVAL 95
   /MISSING LISTWISE
   /NOTOTAL.
```

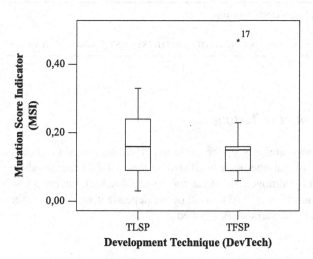

Fig. 8.1 Boxplot for MSI – selective analysis

```
Listing 8.2: Related SPSS syntax

EXAMINE
   VARIABLES=MSI BY DevTech /PLOT=BOXPLOT/STATISTICS=NONE/NOTOTAL.
```

SD = 0.18) is higher than in the TLSP one (M = 0.57, SD = 0.14). To answer the question whether the impact of the TF practice on mutation score indicator and branch coverage is significant or not, statistical tests are performed, preceded by the testing of the underlying assumptions.

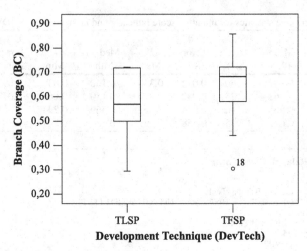

Fig. 8.2 Boxplot for BC – selective analysis

Listing 8.3: Related SPSS syntax

```
EXAMINE
    VARIABLES=BC BY DevTech /PLOT=BOXPLOT/STATISTICS=NONE/NOTOTAL.
```

8.1.2 Assumption Testing

The exploratory analysis of the collected data, necessary to check whether the assumptions of parametric tests (listed in Sect. 4.7.2) are satisfied, starts with Levene's test of homogeneity of variance (see Table 8.2). Levene's test is not statistically significant ($p > 0.05$) for all of the dependent variables, so the assumption of homogeneity of variance is satisfied.

Table 8.2 Levene's test of equality of error variances

DV	F	df1	df2	Sig.
MSI	0.013	1	17	0.910
BC	0.315	1	17	0.582

The assumption of normality was checked by means of the Kolmogorov–Smirnov and the Shapiro–Wilk tests presented in Table 8.3.

It turned out that the assumption of normality is not satisfied, as the significance (Sig.) values for MSI in the TFSP group were lower than 0.05 according to both statistics (see Table 8.3). Therefore, a non-parametric analysis is performed in Sect. 8.1.3.

Table 8.3 Tests of normality

DV	DevTech	Kolmogorov–Smirnov[1]			Shapiro–Wilk		
		Statistic	df[2]	Sig.	Statistic	df[2]	Sig.
MSI	TLSP	0.188	10	0.200[3]	0.943	10	0.590
	TFSP	0.303	9	0.017	0.767	9	0.008
BC	TLSP	0.166	10	0.200[3]	0.926	10	0.412
	TFSP	0.259	9	0.083	0.918	9	0.374

[1] Lilliefors Significance Correction.
[2] Degrees of freedom.
[3] This is a lower bound of the true significance.

8.1.3 Mann–Whitney Test

Table 8.4 shows the Mann–Whitney test statistics for the two dependent variables.

Table 8.4 Mann–Whitney test statistics (TLSP vs. TFSP)[1](DV: MSI, BC)

	MSI	BC
Mann–Whitney U	40.000	31.000
Wilcoxon W	85.000	86.000
Z	−0.410	−1.143
Asymp. Sig. (2-tailed)	0.682	0.253
Exact Sig. (2-tailed)	0.703	0.278
Exact Sig. (1-tailed)	0.351	0.139

[1] Grouping Variable: DevTech.

Listing 8.4: Related SPSS syntax

```
NPAR TESTS
  /M-W = MSI BC BY DevTech(1  2)
  /STATISTICS = DESCRIPTIVES
  /MISSING ANALYSIS
  /METHOD = EXACT TIMER(5).
```

The Mann–Whitney tests have been conducted to compare the MSI and BC data between the TLSP and the TFSP group. Both tests produce two-tailed significance (Sig.) values that are higher than 0.05. As a result, the specific hypotheses $H_{0,MSI,TLSP/TFSP}^{SUBMISSION}$ and $H_{0,BC,TLSP/TFSP}^{SUBMISSION}$ cannot be rejected.

8.1.3.1 Calculating Effect Size

The effect sizes for both dependent variables are calculated in this section from the Z scores on the basis of Eq. (5.3):

$$r_{MSI} = \sqrt{\frac{-0.410^2}{19}} = 0.09 \tag{8.1}$$

This represents a small effect (in accordance with Kempenes et al.'s [133] benchmark presented in Table 4.2) which tells us that there is not much difference between TFSP and TLSP with respect to MSI.

$$r_{BC} = \sqrt{\frac{-1.143^2}{19}} = 0.26 \tag{8.2}$$

This represents a medium effect, which tells us that the result of using or not using TF by the solo programmers was a substantive effect – that is the TFSP subjects achieved substantially higher branch coverage.

8.1.3.2 Summary

BC was not significantly higher in the TFSP (Mdn $= 0.68$) than in the TLSP (Mdn $= 0.57$) group ($U = 31.00$, $p = 0.28$, $r = 0.26$). However, the effect size was medium and therefore the effect of TF on branch coverage is considered a substantive effect. TLSP (Mdn $= 0.16$) and TFSP (Mdn $= 0.15$) did not significantly differ in MSI ($U = 40.00$, $p > 0.05$, $r = 0.09$). Furthermore, the effect size was small.

   In conclusion, the TF practice in this context proves to be visibly superior over the TL practice from the point of view of branch coverage. However, as far as mutation score indicator is concerned, the TF practice superiority is called into question. Plausible mechanisms behind the results are discussed in Sect. 10.3.

Chapter 9
Meta-Analysis

The more one analyses people, the more all reasons for
analysis disappear.
Sooner or later one comes to that dreadful universal thing
called human nature.

Oscar Wilde

Empirical investigation seeks unambiguous and reliable conclusions. Whenever the results of analysed empirical studies are different or even contradictory, arriving at a single, tenable conclusion becomes problematic, though. Moreover, personal commitment into conducted research is another factor hindering any possibly unbiased summary or interpretation of one's own results. In other words, the analysis of one's own investigation is as much a driving force as a threat to scientific objectivity. Fortunately, meta-analysis can be used to merge results of several empirical studies that address the same (or closely related) research questions. Meta-analysis is a statistical technique that has been designed to combine results from a series of studies, which alone had insufficient statistical power to accept or reject the null hypothesis in a reliable way. The results come from independent studies and can be combined and summarized in a quantitative manner for the purpose of integrating the findings and delivering more objective synthesis of previously produced empirical evidence than discursive reviews or conclusions. Hence, the use of meta-analysis, which is a kind of analysis of analyses, is accelerating [75].

This chapter consists of three sections. Introduction to meta-analysis is provided in Sect. 9.1 where the most important concepts (e.g. combining *p*-values, combining effect sizes, a fixed effects model, a random effects model) and calculations used throughout the chapter are put forward. The preliminary meta-analysis based on the results of the three experiments is presented in Sect. 9.2, while the selective meta-analysis of the last two experiments, where more experienced and more homogeneous subjects were used, is shown in Sect. 9.3. The latter meta-analysis minimizes the threat of inadequate conceptualization of the problem (see Sect. 10.5.5.1) which refers to the fact that it is difficult to interpret the aggregated empirical results that include too dissimilar subjects and treatments.

L. Madeyski, *Test-Driven Development*,
DOI 10.1007/978-3-642-04288-1_9, © Springer-Verlag Berlin Heidelberg 2010

9.1 Introduction to Meta-Analysis

The calculations in this chapter concern the comparison between the TFSP and the TLSP development technique and are described in Sects. 9.1.1 and 9.1.2. All of the calculations were preformed in SPSS with the help of additional macros by Marta Garcia-Granero.

9.1.1 Combining p-Values Across Experiments

Whenever several data sets relating to a specific subject are gathered, a common question that arises is whether the combined evidence within them supports a particular statistical hypothesis.

For combining p-values, so-called Fisher's procedure has been followed. Given different p-levels of the experiments we check the heterogeneity of the Z-scores corresponding to each p-level by calculating

$$\chi^2 = \sum_{i=1}^{k} (Z_i - \overline{Z})^2 \tag{9.1}$$

which is distributed as χ^2 with $k - 1$ degrees of freedom (where k is the number of combined studies, Z_i is the Z for each study and $\overline{Z}$ is the mean of all the Z-scores). If the test for homogeneity for the p-values results in $p > 0.05$, we cannot reject the null hypothesis that our p-values, coming from different experiments, are homogeneous. This means that we can combine the p-values according to Fisher's procedure. It is a convenient way to combine the results from a variety of independent tests bearing upon the same overall hypothesis (e.g. $H_{0,\text{PATP},TLSP/TFSP}$) as if in a single large test. Fisher's method combines p-values into one test statistic having a χ^2 distribution. We reject the null hypothesis (e.g. $H_{0,\text{PATP},TLSP/TFSP}^{\text{ACCOUNTING,SUBMISSION,SMELLS\&LIBRARY}}$) for the combined tests if

$$P = -2 * \sum_{i=1}^{k} \ln p_i \geq C \tag{9.2}$$

where p_i is a p-value obtained in the experiment i, C is obtained from the χ^2-distribution with $2k$ degrees of freedom and k is the number of combined studies. Some comments to Fisher's procedure are presented in Box 9.1, while useful snippet of SPSS syntax for Z-scores calculation based on p-values is given in Box 9.2.

The p-values from Experiments ACCOUNTING, SUBMISSION and SMELLS& LIBRARY, as well as the effect sizes, related to the impact of TFSP vs. TLSP on PATP are presented in Table 9.1.

Table 9.1 P-values and effect sizes related to impact of TFSP vs. TLSP on PATP

Experiment	Analysis	Obser-vations	Sig. p	Effect Size r	ES_{Zr}	Weight w	$w \times ES_{Zr}$
ACCOUNTING	Selective[1]	47	0.196	−0.1904	−0.1927	44	−8.4796
SUBMISSION	Selective[2]	20	0.311	−0.2182	−0.2218	17	−3.7703
SMELLS&LIBRARY	Selective[3]	44	0.874	0.0270	0.0270	41	1.1067

[1] Based on the results of the selective analysis presented in Sect. 5.1.2.4.
[2] Based on the results of the selective analysis presented in Sect. 5.2.2.4.
[3] Based on the results of the selective analysis presented in Sect. 5.3.2.

9.1.2 Combining Effect Sizes Across Experiments

Combining p-values does not yield information about the overall magnitude of the TF effect or the consistency of the effects across experiments [212]. Therefore, combining effect sizes is much more important.

There are many different measures of an effect size (e.g. the Pearson product-moment correlation coefficient r, Cohen's effect size index d, odds ratio OR). However, a correlation coefficient (r) is used most often [148], hence the meta-analysis procedure, presented in this section, is based on correlations. The procedure follows the guidelines given by Hedges and Olkin [99], DerSimonian and Laird [62], Rosenthal and Rubin [212], Lipsey and Wilson [151] as well as Hedges and Vevea [100].

Box 9.1 Comments to Fisher's procedure

It is worth mentioning that none of the individual tests may be significant when considered alone, but Fisher's approach can potentially offer more power, and, therefore, it can generate a significant result when all the tests are combined. However, there are certain rules that have to be obeyed in applying Fisher's procedure [27]:

- The samples have to be independent.
- For one-tailed tests, all the p-values must refer to the same tail, i.e. if the observed difference between the means is in the opposite direction than implied by an alternative hypothesis (H_1), then the p-value should be subtracted from unity before combining it in Fisher's expression.
- For two-tailed tests, several approaches were proposed but a conservative approach is to convert two-tailed p-values into one-tailed p-values, use them to obtain the combined one-tailed p and then double it for the final overall two-tailed p-value.

Useful Chi-Square Calculators are available online, e.g. http://www.stat.tamu.edu/~west/applets/chisqdemo.html or http://www.danielsoper.com/statcalc/calc11.aspx. In addition to Fisher's procedure, which is the most popular method for combining p-values, there are also other methods of combining p-values into a single test of a common hypothesis (e.g. Stouffer's method [236], Mudholkhar and George's method [182]).

Box 9.2 Useful snippet of SPSS Syntax for Z-scores calculation based on p-values

COMPUTE zscore=IDF.NORMAL(1-onesignedpvalue, 0, 1).

Note: Online Z-score calculators (e.g. `http://www.fourmilab.ch/rpkp/experiments/analysis/zCalc.html`) can also be used to determine the Z-score.

There are two main ways to combine the effect sizes from individual experiments. The first, called a "fixed effects model" and presented in Sect. 9.1.2.1, assumes that the effect size in the population is the same for all studies included in a meta-analysis [112]. The second, called a "random effects model", assumes that the population effect sizes vary randomly from study to study. In fact, a mixed model is possible, too.

If we want to make inferences that extend to the experiments included in the meta-analysis, then the fixed effects model is appropriate. However, if we want to generalize beyond the experiments included in the meta-analysis, then the random effects model is more appropriate [100].

9.1.2.1 Fixed Effects Model

The standard error is needed for the inverse variance weight in a meta-analysis. However, according to Lipsey and Wilson [151], the product-moment correlation coefficient has a problematic standard error formulation. Therefore, Fisher's r-to-Z transformation is a convenient solution:

$$ES_{Zr_i} = 0.5 \ln \frac{1 + r_i}{1 - r_i} \tag{9.3}$$

The transformed effect sizes are then used to calculate the mean in which each effect size ES_{Zr_i} is weighted.

Hedges showed that the optimal weights for meta-analysis are the so-called inverse variance weights w. For correlation coefficients, the individual variance v_i is the inverse of the sample size minus three [99]:

$$w_i = \frac{1}{v_i} = \frac{1}{\frac{1}{n_i - 3}} = n_i - 3 \tag{9.4}$$

The weighted mean effect size can be calculated as follows:

$$\overline{ES_{Zr}} = \frac{\sum_{i=1}^{k}(w_i \times ES_{Zr_i})}{\sum_{i=1}^{k} w_i} = \frac{\sum_{i=1}^{k}((n_i - 3) \times ES_{Zr_i})}{\sum_{i=1}^{k}(n_i - 3)} \tag{9.5}$$

The standard error of the mean effect size ($SE_{\overline{ES_{Zr}}}$) is the square root of 1 divided by the sum of the weights:

$$SE_{\overline{ES_{Zr}}} = \sqrt{\frac{1}{\sum_{i=1}^{k} w_i}} = \sqrt{\frac{1}{\sum_{i=1}^{k}(n_i - 3)}} \tag{9.6}$$

Furthermore, 95% confidence intervals (95% CI) can be calculated as follows:

$$\overline{ES}_{Lower} = \overline{ES_{Zr}} - 1.96 \times SE_{\overline{ES_{Zr}}} \tag{9.7}$$

$$\overline{ES}_{Upper} = \overline{ES_{Zr}} + 1.96 \times SE_{\overline{ES_{Zr}}} \tag{9.8}$$

As shown in [151], a direct test of the significance of the mean effect size can be obtained in the following way:

$$Z = \frac{|\overline{ES}|}{SE_{\overline{ES}}} \tag{9.9}$$

where $|\overline{ES}|$ is the absolute value of the mean effect size and $SE_{\overline{ES}}$ is the standard error calculated in a way described above. The result of this formula is distributed as a standard normal variate (i.e. if it exceeds 1.96, it is statistically significant with $p \leq 0.05$).

9.1.2.2 Homogeneity Analysis

Undoubtedly, homogeneity analysis should be conducted to test the validity of the assumption that all of the effect sizes estimate the same population mean. If homogeneity is rejected, the distribution of effect sizes is assumed to be heterogeneous. In such case, a single mean effect size is not a good descriptor of distribution, since there are real differences between the studies and, consequently, the studies estimate different population mean effect sizes.

The homogeneity test is based on the Q statistic, which is distributed as a χ^2 with $k - 1$ degrees of freedom, where k is the number of effect sizes [99]:

$$Q = \sum_{i=1}^{k} w_i (ES_{Zr_i} - \overline{ES_{Zr}})^2 \tag{9.10}$$

where w_i is the weight for the individual effect size ES_{Zr_i}, while $\overline{ES_{Zr}}$ is the weighted mean effect size over the k effect sizes.

An algebraically equivalent formula for Q is [151]:

$$Q = (\sum_{i=1}^{k} w_i E S_{Zr_i}^2) - \frac{(\sum_{i=1}^{k} w_i E S_{Zr_i})^2}{\sum_{i=1}^{k} w_i} \tag{9.11}$$

Q is distributed as a Chi-Square with df equal to one less than the number of meta-analysed studies (combined effect sizes). Critical value for a Chi-Square with df equal to the number of studies decreased by one and assumed significance level can be obtained from a table of critical values of χ^2 distribution. If our calculated Q is lower than the critical value, we cannot reject the null hypothesis of homogeneity (i.e. the variability across effect sizes does not exceed what would be expected based on sampling error) and, in consequence, the fixed effects model is considered appropriate. If otherwise, distributions are heterogeneous and one of possible solutions is to assume random variability and fit the random effects model.

9.1.2.3 Random Effects Model

The procedure for a random effects model is described by Hedges and Olkin [99], DerSimonian and Laird [62] and Hedges and Vevea [100]. The difference between the fixed and the random effects model is that in the latter model the weights (used to calculate the average effect size and its associated standard error) include not only the within-study variance component (v_i) but also the between-study variance component (denoted by τ^2). Hence, both are added to calculate weights:

$$w_i = \frac{1}{v_i + \tau^2} \tag{9.12}$$

These weights can be used to calculate the weighted mean effect size $\overline{E S_{Zr}}$ and the standard error of the mean effect size $SE_{\overline{E S_{Zr}}}$ in the same way as for the fixed effects model.

The between-study variance component (τ^2) may be estimated on the basis of the weighted sum of squared errors (Q), the number of studies combined in the meta-analysis (k) as well as an additional constant c:

$$\tau^2 = \frac{Q - (k - 1)}{c} \tag{9.13}$$

where

$$c = \sum_{i=1}^{k} w_i - \frac{\sum_{i=1}^{k} w_i^2}{\sum_{i=1}^{k} w_i} \tag{9.14}$$

If Q is lower than $k - 1$, the estimate of between-study variance, τ^2, yields a negative value and is set at zero, as the variance between-studies cannot be negative.

Relying on Eqs. (9.14) and (9.4):

$$c = \sum_{i=1}^{k} (n_i - 3) - \frac{\sum_{i=1}^{k} (n_i - 3)^2}{\sum_{i=1}^{k} (n_i - 3)} \qquad (9.15)$$

9.2 Preliminary Meta-Analysis

The preliminary meta-analysis is based on the results of the three experiments (ACCOUNTING, SUBMISSION and SMELLS&LIBRARY).

9.2.1 Combining Effects on the Percentage of Acceptance Tests Passed (PATP)

The aim of this section is to provide a single, and as reliable as possible, conclusion on the effect of TF on PATP on the basis of a meta-analysis of the results of the conducted experiments presented in Table 9.1. In this meta-analysis, the results of all the selective analyses of Experiments ACCOUNTING, SUBMISSION and SMELLS&LIBRARY are combined.

It is worth mentioning that combining the effect sizes based on parametric and non-parametric statistics may have led to less precise results and, for that reason, they could be questionable. However, Rosenthal [212, p. 19] showed that an effect size r can be calculated on the basis of t (see Eq. (5.13)) or F (see Eq. (5.58)) statistics, or can be obtained from a p-level (converted to a Z-score) and the size of the study (see Eq. (5.3)). He declared that it makes no difference whether the data are ranked, or whether they are in a continuous or dichotomous form, and thus correlations (e.g. Pearson's r, point biserial r) are interpreted in exactly the same way [212, p. 19]. Moreover, Rosenthal and Rubin argued that the effect sizes from a variety of designs and analyses can be made comparable by transforming them into correlations [213]. Hence, the proposed approach seems to be justified.

9.2.1.1 Combining p-Values Across Experiments

For combining p-values, so-called Fisher's procedure (described in Sect. 9.1.1) has been followed. Given the three p-levels of our experiments (ACCOUNTING, SUBMISSION and SMELLS&LIBRARY) we check the heterogeneity of the Z-scores corresponding to each p-level by calculating

$$\chi^2 = \sum_{i=1}^{3} (Z_i - \overline{Z})^2 = (1.2930 - 0.8216)^2 + (1.0131 - 0.8216)^2$$

$$+ (0.1586 - 0.8216)^2 = 0.6985 \qquad (9.16)$$

which is distributed as χ^2 with 2 degrees of freedom.

The test for homogeneity for p-values results in $p = 0.7052 > 0.05$. Therefore, we cannot reject the null hypothesis that our p-values, coming from the experiments (ACCOUNTING, SUBMISSION and SMELLS&LIBRARY), are homogeneous. That means that we can can combine the p-values from a variety of independent tests bearing upon the same overall hypothesis as if in a large single test. We reject the null hypothesis $H_{0,PATP,TLSP/TFSP}^{ACCOUNTING,SUBMISSION,SMELLS\&LIBRARY}$ for the combined tests if

$$P = -2 \times \sum_{i=1}^{k} \ln p_i = -2 \times (\ln 0.098 + \ln 0.1555 + \ln 0.437) = 10.0234 \geq C$$

(9.17)

On the basis of χ^2 distribution, this value of P results in a two-tailed p-value $p = 2 \times 0.1237 = 0.2473 > 0.05$. Hence, we can conclude that the resulting combination of Experiments ACCOUNTING, SUBMISSION and SMELLS&LIBRARY revealed that the developers using the TFSP technique did not have a significantly different PATP than the developers using the TLSP technique.

It is worth mentioning that Mudholkar and George's method [182] (based on transforming p-values into logits) and Stouffer's method [236] (based on Z-values) have led to the same conclusion. Mudholkar and George's method returned a two-tailed $p = 0.1772$. Stouffer's methods (unweighted, weighted by weighting factors and weighted by square roots of weighting factors) returned the following two-tailed p-values: $p = 0.1547$, $p = 0.1971$ and $p = 0.1728$, respectively. Hence, we cannot reject the null hypothesis $H_{0,PATP,TLSP/TFSP}^{ACCOUNTING,SUBMISSION,SMELLS\&LIBRARY}$.

9.2.1.2 Combining Effect Sizes Across Experiments – Fixed Effects Model

However, combining p-values does not yield information about the overall magnitude of the TF effect or the consistency of effects across the experiments. Therefore, combining effect sizes is much more important. The standard error is needed for the inverse variance weight in meta-analysis. However, as mentioned before in Sect. 9.1.2.1, correlation has a problematic standard error formulation [151]. Therefore, Fisher's r-to-Z transformation (i.e. the meta-analysis performed on Fisher's Zr transformed correlations) is a convenient solution:

$$ES_{Zr_i} = 0.5ln\frac{1 + r_i}{1 - r_i}$$

(9.18)

The transformed effect sizes are then used to calculate a mean in which each effect size ES_{Zr_i} is weighted.

Hedges [99] showed that the optimal weights for meta-analysis are the so-called inverse variance weights w. For correlation coefficients, the individual variance is the inverse of the sample size minus three (see Eq. (9.4)), so $w_i = \frac{1}{v_i} = \frac{1}{\frac{1}{n_i-3}} = n_i - 3$ [99].

The weighted mean effect size can be calculated on the basis of Eq. (9.5):

$$
\begin{aligned}
\overline{ES} &= \frac{\sum_{i=1}^{k}(w_i \times ES_{Zr_i})}{\sum_{i=1}^{k} w_i} \\
&= \frac{\sum_{i=1}^{k}((n_i - 3) \times ES_{Zr_i})}{\sum_{i=1}^{k}(n_i - 3)} \\
&= \frac{-8.4796 - 3.7703 + 1.1067}{44 + 17 + 41} = -0.1092
\end{aligned}
\tag{9.19}
$$

It means that the mean effect size of the test-first programming (TF) practice on the percentage of acceptance tests passed (PATP) represents a small effect.

The standard error of the mean effect size (SE$_{\overline{ES}}$) is the square root of 1 divided by the sum of the weights:

$$
\mathrm{SE}_{\overline{ES}} = \sqrt{\frac{1}{\sum_{i=1}^{k} w_i}} = \sqrt{\frac{1}{\sum_{i=1}^{k}(n_i - 3)}} = \sqrt{\frac{1}{102}} = 0.0990
\tag{9.20}
$$

Furthermore, 95% confidence intervals (95% CI) can be calculated as follows:

$$
\overline{ES}_{Lower} = \overline{ES} - 1.96 \times \mathrm{SE}_{\overline{ES}} = -0.1092 - 1.96 \times 0.0990 = -0.3033
\tag{9.21}
$$

$$
\overline{ES}_{Upper} = \overline{ES} + 1.96 \times \mathrm{SE}_{\overline{ES}} = -0.1092 + 1.96 \times 0.0990 = 0.0848
\tag{9.22}
$$

The Z-score of the mean effect size can be obtained as follows:

$$
Z = \frac{|\overline{ES}|}{\mathrm{SE}_{\overline{ES}}} = \frac{0.1092}{0.0990} = 1.1033
\tag{9.23}
$$

where $|\overline{ES}|$ is the absolute value of the mean effect size and SE$_{\overline{ES}}$ is the standard error calculated, as mentioned before in Sect. 9.1.2.1.

The results of the meta-analysis of correlations using the fixed effects model by Hedges and Olkin [99] are presented by the Forest plot shown in Fig. 9.1. The figure illustrates the benefits of the meta-analysis, as the width of the 95% confidence interval is much narrower.

The homogeneity test is based on the Q statistic, which is distributed as a χ^2 with $k - 1$ degrees of freedom, where k is the number of effect sizes [99]:

$$
Q = \sum_{i=1}^{k} w_i (ES_{Zr_i} - \overline{ES})^2 = 1.2829
\tag{9.24}
$$

where w_i is the weight for the individual effect size ES_{Zr_i}, while $\overline{ES}$ is the weighted mean effect size over the k effect sizes.

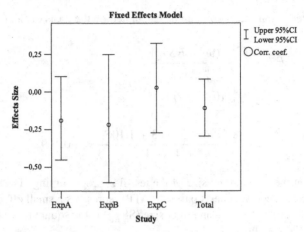

Fig. 9.1 Forest plot with individual and aggregated effect sizes for PATP – preliminary meta-analysis using fixed effects model

Q is distributed as a Chi-Square with df equal to the number of the combined effect sizes decreased by one (i.e. $3-1 = 2$). Based on the χ^2 distribution, this value of Q results in a one-tailed p-value of $p = 0.5265$ (critical value for a Chi-Square with $df = 2$ and one-tailed $p = 0.05$ is 5.99, while our calculated $Q = 1.2829$ is lower than the aforesaid critical value). Hence, we cannot reject the null hypothesis of homogeneity and, therefore, the fixed effects model is considered appropriate. However, to allow inferences that generalize beyond the experiments included in the meta-analysis, the random effects model will be employed [100].

9.2.1.3 Combining Effect Sizes Across Experiments – Random Effects Model

Following the procedure described in Section 9.1.2.3, the between-study variance component (τ^2) may be estimated on the basis of Eq. (9.13):

$$\tau^2 = \frac{Q - (k - 1)}{c} \tag{9.25}$$

Since Q is lower than $k - 1 = 2$, the estimate of between-study variance, τ^2, yields a negative value. Therefore, as already explained in Sect. 9.1.2.3, τ^2 is set at zero. That means that the fixed and random effects models yield identical results.

9.2.1.4 Summary

The null hypothesis $H_{0,PATP,TLSP/TFSP}^{ACCOUNTING,SUBMISSION,SMELLS\&LIBRARY}$ for the combined experiments (ACCOUNTING, SUBMISSION and SMELLS&LIBRARY) cannot be rejected ($\chi^2(6) = 10.0234$, two-tailed $p = 0.2473$). The mean effect size of the TF practice on the percentage of acceptance tests passed (PATP) represents a small effect ($\overline{ES} = -0.1092$, 95% confidence interval: -0.303 to 0.085).

9.2.2 Combining Effects on the Number of Acceptance Tests Passed Per Development Hour (NATPPH)

The aim of this section is to provide a single and reliable conclusion on the effect of TF on NATPPH on the basis of a meta-analysis of the results of the conducted experiments presented in Table 9.2.

Table 9.2 *P*-values and effect sizes related to impact of TFSP vs. TLSP on NATPPH

Expe- riment	Analysis	Obser- vations	Sig. (2-tailed)	Effect Size *r*
ACCOUNTING	Selective[1]	47	0.196	−0.1904
SUBMISSION	Selective[2]	20	0.572	−0.1270
SMELLS&LIBRARY	Selective[3]	44	0.463	0.1150

[1] Based on the results of the selective analysis presented in Sect. 6.1.
[2] Based on the results of the selective analysis (rank-transformed ANCOVA) in Sect. 6.2.3.2.
[3] Based on the results of the selective, non-parametric analysis presented in Sect. 6.3.

9.2.2.1 Combining *p*-Values Across Experiments

Combining *p*-values across experiments by means of Fisher's method (presented in Sect. 9.1.1) has given the following results:

- We cannot reject the null hypothesis that our *p*-values, coming from Experiments ACCOUNTING, SUBMISSION and SMELLS&LIBRARY, are homogeneous ($\chi^2(k - 1) = 0.2903$ where $k = 3$ is the number of meta-analysed experiments, $p = 0.8649$). Consequently, we can combine the *p*-values from the independent studies.
- We cannot reject the null hypothesis $H_{0,\text{NATPPH},TLSP/TFSP}^{\text{ACCOUNTING,SUBMISSION,SMELLS\&LIBRARY}}$ for the combined tests ($\chi^2(2k) = 10.0755$, the two-tailed $p = 0.2430$).

It is worth mentioning that Mudholkar and George's method [182] has led to the same conclusion (two-tailed $p = 0.1610$, $t(5k + 4) = 1.4586$). Stouffer's unweighted, weighted by weighting factors and weighted by square roots of weighting factors methods returned the following two-tailed *p*-values: $p = 0.1345$ ($r = 0.1482$), $p = 0.1222$ ($r = 0.1530$) and $p = 0.1223$ ($r = 0.1530$), respectively. In conclusion, we cannot reject the null hypothesis $H_{0,\text{NATPPH},TLSP/TFSP}^{\text{ACCOUNTING,SUBMISSION,SMELLS\&LIBRARY}}$, owing to the fact that all the methods returned two-tailed *p*-values greater than 0.05.

9.2.2.2 Combining Effect Sizes Across Experiments – Fixed Effects Model

The effect sizes from the conducted experiments (ACCOUNTING, SUBMISSION and SMELLS&LIBRARY), as well as the aggregated effect size of TF on NATPPH, calculated by means of the fixed effects model by Hedges and Olkin [99] are presented by the Forest plot shown in Fig. 9.2.

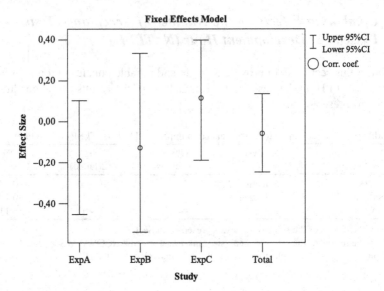

Fig. 9.2 Forest plot with individual and aggregated effect sizes for NATPPH – preliminary meta-analysis using fixed effects model

The weighted mean effect size is calculated as shown in Eq. (9.19):

$$\overline{ES} = -0.058 \tag{9.26}$$

95% confidence intervals (95% CI), calculated as demonstrated in Eqs. (9.21) and (9.22), are as follows:

$$\overline{ES}_{\text{Lower}} = -0.247 \tag{9.27}$$

$$\overline{ES}_{\text{Upper}} = 0.135 \tag{9.28}$$

9.2.2.3 Combining Effect Sizes Across Experiments – Random Effects Model

Following the procedure described in Sect. 9.1.2.3, the between-study variance component (τ^2) has been estimated:

$$\tau^2 = 0.002 \tag{9.29}$$

The effect sizes from the conducted experiments (ACCOUNTING, SUBMISSION and SMELLS&LIBRARY), as well as the aggregated effect size of TF on NATPPH, calculated by means of the random effects model by Hedges and Olkin [99] are presented by the Forest plot shown in Fig. 9.3.

The weighted mean effect size is calculated as shown in Eq. (9.19):

$$\overline{ES} = -0.058 \tag{9.30}$$

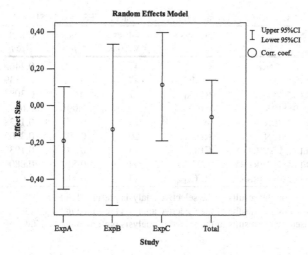

Fig. 9.3 Forest plot with individual and aggregated effect sizes for NATPPH – preliminary meta-analysis using random effects model

95% confidence intervals (95% CI), calculated as presented in Eqs. (9.21) and (9.22), are as follows:

$$\overline{ES}_{\text{Lower}} = -0.253 \tag{9.31}$$

$$\overline{ES}_{\text{Upper}} = 0.142 \tag{9.32}$$

9.2.2.4 Summary

The null hypothesis $H_{0,\text{NATPPH},TLSP/TFSP}^{\text{ACCOUNTING,SUBMISSION,SMELLS\&LIBRARY}}$ for the combined studies cannot be rejected ($\chi^2(6) = 10.0755$, two-tailed $p = 0.2430$). On the basis of the random effects model, the mean effect size of the TF practice on the number of acceptance tests passed per hour (NATPPH) represents a small effect ($\overline{ES} = -0.058$, 95% confidence interval: -0.253 to 0.142).

9.2.3 Combining Effects on Design Complexity

The aim of this section is to provide a single and reliable conclusion on the effect of TF on CBO_{Mean}, WMC_{Mean} and RFC_{Mean} on the basis of a meta-analysis of the results of the three conducted experiments presented in Table 9.3.

9.2.3.1 Combining p-Values Across Experiments

The significance values related to the three dependent variables (CBO_{Mean}, WMC_{Mean} and RFC_{Mean}) are combined in the forthcoming sections.

Table 9.3 P-values and effect sizes related to impact of TFSP vs. TLSP on NATPPH

Expe- riment	Analysis	Obser- vations	Sig. p	Effect Size r
ACCOUNTING	CBO_{Mean}[1]	47	0.002	0.4466
ACCOUNTING	WMC_{Mean}[1]	47	0.442	0.1139
ACCOUNTING	RFC_{Mean}[1]	47	0.034	0.3084
SUBMISSION	CBO_{Mean}[2]	20	0.001	0.6719
SUBMISSION	WMC_{Mean}[2]	20	0.574	0.1338
SUBMISSION	RFC_{Mean}[2]	20	0.198	0.3002
SMELLS&LIBRARY	CBO_{Mean}[3]	44	0.191	0.1933
SMELLS&LIBRARY	WMC_{Mean}[3]	44	0.549	−0.0806
SMELLS&LIBRARY	RFC_{Mean}[3]	44	0.911	−0.0154

[1] Based on the results of the selective analysis presented in Sect. 7.2.
[2] Based on the results of the selective analysis presented in Sect. 7.3.
[3] Based on the results of the selective analysis presented in Sect. 7.4.

Coupling Between Object Classes (CBO_{Mean})

Combining p-values across the experiments, by means of Fisher's method (see Sect. 9.1.1), has given the following results:

- We cannot reject the null hypothesis that our p-values, coming from Experiments ACCOUNTING, SUBMISSION and SMELLS&LIBRARY, are homogeneous ($\chi^2(k - 1) = 2.3832$ where $k = 3$ is the number of the meta-analysed experiments, $p = 0.3037$). Consequently, we can combine the p-values from independent studies ACCOUNTING, SUBMISSION and SMELLS&LIBRARY.
- We can reject the null hypothesis $H_{0,CBO_{Mean},TLSP/TFSP}^{ACCOUNTING,SUBMISSION,SMELLS\&LIBRARY}$ for the combined tests ($\chi^2(2k) = 33.7146$, two-tailed $p = 0.0000$).

It is worth mentioning that Mudholkar and George's method [182] and Stouffer's method [236] have led to the same conclusion. Mudholkar and George's method returned a two-tailed $p = 0.0000$ ($t(5k + 4) = 5.6384$). Stouffer's unweighted, weighted by weighting factors and weighted by square roots of weighting factors methods returned the following two-tailed p-values: $p = 0.0000$ ($r = 0.4395$), $p = 0.0001$ ($r = 0.3890$) and $p = 0.0000$ ($r = 0.4161$), respectively. Hence, we may conclude that, in fact, we can reject the null hypothesis $H_{0,CBO_{Mean},TLSP/TFSP}^{ACCOUNTING,SUBMISSION,SMELLS\&LIBRARY}$.

Weighted Methods per Class (WMC_{Mean})

Combining p-values across the experiments, by means of Fisher's method (see Sect. 9.1.1), has given the following results:

- We cannot reject the null hypothesis that our p-values, coming from Experiments ACCOUNTING, SUBMISSION and SMELLS&LIBRARY, are homogeneous ($\chi^2(k - 1) = 0.0243$ where $k = 3$ is the number of the analysed experiments,

$p = 0.9879$). Consequently, we can combine the p-values from independent studies ACCOUNTING, SUBMISSION and SMELLS&LIBRARY.

- We cannot reject the null hypothesis $H_{0,\text{WMC}_{\text{Mean}},TLSP/TFSP}^{\text{ACCOUNTING,SUBMISSION,SMELLS\&LIBRARY}}$ for the combined tests ($\chi^2(2k) = 8.1013$, two-tailed $p = 0.4615$).

It is worth mentioning that Mudholkar and George's method [182] and Stouffer's method [236] have led to the same conclusion. Mudholkar and George's method returned a two-tailed $p = 0.3037$ ($t(5k + 4) = 1.0572$). Stouffer's unweighted, weighted by weighting factors and weighted by square roots of weighting factors methods returned the following two-tailed p-values: $p = 0.2651$ ($r = 0.1103$), $p = 0.2769$ ($r = 0.1077$) and $p = 0.2651$ ($r = 0.1103$), respectively. Hence, we may conclude that we cannot indeed reject the null hypothesis $H_{0,\text{WMC}_{\text{Mean}},TLSP/TFSP}^{\text{ACCOUNTING,SUBMISSION,SMELLS\&LIBRARY}}$.

Response for a Class (RFC_{Mean})

Combining p-values across the experiments, by means of Fisher's method (see Sect. 9.1.1), has given the following results:

- We cannot reject the null hypothesis that our p-values, coming from Experiments ACCOUNTING, SUBMISSION and SMELLS&LIBRARY, are homogeneous ($\chi^2(k-1) = 2.0362$ where $k = 3$ is the number of the analysed experiments, $p = 0.3613$). Therefore, we can combine the p-values from independent studies ACCOUNTING, SUBMISSION, and SMELLS&LIBRARY.
- We cannot reject the null hypothesis $H_{0,RFC_{\text{Mean}},TLSP/TFSP}^{\text{ACCOUNTING,SUBMISSION,SMELLS\&LIBRARY}}$ for the combined tests ($\chi^2(2k) = 14.3471$, two-tailed $p = 0.0520$).

It is worth mentioning that Mudholkar and George's method [182] has led to the opposite conclusion and returned a two-tailed $p = 0.0430$ ($t(5k + 4) = 2.1686$). Stouffer's unweighted, weighted by weighting factors and weighted by square roots of weighting factors methods returned the following two-tailed p-values: $p = 0.0422$ ($r = 0.2012$), $p = 0.0554$ ($r = 0.1897$) and $p = 0.0467$ ($r = 0.1969$), respectively. We cannot reject the null hypothesis $H_{0,RFC_{\text{Mean}},TLSP/TFSP}^{\text{ACCOUNTING,SUBMISSION,SMELLS\&LIBRARY}}$ on the basis of Fisher's test recommended by Hedges and Olkin [99], as the two-tailed p-value is slightly greater than 0.05. However, the logit method (which is considered nearly optimal for a variety of situations, according to Mudholkar and George [182]) suggests the opposite conclusion. Therefore, both results are reported and further investigation is needed to establish evidence.

9.2.3.2 Combining Effect Sizes Across Experiments – Fixed Effects Model

The effect sizes related to the three dependent variables (CBO_{Mean}, WMC_{Mean} and RFC_{Mean}) are combined in the forthcoming sections using the fixed effects model [99].

Coupling Between Object Classes (CBO_Mean)

Effect sizes from the conducted experiments (ACCOUNTING, SUBMISSION and SMELLS&LIBRARY), as well as the aggregated effect size of the TF practice on CBO_Mean, calculated by means of the fixed effects model are presented by the Forest plot shown in Fig. 9.4.

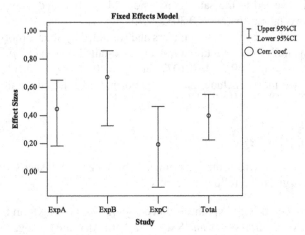

Fig. 9.4 Forest plot with individual and aggregated effect sizes for CBO_Mean – preliminary meta-analysis using fixed effects model

The weighted mean effect size is calculated as shown in Eq. (9.19):

$$\overline{ES} = 0.398 \tag{9.33}$$

95% confidence intervals (95% CI), calculated as demonstrated in Eqs. (9.21) and (9.22), are as follows:

$$\overline{ES}_{\text{Lower}} = 0.224 \tag{9.34}$$

$$\overline{ES}_{\text{Upper}} = 0.548 \tag{9.35}$$

Weighted Methods per Class (WMC_Mean)

The effect sizes from the conducted experiments (ACCOUNTING, SUBMISSION and SMELLS&LIBRARY), as well as the aggregated effect size of TF on WMC_Mean, calculated by means of the fixed effects model are presented by the Forest plot shown in Fig. 9.5.

The weighted mean effect size is calculated as presented in Eq. (9.19):

$$\overline{ES} = 0.039 \tag{9.36}$$

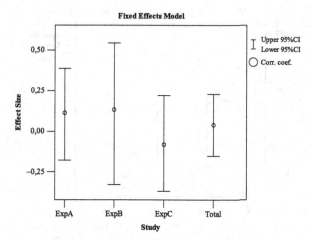

Fig. 9.5 Forest plot with individual and aggregated effect sizes for WMC$_{\text{Mean}}$ – preliminary meta-analysis using fixed effects model

95% confidence intervals (95% CI), calculated as demonstrated in Eqs. (9.21) and (9.22), are as follows:

$$\overline{ES}_{\text{Lower}} = -0.154 \tag{9.37}$$

$$\overline{ES}_{\text{Upper}} = 0.229 \tag{9.38}$$

Response For a Class (RFC_{Mean})

The effect sizes from the conducted experiments (ACCOUNTING, SUBMISSION and SMELLS&LIBRARY), as well as the aggregated effect size of TF on RFC_{Mean}, calculated by means of the fixed effects model are presented by the Forest plot shown in Fig. 9.6.

The weighted mean effect size is calculated as presented in Eq. (9.19):

$$\overline{ES} = 0.181 \tag{9.39}$$

95% confidence intervals (95% CI), calculated as demonstrated in Eqs. (9.21) and (9.22), are as follows:

$$\overline{ES}_{\text{Lower}} = -0.011 \tag{9.40}$$

$$\overline{ES}_{\text{Upper}} = 0.360 \tag{9.41}$$

9.2.3.3 Combining Effect Sizes Across Experiments – Random Effects Model

The effect sizes related to the three dependent variables (CBO$_{\text{Mean}}$, WMC$_{\text{Mean}}$ and RFC$_{\text{Mean}}$) are combined in the forthcoming sections using the random effects model [63, 99].

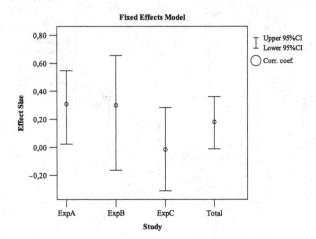

Fig. 9.6 Forest plot with individual and aggregated effect sizes for RFC_{Mean} – preliminary meta-analysis using fixed effects model

Coupling Between Object Classes (CBO_{Mean})

Following the procedure described in Sect. 9.1.2.3, the between-study variance component (τ^2) has been estimated:

$$\tau^2 = 0.045 \tag{9.42}$$

The effect sizes from the conducted experiments (ACCOUNTING, SUBMISSION and SMELLS&LIBRARY), as well as the aggregated effect size of TF on CBO_{Mean}, calculated by means of the random effects model are presented by the Forest plot shown in Fig. 9.7.

The weighted mean effect size is calculated as presented in Eq. (9.19):

$$\overline{ES} = 0.428 \tag{9.43}$$

95% confidence intervals (95% CI), calculated as demonstrated in Eqs. (9.21) and (9.22), are as follows:

$$\overline{ES}_{Lower} = 0.142 \tag{9.44}$$

$$\overline{ES}_{Upper} = 0.648 \tag{9.45}$$

Weighted Methods per Class (WMC_{Mean})

Following the procedure described in Sect. 9.1.2.3, the between-study variance component (τ^2) should be estimated. As $Q = 0.9941$ is lower than $k - 1 = 2$, the estimate of between-study variance, τ^2, yields a negative value. Therefore, as already explained in Sect. 9.1.2.3, τ^2 is set at zero. That points to the fact that the fixed and random effects models yield identical results.

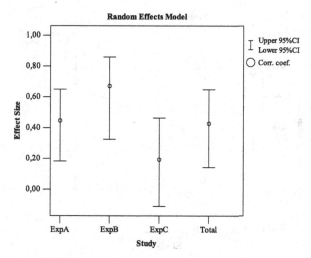

Fig. 9.7 Forest plot with individual and aggregated effect sizes for CBO_{Mean} – preliminary meta-analysis using random effects model

Response for a Class (RFC_{Mean})

Following the procedure described in Sect. 9.1.2.3, the between-study variance component (τ^2) has been estimated:

$$\tau^2 = 0.011 \tag{9.46}$$

The effect sizes from the conducted experiments (ACCOUNTING, SUBMISSION and SMELLS&LIBRARY), as well as the aggregated effect size of TF on RFC_{Mean}, calculated by means of random effects model are presented by the Forest plot shown in Fig. 9.8.

The weighted mean effect size is calculated as presented in Eq. (9.19):

$$\overline{ES} = 0.184 \tag{9.47}$$

95% confidence intervals (95% CI), calculated as demonstrated in Eqs. (9.21) and (9.22), are as follows:

$$\overline{ES}_{Lower} = -0.044 \tag{9.48}$$

$$\overline{ES}_{Upper} = 0.394 \tag{9.49}$$

9.2.3.4 Summary

The null hypothesis $H_{0,CBO_{Mean},TLSP/TFSP}^{ACCOUNTING,SUBMISSION,SMELLS\&LIBRARY}$ for the combined studies can be rejected ($\chi^2(6) = 33.7146$, two-tailed $p = 0.0000$). On the basis of the random effects model, the mean effect size of the TF practice on the mean coupling

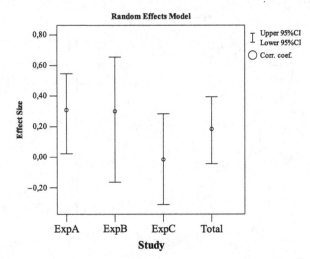

Fig. 9.8 Forest plot with individual and aggregated effect sizes for RFC_{Mean} – preliminary meta-analysis using random effects model

between object classes (CBO_{Mean}) represents a medium (but close to large) effect ($\overline{ES} = 0.428$, 95% confidence interval: 0.142 to 0.628).

The null hypothesis $H_{0,\text{WMC}_{\text{Mean}},TLSP/TFSP}^{\text{ACCOUNTING,SUBMISSION,SMELLS\&LIBRARY}}$ for the combined studies cannot be rejected ($\chi^2(6) = 8.1013$, two-tailed $p = 0.4615$). The mean effect size of TF on weighted methods per class (WMC_{Mean}) represents a small effect ($\overline{ES} = 0.039$, 95% confidence interval: -0.154 to 0.229).

The null hypothesis $H_{0,RFC_{\text{Mean}},TLSP/TFSP}^{\text{ACCOUNTING,SUBMISSION,SMELLS\&LIBRARY}}$ for the combined studies cannot be rejected ($\chi^2(6) = 14.3471$, two-tailed $p = 0.0520$) on the basis of Fisher's method recommended by Hedges and Olkin [99]. However, it should be mentioned that, according to Mudholkar and George's method [182], the null hypothesis can be rejected ($t(19) = 2.1686$, $p = 0.0430$). On the basis of the random effects model, the mean effect size of TF on response for a class (RFC_{Mean}) represents a small (but close to medium) effect ($\overline{ES} = 0.184$, 95% confidence interval: -0.044 to 0.394).

9.3 Selective Meta-Analysis

Experiments SUBMISSION and SMELLS&LIBRARY involved more experienced and more homogeneous subjects (i.e. developers) than Experiment ACCOUNTING. Moreover, as mentioned in Sect. 4.4.7.2, tests were often deferred or even neglected by the subjects in the TL projects in Experiment ACCOUNTING. In order to minimize the threat of an inadequate conceptualization of the problem which arises from the difficulty in the interpretation of the empirical results that come from too dissimilar subjects and treatments (see Sect. 10.5.5.1, it was indispensable to carry out a selective meta-analysis based on the results of Experiments SUBMISSION and SMELLS&LIBRARY.

9.3.1 Combining Effects on the Percentage of Acceptance Tests Passed (PATP)

The aim of this section is to provide a single and reliable conclusion on the effect of TF on PATP on the basis of a meta-analysis of the results of Experiments SUBMISSION and SMELLS&LIBRARY presented earlier in Table 9.1.

9.3.1.1 Combining p-Values Across Experiments

Combining p-values across the experiments, by means of Fisher's method (see Sect. 9.1.1), has given the following results:

- We cannot reject the null hypothesis that our p-values, coming from Experiments SUBMISSION and SMELLS&LIBRARY, are homogeneous ($\chi^2(k-1) = 0.3651$ where $k = 2$ is the number of the meta-analysed experiments, $p = 0.5457$). Therefore, we can combine the p-values from the independent studies.
- We cannot reject the null hypothesis $H_{0,PATP,TLSP/TFSP}^{SUBMISSION,SMELLS\&LIBRARY}$ for the combined tests ($\chi^2(2k) = 5.3779$, two-tailed $p = 0.5014$).

Mudholkar and George's method [182] has led to the same conclusion and returned a two-tailed $p = 0.4264$ ($t(5k + 4) = 8.192$). Stouffer's unweighted, weighted by weighting factors and weighted by square roots of weighting factors methods returned the following two-tailed p-values: $p = 0.4074$ ($r = 0.1088$), $p = 0.5930$ ($r = 0.0702$) and $p = 0.4953$ ($r = 0.0895$), respectively.

In conclusion, we cannot reject the null hypothesis $H_{0,PATP,TLSP/TFSP}^{SUBMISSION,SMELLS\&LIBRARY}$, since all of the aforementioned methods returned two-tailed p-values greater than 0.05.

9.3.1.2 Combining Effect Sizes Across Experiments – Fixed Effects Model

The effect sizes from Experiments SUBMISSION and SMELLS&LIBRARY, as well as the aggregated effect size of the TF practice on PATP, calculated by means of the fixed effects model by Hedges and Olkin [99], are presented by the Forest plot shown in Fig. 9.9.

The weighted mean effect size is calculated as presented in Eq. (9.19):

$$ES = -0.046 \qquad (9.50)$$

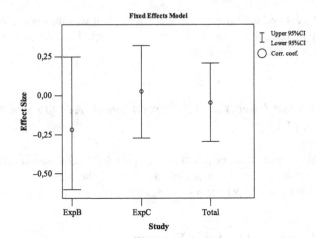

Fig. 9.9 Forest plot with individual and aggregated effect sizes for PATP – selective meta-analysis using fixed effects model

95% confidence intervals (95% CI), calculated as demonstrated in Eqs. (9.21) and (9.22), are as follows:

$$\overline{ES}_{\text{Lower}} = -0.294 \qquad\qquad (9.51)$$

$$\overline{ES}_{\text{Upper}} = 0.208 \qquad\qquad (9.52)$$

The homogeneity test is based on the Q statistic ($\chi^2 = 0.7437$, $p = 0.3885$). We cannot reject the null hypothesis of homogeneity, because $p = 0.3885 > 0.05$. Hence, the fixed effects model is considered appropriate. However, the random effects model, employed in Sect. 9.3.1.3, makes it possible to generalize beyond the studies included in the selective meta-analysis.

9.3.1.3 Combining Effect Sizes Across Experiments – Random Effects Model

Following the procedure described in Sect. 9.1.2.3, the between-study variance component (τ^2) should be estimated. As $Q = 0.7437$ is lower than $k - 1 = 1$, the estimate of between-study variance, τ^2, yields a negative value. Therefore, as already explained in Sect. 9.1.2.3, τ^2 is set at zero. Hence, the fixed and the random effects models yield identical results.

9.3.1.4 Summary

The null hypothesis $H_{0,\text{PATP},TLSP/TFSP}^{\text{SUBMISSION,SMELLS\&LIBRARY}}$ for combined studies cannot be rejected ($\chi^2(4) = 5.3779$, two-tailed $p = 0.5014$). The mean effect size of the TF practice on the percentage of acceptance tests passed (PATP) represents a very small effect ($\overline{ES} = -0.046$, 95% confidence interval: -0.294 to 0.208).

9.3.2 Combining Effects on the Number of Acceptance Tests Passed Per Hour (NATPPH)

The aim of this section is to provide a single and reliable conclusion on the effect of TF on NATPPH on the basis of a meta-analysis of the results of Experiments SUBMISSION and SMELLS&LIBRARY, presented earlier in Table 9.2.

9.3.2.1 Combining p-Values Across Experiments

Combining p-values across experiments, by means of Fisher's method (see Sect. 9.1.1), has given the following results:

- We cannot reject the null hypothesis that our p-values, coming from Experiments SUBMISSION and SMELLS&LIBRARY, are homogeneous ($\chi^2(k-1) = 0.0142$ where $k = 2$ is the number of the analysed experiments, $p = 0.9050$). Consequently, we can combine the p-values from the independent studies.
- We cannot reject the null hypothesis $H_{0,\text{NATPPH},TLSP/TFSP}^{\text{SUBMISSION,SMELLS\&LIBRARY}}$ for the combined tests ($\chi^2(2k) = 5.4299$, two-tailed $p = 0.4919$).

Mudholkar and George's method [182] has led to the same conclusion and returned two-tailed $p = 0.3883$ ($t(5k+4) = 0.8905$). Stouffer's unweighted, weighted by weighting factors and weighted by square roots of weighting factors methods returned the following two-tailed p-values: $p = 0.3583$ ($r = 0.1206$), $p = 0.3711$ ($r = 0.1174$) and $p = 0.3560$ ($r = 0.1212$), respectively.

In conclusion, we cannot reject the null hypothesis $H_{0,\text{NATPPH},TLSP/TFSP}^{\text{SUBMISSION,SMELLS\&LIBRARY}}$, since all of the aforementioned methods returned two-tailed p-values greater than 0.05.

9.3.2.2 Combining Effect Sizes Across Experiments – Fixed Effects Model

The effect sizes from Experiments SUBMISSION and SMELLS&LIBRARY, as well as the aggregated effect size of TF on NATPPH, calculated by means of the fixed effects model by Hedges and Olkin [99] are presented by the Forest plot shown in Fig. 9.10.

The weighted mean effect size is calculated as presented in Eq. (9.19):

$$\overline{ES} = 0.044 \tag{9.53}$$

95% confidence intervals (95% CI), calculated as demonstrated in Eqs. (9.21) and (9.22), are as follows:

$$\overline{ES}_{\text{Lower}} = -0.210 \tag{9.54}$$

$$\overline{ES}_{\text{Upper}} = 0.293 \tag{9.55}$$

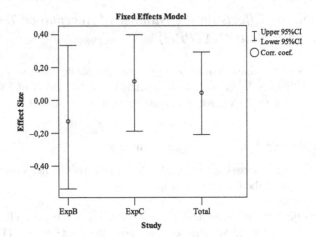

Fig. 9.10 Forest plot with individual and aggregated effect sizes for NATPPH – selective meta-analysis using fixed effects model

The homogeneity test is based on the Q statistic ($\chi^2 = 0.7111$, $p = 0.3991$). We cannot reject the null hypothesis of homogeneity, as $p = 0.3991 > 0.05$. Hence, the fixed effects model is considered appropriate. In addition, Sect. 9.3.2.3 presents the results of the random effects model, which makes it possible to generalize beyond the studies included in the selective meta-analysis.

9.3.2.3 Combining Effect Sizes Across Experiments – Random Effects Model

Following the procedure described in Sect. 9.1.2.3, the between-study variance component (τ^2) should be estimated. As $Q = 0.7111$ is lower than $k - 1 = 1$ the estimate of between-study variance, τ^2, yields a negative value. Therefore, as it was already explained in Sect. 9.1.2.3, τ^2 is set at zero. Hence, the fixed and the random effects models yield identical results.

9.3.2.4 Summary

The null hypothesis $H_{0,\text{NATPPH},TLSP/TFSP}^{\text{SUBMISSION,SMELLS\&LIBRARY}}$ for the combined studies cannot be rejected ($\chi^2(4) = 5.4299$, two-tailed $p = 0.4919$). The mean effect size of the TF practice on the number of acceptance tests passed per hour (NATPPH) represents a very small effect ($\overline{ES} = 0.044$, 95% confidence interval: -0.210 to 0.293).

9.3.3 Combining Effects on Design Complexity

The aim of this section is to provide a single and reliable conclusion on the effect of the TF practice on CBO_{Mean}, WMC_{Mean} and RFC_{Mean} on the basis of a meta-analysis of the results of Experiments SUBMISSION and SMELLS&LIBRARY presented earlier in Table 9.2.

9.3.3.1 Combining p-Values Across Experiments

The significance values (related to CBO_{Mean}, WMC_{Mean} and RFC_{Mean}) from Experiments SUBMISSION and SMELLS&LIBRARY are combined in the forthcoming sections.

Coupling Between Object Classes (CBO_{Mean})

Combining p-values across experiments, by means of Fisher's method (see Section 9.1.1), has given the following results:

- We cannot reject the null hypothesis that our p-values, coming from Experiments SUBMISSION and SMELLS&LIBRARY, are homogeneous ($\chi^2(k-1) = 1.9659$ where $k = 2$ is the number of the analysed experiments, $p = 0.1609$). Therefore, we can combine the p-values from the independent experiments.
- We can reject the null hypothesis $H_{0,CBO_{Mean},TLSP/TFSP}^{SUBMISSION,SMELLS\&LIBRARY}$ for the combined tests ($\chi^2(2k) = 19.8991$, two-tailed $p = 0.0010$).

Mudholkar and George's method [182] has led to the same conclusion and returned a two-tailed $p = 0.0010$ ($t(5k + 4) = 4.1471$). Stouffer's unweighted, weighted by weighting factors and weighted by square roots of weighting factors methods returned the following two-tailed p-values: $p = 0.0011$ ($r = 0.4269$), $p = 0.0136$ ($r = 0.3241$) and $p = 0.0040$ ($r = 0.3783$), respectively.

As a result, we can reject the null hypothesis $H_{0,CBO_{Mean},TLSP/TFSP}^{SUBMISSION,SMELLS\&LIBRARY}$, since all of the aforementioned methods returned a two-tailed p-value lower than 0.05.

Weighted Methods per Class (WMC_{Mean})

Combining p-values across the experiments, by means of Fisher's method (see Section 9.1.1), has given the following results:

- We cannot reject the null hypothesis that our p-values, coming from Experiments SUBMISSION and SMELLS&LIBRARY, are homogeneous ($\chi^2(k-1) = 0.0007$ where $k = 2$ is the number of the analysed experiments, $p = 0.9791$). Consequently, we can combine the p-values from the independent studies.
- We cannot reject the null hypothesis $H_{0,WMC_{Mean},TLSP/TFSP}^{SUBMISSION,SMELLS\&LIBRARY}$ for the combined tests ($\chi^2(2k) = 5.0822$, two-tailed $p = 0.5579$).

Mudholkar and George's method [182] has led to the same conclusion and returned a two-tailed $p = 0.4413$ ($t(5k + 4) = 0.7924$). Stouffer's unweighted, weighted by weighting factors and weighted by square roots of weighting factors methods returned the following two-tailed p-values: $p = 0.4115$ ($r = 0.1078$), $p = 0.4420$ ($r = 0.1010$) and $p = 0.4190$ ($r = 0.1061$), respectively.

In conclusion, we cannot reject the null hypothesis $H_{0,\mathrm{WMC_{Mean}},TLSP/TFSP}^{\mathrm{SUBMISSION,SMELLS\&LIBRARY}}$, owing to the fact that all of the aforementioned methods returned two-tailed p-values greater than 0.05.

Response For a Class (RFC_{Mean})

Combining p-values across the experiments, by means of Fisher's method (see Section 9.1.1), has given the following results:

- We cannot reject the null hypothesis that our p-values, coming from Experiments SUBMISSION and SMELLS&LIBRARY, are homogeneous ($\chi^2(k-1) = 0.6909$ where $k = 2$ is the number of the analysed experiments, $p = 0.4059$). Consequently, we can combine the p-values from the independent studies.
- We cannot reject the null hypothesis $H_{0,\mathrm{WMC_{Mean}},TLSP/TFSP}^{\mathrm{SUBMISSION,SMELLS\&LIBRARY}}$ for the combined tests ($\chi^2(2k) = 6.1980$, two-tailed $p = 0.3697$).

Mudholkar and George's method [182] has led to the same conclusion and returned a two-tailed $p = 0.3319$ ($t(5k+4) = 1.0051$). Stouffer's unweighted, weighted by weighting factors and weighted by square roots of weighting factors methods returned the following two-tailed p-values: $p = 0.3225$ ($r = 0.1299$), $p = 0.5510$ ($r = 0.0783$) and $p = 0.4290$ ($r = 0.1038$), respectively.

In brief, we cannot reject the null hypothesis $H_{0,RFC_{\mathrm{Mean}},TLSP/TFSP}^{\mathrm{SUBMISSION,SMELLS\&LIBRARY}}$, since all of the aforementioned methods returned two-tailed p-values greater than 0.05.

9.3.3.2 Combining Effect Sizes Across Experiments – Fixed Effects Model

This section presents a meta-analysis of the effect sizes from Experiments SUBMISSION and SMELLS&LIBRARY using the fixed effects model by Hedges and Olkin [99].

Coupling Between Object Classes (CBO$_{\mathrm{Mean}}$)

The effect sizes from Experiments SUBMISSION and SMELLS&LIBRARY, as well as the aggregated effect size of the TF practice on CBO_{Mean}, calculated by means of the fixed effects model are presented by the Forest plot shown in Fig. 9.11.

The weighted mean effect size is calculated as presented in Eq. (9.19):

$$\overline{ES} = 0.360 \tag{9.56}$$

95% confidence intervals (95% CI), calculated as demonstrated in Eqs. (9.21) and (9.22), are as follows:

$$\overline{ES}_{Lower} = 0.119 \tag{9.57}$$

$$\overline{ES}_{Upper} = 0.561 \tag{9.58}$$

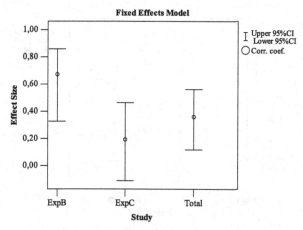

Fig. 9.11 Forest plot with individual and aggregated effect sizes for CBO_{Mean} – selective meta-analysis using fixed effects model

The homogeneity test is based on the Q statistic ($\chi^2 = 4.5970$, $p = 0.0320$). We can reject the null hypothesis of homogeneity as $p = 0.0320 < 0.05$. Hence, the fixed effects model is not considered appropriate and we assume that variability is random and fits the random effects model presented in Sect. 9.3.3.3.

Possible sources of variability between Experiments SUBMISSION and SMELLS&LIBRARY can be the differences in duration and size of the projects. For example, in Experiment SUBMISSION, 2–3 times more non-commented lines of code were produced on average ($NCLOC_{Mean}$) than in Experiment SMELLS& LIBRARY. Moreover, Experiment SUBMISSION consisted of 9-week projects, whereas Experiment SMELLS&LIBRARY covered shorter, 4-week projects. Hence, it seems reasonable that the differences in CBO_{Mean} between the TLSP and the TFSP group are more visible in longer and larger software projects in Experiment SUBMISSION.

Weighted Methods per Class (WMC_{Mean})

The effect sizes from Experiments SUBMISSION and SMELLS&LIBRARY, as well as the aggregated effect size of TF on WMC_{Mean}, calculated by means of the fixed effects model are presented by the Forest plot shown in Fig. 9.12.

The weighted mean effect size is calculated as presented in Eq. (9.19):

$$\overline{ES} = -0.018 \tag{9.59}$$

95% confidence intervals (95% CI), calculated as demonstrated in Eqs. (9.21) and (9.22), are as follows:

$$\overline{ES}_{Lower} = -0.268 \tag{9.60}$$

$$\overline{ES}_{Upper} = 0.235 \tag{9.61}$$

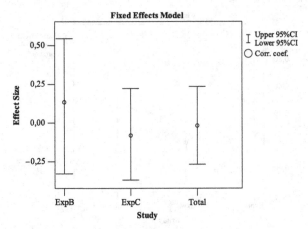

Fig. 9.12 Forest plot with individual and aggregated effect sizes for WMC_{Mean} – selective meta-analysis using fixed effects model

The homogeneity test is based on the Q statistic ($\chi^2 = 0.5578$, $p = 0.4552$). We cannot reject the null hypothesis of homogeneity, as $p = 0.4552 > 0.05$. Hence, the fixed effects model is considered appropriate. However, the random effects model, considered in Sect. 9.3.3.3, makes it possible to generalize beyond the studies included in the selective meta-analysis.

Response for a Class (RFC_{Mean})

The effect sizes from Experiments SUBMISSION and SMELLS&LIBRARY, as well as the aggregated effect size of TF on RFC_{Mean}, calculated by means of the fixed effects model are presented by the Forest plot shown in Fig. 9.13.

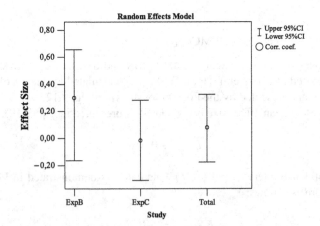

Fig. 9.13 Forest plot with individual and aggregated effect sizes for RFC_{Mean} – selective meta-analysis using fixed effects model

The weighted mean effect size is calculated as presented in Eq. (9.19):

$$\overline{ES} = 0.080 \qquad\qquad (9.62)$$

95% confidence intervals (95% CI), calculated as demonstrated in Eqs. (9.21) and (9.22), are as follows:

$$\overline{ES}_{\text{Lower}} = -0.176 \qquad\qquad (9.63)$$
$$\overline{ES}_{\text{Upper}} = 0.325 \qquad\qquad (9.64)$$

The homogeneity test is based on the Q statistic ($\chi^2 = 1.2704$, $p = 0.2597$). We cannot reject the null hypothesis of homogeneity, as $p = 0.2597 > 0.05$. Hence, the fixed effects model is considered appropriate. Again, in order to be able to generalize beyond the studies included in the selective meta-analysis, it is vital to consider the random effects model (see Sect. 9.3.3.3).

9.3.3.3 Combining Effect Sizes Across Experiments – Random Effects Model

This section presents a meta-analysis of the effect sizes from Experiments SUBMISSION and SMELLS&LIBRARY, using the random effects model [62, 99].

Coupling Between Object Classes (CBO$_{\text{Mean}}$)

Following the procedure described in Sect. 9.1.2.3, the between-study variance component (τ^2) has been estimated:

$$\tau^2 = 0.150 \qquad\qquad (9.65)$$

The effect sizes from Experiments SUBMISSION and SMELLS&LIBRARY, as well as the aggregated effect size of TF on CBO$_{\text{Mean}}$, calculated by means of the random effects model are presented by the Forest plot shown in Fig. 9.14.

The weighted mean effect size is calculated as presented in Eq. (9.19):

$$\overline{ES} = 0.444 \qquad\qquad (9.66)$$

95% confidence intervals (95% CI), calculated as demonstrated in Eqs. (9.21) and (9.22), are as follows:

$$\overline{ES}_{\text{Lower}} = -0.126 \qquad\qquad (9.67)$$
$$\overline{ES}_{\text{Upper}} = 0.793 \qquad\qquad (9.68)$$

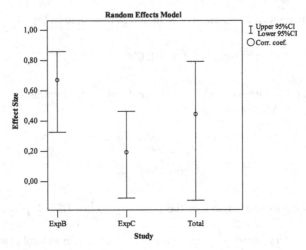

Fig. 9.14 Forest plot with individual and aggregated effect sizes for CBO_{Mean} – selective meta-analysis using random effects model

Weighted Methods per Class (WMC_{Mean})

Following the procedure described in Sect. 9.1.2.3, the between-study variance component (τ^2) may be estimated on the basis of Eq. (9.13):

$$\tau^2 = \frac{Q - (k - 1)}{c} \tag{9.69}$$

As $Q = 0.5578$ is lower than $k - 1 = 1$, the estimate of between-study variance, τ^2, yields a negative value. Therefore, as already explained in Sect. 9.1.2.3, τ^2 is set at zero. Hence, the fixed and the random effects models yield identical results.

Response For a Class (RFC_{Mean})

Following the procedure described in Sect. 9.1.2.3, the between-study variance component (τ^2) has been estimated:

$$\tau^2 = 0.011 \tag{9.70}$$

The effect sizes from Experiments SUBMISSION and SMELLS&LIBRARY, as well as the aggregated effect size of TF on RFC_{Mean}, calculated by means of the random effects model are presented by the Forest plot shown in Fig. 9.15.

The weighted mean effect size is calculated as presented in Eq. (9.19):

$$\overline{ES} = 0.094 \tag{9.71}$$

95% confidence intervals (95% CI), calculated as demonstrated in Eqs. (9.21) and (9.22), are as follows:

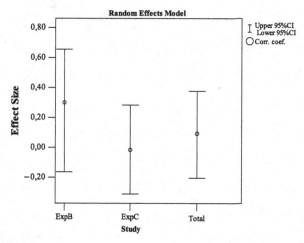

Fig. 9.15 Forest plot with individual and aggregated effect sizes for RFC_{Mean} – selective meta-analysis using random effects model

$$\overline{ES}_{\text{Lower}} = -0.204 \tag{9.72}$$

$$\overline{ES}_{\text{Upper}} = 0.376 \tag{9.73}$$

9.3.3.4 Summary

The null hypothesis $H_{0,\text{CBO}_{\text{Mean}},TLSP/TFSP}^{\text{SUBMISSION,SMELLS\&LIBRARY}}$ for the combined studies (SUBMISSION and SMELLS&LIBRARY) can be rejected ($\chi^2(4) = 19.8991$, two-tailed $p = 0.0010$). On the basis of the random effects model, the mean effect size of TF on the mean value of the coupling between object classes (CBO_{Mean}) represents a medium (but close to large) effect ($\overline{ES} = 0.444$, 95% confidence interval: -0.126 to 0.793).

The null hypothesis $H_{0,\text{WMC}_{\text{Mean}},TLSP/TFSP}^{\text{SUBMISSION,SMELLS\&LIBRARY}}$ for the combined studies (SUBMISSION and SMELLS&LIBRARY) cannot be rejected ($\chi^2(4) = 5.0822$, two-tailed $p = 0.5579$). The mean effect size of TF on weighted methods per class (WMC_{Mean}) represents a small effect ($\overline{ES} = -0.018$, 95% confidence interval: -0.268 to 0.235).

The null hypothesis $H_{0,\text{RFC}_{\text{Mean}},TLSP/TFSP}^{\text{SUBMISSION,SMELLS\&LIBRARY}}$ for the combined studies (SUBMISSION and SMELLS&LIBRARY) can be rejected ($\chi^2(4) = 6.1980$, two-tailed $p = 0.3697$). On the basis of the random effects model, the mean effect size of TF on response for a class (RFC_{Mean}) also represents a small effect ($\overline{ES} = 0.094$, 95% confidence interval: -0.204 to 0.376).

Chapter 10
Discussion, Conclusions and Future Work

Surmounted labours are pleasant.

Marcus Tullius Cicero

The purpose of this section is to present and interpret the findings gathered through-out the experimentation process, including meta-analysis, as well as to compare our findings to those of the previous researchers (Sect. 10.1), to derive some rules of thumb useful for practitioners involved in industrial projects (Sect. 10.2), to explain plausible mechanisms behind the results (Sect. 10.3) and to present the main contributions of the book (Sect. 10.4). Threats to the validity of the results are discussed in Sect. 10.5, while conclusions and future work are presented in Sect. 10.6.

10.1 Overview of Results

The research findings presented in this book are based on three experiments (described in Chap. 4) conducted in academic settings. The purpose of the investigation was to evaluate the impact of the Test-First Programming practice (labelled TF, alternatively TFSP or TFPP when it was important to emphasize whether solo programmers or pairs were considered) versus the Test-Last programming practice (labelled TL, TLSP or TLPP, respectively) on different aspects of software quality, and on the development speed. Keeping in line with the recent APA guidelines [12], as well as the guidelines by Kitchenham et al. [142], not only statistical significance but also effect sizes, which address the issue of practical significance [237, 243], were investigated.

The effect of the TF practice followed by solo programmers on the percentage of acceptance tests passed (PATP) was non-significant according to both preliminary and selective meta-analyses (Sects. 9.2.1.4 and 9.3.1.4). Hence, the null hypothesis $H_{0,PATP,ITLSP/ITFSP}$, posed in Sect. 4.2, cannot be rejected. Moreover, the mean effect size represents a small but negative effect. The aforementioned results do not appear to replicate the findings of Ynchausti [268]. However, the findings of Ynchausti come from a different (i.e. industrial) environment. Moreover, the study involved only one solo developer and two pairs [268]. Also George and Williams [87, 88] reported slight increase in functional tests passed. It is worth mentioning that the results from those studies were not analysed with respect to statistical significance and effect sizes. Moreover, Gupta and Jalote [94] found in one of the two

L. Madeyski, *Test-Driven Development*,
DOI 10.1007/978-3-642-04288-1_10, © Springer-Verlag Berlin Heidelberg 2010

experimental tasks that the impact of TF was statistically significant, but they argued that the result was affected by the actual testing efforts.

Our results are consistent with the findings of Pančur et al. [201] and Erdogmus et al. [72] Furthermore, Müller and Hagner [187] reported that this negative effect of TF is statistically significant. In conclusion, results obtained through the meta-analysis preformed in Chapter 9 and summarized below as Finding 10.1 are, to a large extent, consistent with the results reported by other researchers (though, as mentioned before, some of the researchers reported more positive and more negative effects of TF).

> **Findings 10.1: The impact of the TF practice on the percentage of acceptance tests passed is small and negative according to the meta-analysis performed in Chap. 9.**

The effect of the TF practice followed by solo programmers on the number of acceptance tests passed per hour (NATPPH) was non-significant according to both preliminary and selective meta-analyses (see Sects. 9.2.2.4 and 9.3.2.4). For this reason, the null hypothesis $H_{0,NATPPH,TLSP/TFSP}$, formulated in Sect. 4.2, cannot be rejected. Moreover, the mean effect size represents a small effect. As far as productivity is concerned, our results are consistent with the findings of Ynchausti [268], Müller and Hagner [187], George and Williams [87, 88], Geras et al. [89], Flohr and Schneider [79], Canfora et al. [40], Bhat and Nagappan [28] and Nagappan et al. [192]. However, it is worth mentioning that different dependent variables were used in particular studies. The results of the meta-analysis conducted in Chap. 9 and summarized in Finding 10.2 do not appear to replicate some of the findings [94, 167]. However, the improvements in productivity in both studies [94, 167] were rather small and not statistically significant. Moreover, the former study [167] involved only one developer.

> **Findings 10.2: The impact of the TF practice on the number of acceptance tests passed per hour is small and negative according to the meta-analysis performed in Chap. 9.**

The effect of the TF practice on internal quality indicators was measured by three dependent variables selected on the basis of the empirical evidence that coupling between object classes, weighted methods per class and response for a class are very significant for assessing fault content and fault-proneness (see Sect. 3.3.2.2).

The main result of the meta-analysis performed in Chap. 9 was that the TF practice followed by solo programmers significantly affected the mean coupling between object classes (CBO_{Mean}) according to both preliminary and selective meta-analyses (see Sects. 9.2.3.4 and 9.3.3.4). Furthermore, the mean effect size represents a medium (but close to large) positive effect, which is highlighted in Finding 10.3. Therefore, apart from being statistically significant, this effect is fairly large and, as such, it represents a substantive finding. Our results are consistent with the findings of Siniaalto and Abrahamsson [230] but the differences in their study seem to be smaller, although not analysed with respect to statistical significance or effect size. Janzen and Saiedian [126] have presented diverse results concerning coupling, with no conclusive answer.

Findings 10.3: The effect of the TF practice on the mean coupling between object classes is medium (but close to large) and positive according to the meta-analysis performed in Chap. 9.

The mean value of weighted methods per class (WMC_{Mean}) was not significantly affected by the TF practice according to both preliminary and selective meta-analyses (see Sects. 9.2.3.4 and 9.3.3.4). The mean effect size represents a small effect, which is highlighted in Finding 10.4. It is consistent with the findings of Siniaalto and Abrahamsson [230]. However, our results do not appear to replicate the findings by Janzen and Saiedian [126], who reported lower values of weighted methods per class in all but one study. Nevertheless, their definition of weighted methods per class is different than ours and corresponds to a different metric. Our definition, presented in Sect. 3.3.2.2, is consistent with the definition by Basili et al. [19], which in turn is based on the definition by Chidamber and Kemerer [43].

Findings 10.4: The effect of the TF practice on the mean value of weighted methods per class is small according to the meta-analysis performed in Chap. 9.

According to both preliminary and selective meta-analyses, presented in Sects. 9.2.3.4 and 9.3.3.4, the mean value of response for a class (RFC_{Mean}) was not significantly affected by the TF programming practice. Much more important is, however, that the mean effect size represents a small effect, which is emphasized in Finding 10.5. Our results are consistent with the findings of Siniaalto and Abrahamsson [230].

Findings 10.5: The effect of the TF practice on the mean value of response for a class is small according to the meta-analysis performed in Chap. 9.

The effect of the TF practice on unit tests was measured by two dependent variables: mutation score indicator (MSI) and branch coverage (BC). Both effects were non-significant. However, relying on the preliminary results reported in Sect. 8.1.3.2, the effect of the TF practice on branch coverage was medium in size, which is a substantive finding highlighted in Finding 10.6.

> **Findings 10.6: The effect of the TF practice on branch coverage turned out to be positive and medium in size according to the preliminary analysis performed in Sect. 8.1.3.2.**

10.2 Rules of Thumb for Industry Practitioners

The title of this section has been chosen on purpose because a number of the rules and recipes given here are simply practical expedients, not too closely scientific. The idea is to supply practical and useful information in language as free from technicalities as possible, and leave out the academic and scientific jargon on the results in order to adapt it to practitioners involved in industrial projects, some of whom might have had no scientific training or background in statistics. Some of the rules of thumb (or simply "Thumb-Rules") are derived from related work (discussed in Chapter 2); the others have been found in course of the experiments presented in this book.

It is worth mentioning that a rule of thumb, according to the definition [54], is a principle with a broad application that is not intended to be strictly accurate or reliable in every situation. As a result, the rules of thumb presented below are not meant to be 100% accurate in every situation.

The findings derived from the empirical research cited, as well as presented in detail, throughout this book are summarized in Fig. 10.1.

The rules of thumb on the effects of the TF practice stem from the findings supported by meta-analyses of empirical studies or several empirical studies (but not single-subject studies, which are not considered reliable enough) coming to the same conclusion:

Thumb-Rule TF1: The TF practice has a positive impact on defect rate – supported by industrial empirical studies in Microsoft [28, 192], IBM [174, 192, 217, 255] and StatoilHydro ASA (Statoil merged with Hydro creating StatoilHydro ASA in 2007) [232] discussed in Sect. 2.1.

Thumb-Rule TF2: The TF practice has a little impact on the percentage of acceptance tests passed – supported by meta-analysis presented in Chap. 9.

Thumb-Rule TF3: The TF practice has a little impact on the number of acceptance tests passed per hour – supported by meta-analysis presented in Chap. 9.

Thumb-Rule TF4: The TF practice has a medium (but close to large) and positive impact on the mean coupling between object classes – supported by meta-analysis presented in Chap. 9.

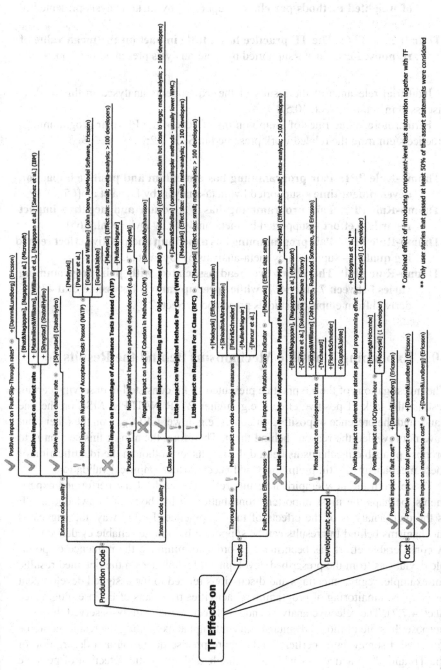

Fig. 10.1 Mind-map from empirical research to thumb-rules

Thumb-Rule TF5: The TF practice has a little impact on the mean value of weighted methods per class – supported by meta-analysis presented in Chap. 9.

Thumb-Rule TF6: The TF practice has a little impact on the mean value of response for a class – supported by meta-analysis presented in Chap. 9.

Industrial relevance of the results of the experiments analysed in this book is discussed in detail in Sect. 10.5.4.

Furthermore, some rules of thumb on the effects of the PP (pair programming) practice stem from the related work presented in Sect. 2.2:

Thumb-Rule PP1: Pair programming has a medium and positive impact on development time – supported by meta-analysis by Dybå et al. [65].

Thumb-Rule PP2: Pair programming has a medium and negative impact regarding effort – supported by meta-analysis by Dybå et al. [65].

Thumb-Rule PP3: Pair programming has a medium and positive effect regarding quality – supported by meta-analysis by Dybå et al. [65].

Thumb-Rule PP4: The effort overhead associated with pair programming varies between 7 and 84%, while speedup ratio is between 8 and 47% – derived from empirical studies presented in Sect. 2.2).

10.3 Explaining Plausible Mechanisms Behind the Results

The investigations of the TF practice presented so far consisted in observing certain results (the lack of positive effects, e.g. higher PATP, NATPPH, MSI, on the one hand, and the presence of positive outcomes, e.g. lower CBO_{Mean}, on the other), but have not revealed the reasons behind them. Therefore, the aim of this section is to propose plausible mechanisms behind the results, even though the identification of these mechanisms is still preliminary and needs further empirical validation.

Aside from the new empirical results related to each of the performed experiments, perhaps the most important contribution to the body of knowledge in SE is the meta-analysis of the effects of the TF practice. In that way, the suggested mechanisms behind the results can be supported by a more reliable evidence base. A considerable effort has been made in order to minimize the influence of possible deviations from the prescribed development techniques on the obtained results: for example, regular meetings and discussions related to the assigned development techniques, monitoring of programmers' activities by means of Eclipse plugin (see Sect. 4.7.7). The selective analysis and the selective meta-analysis served the same purpose. In spite of those advantages, this attempt at explaining the results could be considered somewhat superficial and a more precise definition and description of the TF and TL practices, as well as a reliable and automatic detection of possible discrepancies from the aforementioned techniques, would be a valuable direction of future research. Nevertheless, some explanations of the obtained results which are plausible and help to build a broader theoretical foundation of the work will be presented in this section. After all, explaining mechanisms, and then building theories based on these mechanisms, is a method of acquiring and accumulating knowledge that may be used in different settings [227].

The first plausible explanation of the obtained results is that *pre-existing differences* between the subjects are more important predictors of the outcome than development technique. This explanation is supported by the obtained results (e.g. the effect size estimations of covariates were usually much higher than those of development technique). In fact, covariates explained a large part of the variance in the dependent variables (e.g. see Sects. "Adjusting for pre-Intervention Scores" (p. 80), "Covariate Included in Analysis" (p. 97), "ANCOVA Results" (p. 107), "ANCOVA Results" (p. 114) and "Covariance Included in Analysis" (p. 135)). The mechanism of *pre-existing differences* is also consistent with the claim, cited by Maxwell and Delaney [178], that most researchers in the behavioural sciences today expect that individual differences between subjects are at least as important predictor of the outcome as any treatment variable. Therefore, an interesting alternative to the between-subjects experimental design (used in Experiments ACCOUNTING and SUBMISSION) is the repeated measures design (used in Experiment SMELLS&LIBRARY) where we effectively reduce subject-induced variation in the results. The differences between the results of the first two experiments (ACCOUNTING and SUBMISSION) and the last experiment (SMELLS&LIBRARY) are visible in the meta-analysis of the effects of TF on the percentage of acceptance tests passed in Sect. 9.2.1, the number of acceptance tests passed in Sect. 9.2.2 and also on the internal quality metrics in Sect. 9.2.3. The aforementioned differences can be, to some extent, attributed to the mechanism of *pre-existing differences*, as the impact of differences between the subjects was reduced in Experiment SMELLS&LIBRARY. Both the between-subjects and the repeated measures experimental design have been used due to their particular advantages and disadvantages described in Sect. 1.2.2.4.

Another plausible mechanism concerns *relative difficulty* of the TF practice. *Relative difficulty* of the TF versus the TL practice was revealed by questionnaire results (see Box 4.7.7). Such difficulty can be overcome by more skilful subjects and only these subjects would benefit from TF in short-term experiments. In other words, the positive effects of the TF practice may be masked, to some extent, by the relative difficulty of the technique. Therefore, long-term (but, unfortunately, also more expensive) empirical studies may be necessary to establish more complete, evidence-based recommendations.

The Quality Model Framework Lifecycle of ISO/IEC 9126 [121] can also be helpful in explaining mechanisms behind the results. According to the aforementioned life cycle, process quality influences internal quality which in turn influences external quality, which influences quality in use [30]. The aforementioned *life cycle* mechanism provides partial explanation why coupling between object classes is the first visible and immediate effect of the TF practice, while further effects might be visible in a long-run perspective. If the *life cycle* and the *relative difficulty* mechanisms are influential indeed, then we should observe other effects (e.g. effect on external code quality indicators) in long-term empirical studies.

Tests are perceived as another form of communication and a kind of a live documentation which can be even more useful in long-term projects, since unit tests show concrete examples of how to exercise the class's functionality and, therefore, become a critical part of documentation [36]. Suites of unit tests are a kind of a safety net and repository of design decisions [179] which is invaluable in longer projects where staff turnover is a serious threat. Hence, further empirical investigation of longer and larger projects would reveal additional mechanisms of the influence of the aforementioned factors (i.e. safety net and repository of design decisions) on software quality or productivity.

One may argue that there is a confounding effect of class or project size (similar problem has been presented in Sect. 7.1) on object-oriented metrics: in other words, that smaller (immature) projects and classes have different (usually lower) values of object-oriented metrics. However, the impact of the TF projects on the percentage of acceptance tests passes was not significant and the mean effect size was small. Hence, the TF projects seem to be matured to a similar extent as the TL projects; but, on the other hand, they exhibited lower coupling between object classes. Moreover, the difference was statistically significant and the mean effect size was fairly large.

According to the preliminary results, the TF practice has positive effect on branch coverage. A plausible explanation of this phenomenon can be based on a mechanism of *interrelation between testing and code coverage*. In the TF projects, up-to-date and frequently run tests, written for any piece of the production code that could possibly break [129], help to ensure a certain level of code coverage.

As mentioned before, the main result is that the Test-First programmers produce code that is significantly less coupled. A plausible explanation of this phenomenon can be based on a mechanism of *interrelation between testing and coupling*. According to Chidamber and Kemerer [43], a measure of coupling is useful to determine how complex the testing of various parts of the software systems is likely to be. It seems probable that coupling in the software products developed in accordance with the TF practice was low because, otherwise, it would be difficult to write unit tests on a regular basis, which is an essential feature of the TF practice. In other words, the TF practice reduces the coupling in order to streamline and accelerate the development of unit tests. Moreover, tests provide a useful context in which low-level design decisions (e.g. what interfaces are provided, how classes and methods are used) are made [72].

Another explanation of the phenomenon of lower coupling in the TF projects can be based on a mechanism of *interrelation between refactoring and coupling*. Refactoring is a part of the TF practice, as mentioned in Sect. 3.3.1.1. Moreover, maintaining up-to-date tests by following TF gives courage to refactor [81, 137] in order to keep the design simple and to avoid needless coupling. The importance of the aforementioned mechanisms needs further empirical evaluation.

10.4 Contributions

The main contributions of this book to the body of knowledge in software engineering correspond to the research questions (RQ1, RQ2, RQ3 and RQ4) and are as
follows:

C1 Increased understanding of the impact of TF on the percentage of acceptance
   tests passed (PATP), an indicator of external code quality.
C2 Increased understanding of the impact of TF on the number of acceptance
   tests passed per development hour (NATPPH), an indicator of software
   development speed.
C3 Increased understanding of the impact of TF on internal code quality indica-
   tors, which have been found very significant for assessing fault-proneness
   [19, 32, 33, 95, 200, 238]
   C3a Increased understanding of the impact of TF on the mean value of
      coupling between object classes (CBO_{Mean}).
   C3b Increased understanding of the impact of TF on the mean value of
      weighted methods per class (WMC_{Mean}).
   C3c Increased understanding of the impact of TF on the mean value of
      response for a class (RFC_{Mean}).
C4 Increased understanding of the impact of TF on indicators of the fault detection
   effectiveness and the thoroughness of unit tests
   C4a Increased understanding of the impact of TF on mutation score indicator
      (MSI).
   C4b Increased understanding of the impact of TF on branch coverage (BC).

Probably the most substantial finding relates to the contribution **C3a**, as it turned
out that the TF programmers produce code which is significantly less coupled
than that produced by the TL programmers. Apart from being statistically significant, the effect is fairly large and, as such, it represents a substantive finding (see
Sect. 9.3.3.4).

Furthermore, practical contributions are related to new measurement tools which
have been developed to support the experiments:

- ActivitySensor and SmartSensor Eclipse plugins [1, 167] contributed to reducing
  some threats to validity (e.g. threat to process conformance, threat to reliability
  of treatment implementation, treatment diffusion).
- Judy [160, 161, 163, 164] mutation testing tool greatly contributed to obtaining unique results concerning the impact of the TF practice on mutation score
  indicator (an indicator of the fault detection effectiveness of unit tests).
- Aopmetrics [3, 159, 166] made it possible to collect design complexity metrics
  from a large number of software projects.

The main contributions are based on the individual, minor contributions coming
from the whole empirical research process including the following:

- presenting an overview (state-of-the-art) of the empirical studies concerning the effects of the TF and PP practices,
- formalization of the TF and TL practices, as well as *Obvious Implementation*, *Fake It*, and *Triangulation* green bar patterns which facilitated automatic measurement of TF conformance by means of SmartSensor Eclipse plugin,
- the defining of experiments using goal definition template,
- the planning of experiments, e.g. development of the conceptual model that drives the research, selection of variables, hypotheses formulation, design of experiments, arrangement of experimental and pre-experimental tasks and materials, preparation of measurement infrastructure including the new measurement tools developed for the sake of experiments (Aopmetrics, ActivitySensor and SmartSensor Eclipse plugins, Judy mutation testing tool),
- the operation of experiments, i.e. preparation and execution phases,
- the descriptive and statistical analysis of consecutive experiments indicating the statistical, as well as practical, significance of the results via effect size estimations,
- the meta-analysis of the experimental results in order to get more reliable and unbiased conclusions based on the merged results of the three performed experiments that address the same research questions.

10.5 Threats to Validity

The usefulness of experimental results depends on the following two aspects: their importance and their validity. The importance of TF as one of the key software development practices popularized by XP has been stressed in Chap. 1. Chapter 2 points to the growing interest in the TF practice effects, on behalf of both the industrial and the academic environment, which is confirmed by empirical studies all over the world. Bearing that in mind, the investigation presented in this work relates to an important and noteworthy – from the practical, as well as scientific, point of view – Test-First programming practice.

Due to the fact that when conducting experiments one has to deal with threats to the validity of the results [225], the issue should not be disregarded. Therefore, the aim of this section is to discuss the threats that might have had an impact on the validity of the obtained results. The possible threats are discussed on the basis of a comprehensive classification of threats to validity given by Cook and Campbell [52], popularized in the empirical software engineering community by Wohlin et al. [259], and further refined by Shadish et al. [225]. This classification consists of four related components: statistical conclusion validity, internal validity, construct validity and external validity, all discussed in the forthcoming sections.

10.5.1 Statistical Conclusion Validity

Threats to statistical conclusion validity relate to the issues that affect the validity of inferences, i.e. the ability to draw the correct conclusion about relations between the treatment and the outcome (e.g. choice of statistical tests, tools and sample sizes and the care taken in the implementation and measurement of the experiment) [225, 259]. The most popular approach to show the cause-and-effect relationship (which was adopted in this book as well) is null hypothesis significance testing. That, however, does not provide evidence for the intervention's effect magnitude, that is, if the effect is large enough to be of practical significance. In fact, a statistically significant result neither is always of practical significance, nor demonstrates a large effect in the population. Given a sufficiently large sample, even small differences can be found to be statistically significant. An opposite misconception is that non-significance implies a zero effect when it is more often not true [225]. Indeed, practical significance determines whether the difference is large enough to be of value in a practical sense. Therefore, not only statistical significance, but also effect size estimations and 95% confidence intervals were reported in this book. Unlike significance tests, the effect size is much less influenced by sample size and shows how much more effective the new software development practice is. The effect size indicates whether the difference between the practices is substantial and meaningful beyond simple statistical significance.

10.5.1.1 Low Statistical Power

Low power of statistical tests is a threat that affects the ability to reveal a true pattern in the data and to reject an erroneous hypothesis. In order to avert that threat and to increase statistical power, large sample sizes were used (Experiment ACCOUNTING entailed 188 subjects), as well as the repeated measures design (Experiment SMELLS&LIBRARY). Moreover, a statistical technique called meta-analysis has been used to combine results from a series of experiments, because each of them alone might have had insufficient statistical power to reliably accept or reject the null hypotheses.

10.5.1.2 Violated Assumptions of Statistical Tests

Violating the assumptions of statistical tests could lead to incorrect conclusions concerning the significance and size of an effect. Therefore, assumptions of statistical tests have been thoroughly checked and, if they had not been met, non-parametric tests (which do not require many restrictive assumptions on the distribution of the variables being tested) have been used.

10.5.1.3 Fishing and the Error Rate Problem

Fishing and the error rate threat was decreased by describing what tests have been performed and by controlling family wise error rate by means of correction procedures. The Bonferroni correction and its interesting alternatives are explained in Box 5.2.

10.5.1.4 Reliability of Measures

The validity of experiments is dependent on the reliability of the measures which can be divided into objective and subjective ones [259]. Whenever feasible, measures used as dependent variables were selected to be objective rather than subjective (e.g. the ones that do not involve human judgement) [259]. However, unreliability of covariates remains a threat.

10.5.1.5 Restriction of Range

The restriction of the independent or dependent variables to a narrow range brings about, simultaneously, the reduction of the bivariate relations between the variables. It does not seem to be a threat for the dependent variables, which are not restricted by floor or ceiling effects, as results do not cluster near the lowest or the highest possible score. However, following the arguments by Erdogmus et al. [72], the range of the independent variable is restricted to treatments which require tests (TF and TL).

10.5.1.6 Reliability of Treatment Implementation

Treatment implementation, i.e. the application of treatments to subject, is considered not 100% reliable but probably more reliable than in most experiments concerning TF. A risk that the implementation was not similar between different subjects using the same treatment was reduced by controlling treatment implementation (e.g. by means of regular meetings), measuring and analysing treatment implementation (e.g. with the help of ActivitySensor Eclipse plugin and selective analysis, see Sect. 4.7.7).

10.5.1.7 Random Irrelevancies in Experimental Setting

Extraneous variance (random irrelevancies according to Wohlin et al. [259]) in the experimental setting was monitored via regular meetings and post-test questionnaires. The students taking part in the experiment had additional duties, which constitutes another vital source of extraneous variance. However, that is not too dangerous as long as it affected all the subjects, not just those from one experimental group more than the others. For that reason, it is not considered a serious threat.

10.5.1.8 Random Heterogeneity of Subjects

A risk that the variation due to random heterogeneity of subjects is larger than that due to the treatment was minimized, as all the subjects were homogeneous, to some extent. In fact, all of the subjects were graduate M.Sc. students from the same university. Moreover, analysis of covariance and the repeated measures design were used to reduce the influence of pre-existing differences between the subjects.

10.5.1.9 Inaccurate Effect Size Estimation

Inaccurate effect size estimation is a threat, all the more that even famous statisticians' opinions are not consistent with one another, and some of them, according to Dunlap et al. [64], ignore the difference between experimental designs completely or provide incorrect suggestions concerning effect size calculation (see Sect. 7.4.3.1). Therefore, aside from using robust statistical technologies and tools (e.g. SPSS), also the latest advances in effect size estimation procedures (presented, for instance, by Dunlap et al. [64]) were taken into account.

10.5.2 Internal Validity

The internal validity of the experiment concerns the true causes of the outcomes observed in the study. The question is whether the effect is caused by the independent variables or by other factors, i.e. if it could have occurred even in the absence of treatment. Fortunately, according to Shadish et al. [225], random assignment eliminates or reduces plausibility of threats to internal validity.

10.5.2.1 Ambiguous Temporal Precedence

The causal order (i.e. the rule that cause must precede effect for causal relationship) is guaranteed, as the experimental manipulation comes before the measurement of the dependent variables.

10.5.2.2 Selection

The threat of selection concerns natural differences between subjects. However, random assignment to the TF and TL groups eliminates such selection bias, as randomly assigned groups differ only by chance [225].

10.5.2.3 History

History threat concerns events that could have produced outcome in the absence of the treatment. However, as suggested by Shadish et al. [225], this threat was reduced by selecting groups from the same location (WUT) and by ensuring that groups are not being tested at very different times. Moreover, any initial group differences in the experience of events are due to chance when the TF and TL groups are randomly formed.

10.5.2.4 Maturity

Maturation threats regard changes that would occur as time passes even in the absence of treatment. Subjects can be affected negatively (e.g. bored, tired) or positively (e.g. becoming more experienced) during the experiment. According to Shadish et al. [225], maturation threats can be reduced by ensuring that all groups are roughly of the same age (i.e. their maturational status is similar) and by ensuring that groups are from the same location which is the case in Experiments ACCOUNTING, SUBMISSION and SMELLS&LIBRARY. Moreover, any initial group differences in maturity are due to chance when TF and TL groups are randomly formed.

10.5.2.5 Regression Artefacts

Regression artefacts threat occurs in the situation when subjects are selected to receive a treatment because their scores were high or low on some measures [225]. However, this is not the case in Experiments ACCOUNTING, SUBMISSION and SMELLS&LIBRARY.

10.5.2.6 Attrition

Attrition refers to the fact that subjects sometimes fail to complete the outcome measures. It can distort effects if that loss is systematically correlated with conditions. However, it turned out that attrition is not systematically correlated with TFSP and TLSP.

10.5.2.7 Testing

Subjects may respond differently in subsequent investigations since they know how the test is conducted. However, each subject took part in only one experiment.

10.5.2.8 Instrumentation

A measuring instrument may change in a similar manner as a subject. Instrumentation changes are not considered harmful as switching instruments in course of the experiments was avoided. However, it is noteworthy that Eclipse plugin was updated to resolve minor issues submitted by the subjects.

10.5.2.9 Additive and Interactive Effects of Threats

Additive and interactive effects of threats mean that threats to internal validity can operate simultaneously, i.e. can be added or one may depend on the level of another [225].

Fortunately, according to Shadish et al. [225], random assignment to the TF and TL groups eliminated selection bias and reduced the plausibility of the aforementioned threats to internal validity.

10.5.3 Construct Validity

Threats to construct validity concern the extent to which measures accurately reflect the theoretical concepts they are intended to measure. Construct validity is concerned with the relationship between variables. However, many variables are not easily or directly defined and measurable such as age or length. Hence, construct validity is the degree to which a measure adequately captures the construct of interest. A construct can be defined as a characteristic or concept that it is intended to measure (e.g. leadership, expertise). If our variable, based on theory, should be positively related to constructs P_i, negatively related to N_j and unrelated to U_k, then our measure should be positively correlated with measures of P_i, negatively correlated with measures of N_j and uncorrelated with measures of U_k. Therefore, construct validity concerns the ability to generalize from the experimental result to the concept or theory behind the experiment. It is worth mentioning that it can be possible to enhance construct validity when different estimates of a construct are considered together.

Some threats to construct validity relate to the design of the experiment and its ability to reflect the construct under study, while others relate to social factors [259].

10.5.3.1 Mono-Operation Bias

The mono-operation bias relates to a single operationalization of a construct, as it may under-represent the construct of interest and may not reflect the theory well. Where feasible and justified by empirical evidence, different measures of TF effects have been used (e.g. internal code quality indicators in Chap. 7). Experiments ACCOUNTING and SUBMISSION were conducted with single experimental tasks (projects), while Experiment SMELLS&LIBRARY was performed with two experimental tasks. It is worth mentioning that projects consisted of different sets of user stories to introduce requirements.

10.5.3.2 Mono-method Bias

Using a single means of recording response or a single way to present treatments poses a mono-method bias threat. To reduce mono-method threats, the qualitative validation of the quantitative results was performed with no apparent contradiction found. Moreover, to reduce that threat, development techniques were explained by practitioners (e.g. the agile coach) and researchers.

10.5.3.3 Construct Confounding

Construct confounding threat relates to inappropriate representations of constructs, e.g. when some characteristics are not part of the intended construct but are, unfortunately, confounded with it. For example, the confounding effect of class size on the validity of the OO metrics is discussed in Sect. 7.1, while threats to the validity of software quality standards, e.g. ISE/IEC 9126, on which constructs in Software Engineering are commonly based, are discussed in Sect. 1.3.2.3.

10.5.3.4 Confounding Constructs with Levels of Constructs

A threat of confounding constructs with levels of constructs comes from the fact that the effect of the presence of the construct can be confounded with the effect of the level of the construct. For example, the presence or absence of recent industrial experience or the TF treatment may not explain the results, but the difference may depend on the length of recent industrial experience or the TF conformance level, respectively. Therefore, the levels of constructs have been recorded throughout experiments. Some characteristics of subjects are presented in Table 4.1. Moreover, the subjects with low levels of TF conformance were excluded from selective analysis (see Sect. 4.7.7).

10.5.3.5 Reactivity to the Experimental Situation and Hypothesis Guessing

Subjects might try to guess the purpose and intended result of an experiment and adjust their behaviour to their guesses. Therefore, following the suggestions by Shadish et al. [225], the dependent variables were not obvious and measured later, usually with the help of the measurement infrastructure and inside the measurement, not the experimental, setting.

10.5.3.6 Experimenter Expectancies

The experimenter-bias effect demonstrated by Rosenthal [211] involves the impact of the researcher's expectancies and, in particular, the transmission of that expectancy to the subjects in such a way that the dependent variables are affected. However, experimenter's expectancies were not revealed and all treatments were presented as equally interesting alternatives.

10.5.3.7 Compensatory Equalization

Compensatory equalization of treatments is the result of a demand (stemming from an ethical dilemma) that the benefits of the treatment should be extended to the control group. Compensation occurs to the control group in the form of equalizing the control and treatment groups with respect to treatment access. Equalization can also rely on taking benefits away from treatment group. None of the mentioned equalizations was performed and thus the outcome was not affected by compensation.

10.5.3.8 Compensatory Rivalry and Resentful Demoralization

The risk of compensatory rivalry (also called the "John Henry effect") or resentful demoralization of the subjects receiving less desirable treatment must be considered.

The group using the classical method (i.e. TL) may do their very best to show that the old method is competitive. On the other hand, subjects receiving less desirable treatments may perform not as well as they generally do. However, the subjects were informed that the goal of the experiments is to measure different development methods, not the subjects' skills.

10.5.3.9 Treatment Diffusion

Preventing possible diffusion or imitation of treatments is not an easy task. Shadish et al. [225] suggest separating the two treatment conditions as much as possible, either geographically or by using different practitioners in each. The latter was applied during Experiments ACCOUNTING and SUBMISSION. Another possibility is to provide ongoing reminders to subjects about the need not to imitate other treatments [215]. Such reminders were given in a regular manner in course of the experiment. To monitor the extent to which the imitation of treatment has occurred, the ActivitySensor/SmartSensor plugin reports were used. In order to prevent the threat from reaching a level that would seriously undermine the validity of the experiments, the subjects were frequently interviewed.

10.5.4 External Validity

Shadish et al. [225] present threats to external validity to enable estimates of the degree to which a causal relationship holds over variations in subjects (Interaction of Causal Relationship with Units), settings (Interaction of Causal Relationship with Settings), treatments (Interaction of Causal Relationship with Treatment Variations) and outcomes (Interaction of Causal Relationship with Outcomes). Hence, external validity refers to the generalization of research findings, either from a sample to a larger population or to settings, treatments, outcomes and populations other than those studied, e.g. practitioners involved in industrial projects.

10.5.4.1 Generalization to Industrial Setting

With respect to generalization of the results to industrial setting, the largest threat stems from the fact that the subjects were graduate students, who had rather little experience in the assigned development techniques. Their programming experience, recent industrial experience and average sizes of the largest software components written individually in any language, as well as in Java, are reported in Table 4.1. It should be noted that the subjects in Experiment ACCOUNTING had, on average, lower programming experience than the subjects in Experiments SUBMISSION and SMELLS&LIBRARY. Consequently, the results of the experiments might be a conservative measure of the effects of the TF practice, since the subjects had probably not reached their maximum level of efficiency. To minimize this threat, preparation phases lasting several weeks preceded the main experimental tasks in Experiments ACCOUNTING, SUBMISSION and SMELLS&LIBRARY, see Table 4.1. Moreover, selective meta-analysis of Experiments SUBMISSION and SMELLS&LIBRARY (in which more experienced developers were involved) has been carried out in Sect. 9.3. Fortunately, a large portion of subjects (38% in Experiment SUBMISSION and 85% in Experiment SMELLS&LIBRARY) had recent industrial experience. Hence, it can be argued that the results of selective meta-analysis of Experiments SUBMISSION and SMELLS&LIBRARY have higher external validity than the preliminary meta-analysis of Experiments ACCOUNTING, SUBMISSION and SMELLS&LIBRARY carried out in Sect. 9.2 because the subjects in Experiments SUBMISSION and SMELLS&LIBRARY are relatively close to the population of software practitioners involved in industrial projects.

Host et al. [107] found that students may be relevant as subjects in empirical software engineering research. Svahnberg et al. [239] reported that students have a good understanding of the way industry acts in the context of requirements selection, and they may work well as subjects in empirical studies in this area. Furthermore, Runeson [216] identified similar improvement trends amongst freshmen students, graduate students and professionals. The dispersion was larger in the freshmen group, but graduate students did the tasks in a significantly shorter time than the freshmen students.

Further arguments why it is acceptable to use students as subjects are given by Tichy [242] and Kitchenham et al. [142]. Tichy argues that students are acceptable when used to establish a trend. An important argument given by Tichy is that when an empirical study compares two methods to see which is better, then if one method has a clear relative advantage over the other with students as subjects, it may be argued that there will be a difference in the same direction (although perhaps of a different magnitude) for professionals [242]. Hence, it is plausible to expect lower coupling between object classes (see Thumb-Rule 4) due to the TF practice in an industrial setting as well.

It is also worth mentioning that student subjects are useful to eliminate alternative hypotheses, as it is difficult to find professional subjects if there is no evidence of difference between the compared methods. Tichy maintains that it is unlikely that a large effect will surprisingly appear in a professional setting if it is absent in an academic environment [242]. Hence, it is implausible to expect large effects of the TF practice on the percentage of acceptance tests passed (see Thumb-Rule 2), the number of acceptance tests passed per hour (see Thumb-Rule 3), the mean value of weighted methods per class (see Thumb-Rule 5) or the mean value of response for a class (see Thumb-Rule 6) in a professional setting.

In consequence, results with students help practitioners involved in industrial projects to get better understanding of the compared methods and to focus on the most promising approaches. In fact, the empirical studies with students are a prerequisite for getting professionals to participate, and having an empirical validation with students is better than no validation at all. Unfortunately, too many Software Engineering techniques are introduced in industrial environments without any kind of empirical assessment [41]. Furthermore, software engineering students are technically up to date and much closer to the world of software professionals than, for example, psychology students are to the general population [242]. Kitchenham et al. [142] also state that students are the next generation of software professionals and, thus, are relatively close to the population of interest. It is also important to note that TF is a rather new development practice and long-term experience in TF is probably rare, even in industry.

The software systems developed during the experiments were rather small, as shown in Table 4.1, compared with industrial object-oriented software systems, but probably larger than usually developed by way of experiments in software engineering. Nevertheless, it is possible that the effects of the TF practice would have been different in more complex and longer projects, as mentioned in Sect. 10.3. The interaction of the causal relationship with setting was reduced by making the experimental setting and material as realistic and close to the industrial one as possible.

10.5.4.2 Relevance to Industry

An important issue that pertains to all software engineering research is its relevance to industry. One may divide the relevance of a study into the investigated topic and the implications of the results [26]. The topics being addressed are very influential in determining a relevance in the eyes of practitioners [26]. The effects of the TF practice are perceived to be of relevance to industry for several reasons. According to Kitchenham et al. [143], agile methods or practices are good examples of topics to be studied as they are not specified at too high a level of abstraction. Even more importantly, TF has gained much and recent attention in professional settings. A number of books written by practitioners [15, 22, 23, 97, 144, 195] give compelling evidence of the attention to the topic. A thorough description of empirical studies on the impact of the TF practice in industrial environment [28, 40, 56, 57, 87, 88, 126, 174, 192, 217, 255, 268] presented in Chap. 2 should attract practitioners' attention to the book as well. Section 10.2 presents the results of Experiments ACCOUNTING, SUBMISSION and SMELLS&LIBRARY in a way that is comprehensible to decision makers in industry, i.e. leaving out the academic and scientific jargon. Although the thumb-rules by definition denote the guidelines that are not strictly accurate in every situation, the ones formulated in Sect. 10.2 stem from empirical evidence rather than fashion or hype.

However, relevancy is assured not only through the selection of a "relevant" topic [26]. The implications of the results and the possibility to implement the TF practice are important as well. Therefore, the implications of the main findings are discussed in the next paragraph.

Excessive coupling between object classes is detrimental to modular design, prevents reuse, hinders maintenance and increases complexity of the testing [43]. Tightly coupled components are "harder to maintain" [155], and thus imply higher maintenance costs. The importance of software maintenance in managing the life cycle costs of a system cannot be overemphasized due to the fact that software maintenance costs typically constitute about half the total cost spent on a software system during its useful life [49]. The TF practice, which has a positive impact on the mean coupling between object classes (see Finding 10.3 and Thumb-Rule TF4), can be seen as a kind of remedy for increased maintenance costs. Furthermore, a safety net of unit tests and high code coverage, which is a side effect of the TF practice, reduce the time to detect errors introduced in the maintenance phase and, as a result, further facilitate maintenance and decrease the maintenance costs. Without this safety net, maintenance would be much more difficult [179].

The TF practice can be implemented in an industrial environment, as confirmed in many empirical studies mentioned earlier. Last but not least, the book synthesizes existing body of research and summarizes major findings related to the effects of the TF practice. This can be attractive to some practitioners too [26].

10.5.5 Threats to Validity of Meta-Analysis

Although meta-analysis is a statistical technique which allows the aggregation of research results, there has been some criticism about its use [90, 152]. The most common criticisms are discussed in the forthcoming sections.

There is also a question whether it is appropriate to perform a meta-analysis with a small meta-sample (in our case a meta-sample of three experiments). However, according to Kramer and Rosenthal [145], meta-analyses can be carried out with as few as two studies, and the procedures are the same. Kramer and Rosenthal [145] have given an example of a meta-analysis of only two small, pilot studies published in *Science* [47].

Yet another question might be raised: why not simply combine the raw data from several studies and then find the overall effect size of this combined data set rather than meta-analytically combining study's effect sizes? The answer to this question has been called Simpson's or Yule's paradox after the researchers who showed the importance of computing effect sizes separately for each study and then combining the effect sizes via meta-analysis instead of pooling raw data [229, 269].

10.5.5.1 Inadequate Conceptualization of the Problem

Inadequate conceptualization of the problem refers to the fact that it is difficult to interpret aggregated empirical results that include different measurement techniques, definitions of variables and subjects when they are too dissimilar. This threat is vividly characterized as "combining apples and oranges" [152]. Measurement techniques and definitions of variables were similar across experiments. However, to avoid the threat that subjects are too dissimilar, i.e. that the subjects in Experiment ACCOUNTING and the subjects in Experiments SUBMISSION and SMELLS&LIBRARY are too dissimilar (see Table 4.1), a selective meta-analysis has been performed in Sect. 9.3.

10.5.5.2 Inadequate Assessment of Study Quality

Inadequate assessment of study quality means that results of a meta-analysis cannot be reliably interpreted if results from "weak" studies (e.g. studies with implementation problems) are included in the meta-analysis. As mentioned in Sect. 4.4.7.2, tests were often deferred for too long or even neglected in the TL projects in Experiment ACCOUNTING. The situation changed in Experiments SUBMISSION and SMELLS&LIBRARY where Eclipse plugin helped to monitor development techniques. Therefore, to minimize the threat, a selective meta-analysis has been performed in Sect. 9.3.

10.5.5.3 Publication Bias

Publication bias refers to the fact that published research is biased, as statistically significant results are more likely to be published than null findings. This is also known as outcome reporting bias. However, publication bias does not play a role in our case.

10.5.5.4 Dissemination Bias

Dissemination bias is related to issues of language, availability, familiarity and cost of research reports [152]. However, dissemination bias do not apply here.

10.6 Conclusions and Future Work

The Test-First programming practice has been evaluated through a series of experiments conducted with graduate students. The statistical technique of meta-analysis was used to get more reliable and unbiased conclusions based on the performed experiments. The evaluation focused on the key aspect of the Test-First approach, i.e. incremental implementation of small pieces of functionality by writing unit test *before* writing the corresponding production code.

The main result is that Test-First programmers produce a code that is significantly less coupled. The null hypothesis $H_{0,\text{CBO}_{\text{Mean}},TLSP/TFSP}^{\text{ACCOUNTING,SUBMISSION,SMELLS\&LIBRARY}}$ for combined Experiments ACCOUNTING, SUBMISSION and SMELLS&LIBRARY can be rejected ($\chi^2(6) = 33.71$, two-tailed $p = 0.00$), while the mean effect size represents a medium (but close to large) effect ($\overline{ES} = 0.43$, 95% confidence interval: 0.14 to 0.63). The aforementioned result was confirmed in the selective meta-analysis carried out in Sect. 9.3, as the null hypothesis $H_{0,\text{CBO}_{\text{Mean}},TLSP/TFSP}^{\text{SUBMISSION,SMELLS\&LIBRARY}}$ for combined Experiments SUBMISSION and SMELLS&LIBRARY can be rejected as well ($\chi^2(4) = 19.90$, two-tailed $p = 0.00$). Moreover, the mean effect size of TF on CBO_{Mean} also represents a similar effect ($\overline{ES} = 0.44$, 95% confidence interval: -0.13 to 0.79) and therefore is a substantial finding. According to Chidamber and Kemerer [43], lower CBO suggests better modularization (i.e. a more modular design), easier reuse as well as testing, and hence better architecture of developed software solutions. All of those benefits are highly appreciated among software architects, developers and testers.

Other results suggest that the differences between the TF and TL practices with respect to PATP, NATPPH, WMC_{Mean}, RFC_{Mean}, MSI and BC are not statistically significant and the effect sizes are relatively small. Only the effect of TF on BC (i.e. branch coverage) was medium in size and, therefore, can be considered a substantive effect.

In further research, it would be useful to attempt to evaluate the impact of the TF practice on the fault detection effectiveness and the thoroughness of unit tests in other empirical studies. These two characteristics can be affected by the TF practice, as they are, in fact, internal quality measures which, according to the Quality Model Framework Lifecycle of ISO/IEC 9126 standard [121], are directly influenced by development process. Additional empirical studies would give an argument for or against the *life cycle* mechanism presented in Sect. 10.3. It is worth mentioning that the impact of pair programming practice on the aforementioned characteristics of unit tests has been investigated by Madeyski [160, 161]. Furthermore, a new mutation testing tool (called Judy) has been developed [163].

Another interesting direction of further research would be empirical evaluation of the importance of the mechanisms behind the results (i.e. *pre-existing differences, relative difficulty, life cycle, interrelation between testing and code coverage, interrelation between testing and coupling and interrelation between refactoring and coupling*) presented in Sect. 10.3.

With respect to experimental methodology, it has been found very useful to start with a pre-study to check the infrastructure and the instrumentation of the experiment (e.g. ActivitySensor plugin) [166, 167]. However, the experiments can benefit from several improvements before replications are attempted. The most significant ones are securing longer empirical studies with a sample of large enough size to guarantee a high-power design. Additional improvements stem from the fact that even more sophisticated tools and measures could be used. Moreover, further experimentation in different contexts (especially in industry) is needed to establish evidence-based recommendations for the effects of the test-first programming practice. The validity of the results must be considered within the context of the limitations discussed in this chapter.

Appendix A
Structured Abstract Including Statistical Results

All's well that ends well.
a play by William Shakespeare

Background

The quality of the methods used to evaluate new software development techniques, practices, processes, technologies, tools, etc., indicates the maturity of the software engineering research discipline. Consequently, experimentation, as a systematic, disciplined, quantifiable and controlled way of evaluation becomes a fundamental part of both research and practice in software engineering. The importance of properly conducted and replicated experiments has become widely accepted in the software engineering community. Owing to the empirical studies and their analysis or meta-analysis, industry may take advantage of the already accumulated knowledge. The roots of that fundamental shift in software engineering research can, to a large extent, be found in evidence-based medicine. Controlled experiments, quasi-experiments and case studies become the primary research methods by which the choice of software development techniques should be justified. Systematic reviews and meta-analyses are gaining increasing acceptance as the methods of summarizing the results of a number of empirical studies. Evidence-Based Software Engineering (EBSE) undermines anecdotal evidence and unsystematic experience as sufficient grounds for decision making while stressing instead the empirical evidence from software engineering research.

Another interesting shift in software engineering has been created by the agile movement in general, and eXtreme Programming (XP) in particular. Agile teams shape software systems using a collaborative process, with executable software and automated tests at its heart, whilst marginalising the documents. That creates a shift away from tools for managing requirements to tools (originating from the XP values, principles and practices) supporting collaboration and the gradual distillation of requirements into automated test suites [58]. The Test-First Programming (TF) practice, also called Test-Driven Development, is considered the flagship and one of the most influential practices of the XP methodology [15, 23, 144], as well as the one of the most controversial ones [179].

Both the experimentation in software engineering and the agile movement influenced this book. The latter attracted the attention of the author to the agile methodologies, XP and then the flagship XP practice, i.e. TF. The former influenced the way

L. Madeyski, *Test-Driven Development*,
DOI 10.1007/978-3-642-04288-1, © Springer-Verlag Berlin Heidelberg 2010

the research was conducted and reported (e.g. the stress on the effect size estimates and meta-analysis).

Objective

The purpose of this book was to evaluate the effects of the TF agile software development practice with respect to the percentage of acceptance tests passed (considered an external code quality indicator [87, 88]), design complexity metrics (that have been found significant for assessing fault proneness by several researchers [19, 32, 33, 95, 200, 238]) and the number of acceptance tests passed per development hour (which is an indicator of development speed). Moreover, the aim is to present the preliminary evaluation of the impact of the TF practice on mutation score indicator and branch coverage, the indicators of the fault detection effectiveness and the thoroughness of unit tests, respectively.

An additional (but auxiliary) objective of the book was to present how to perform an analysis of experiments in software engineering using the Statistical Package for the Social Sciences (SPSS). Conference or even journal papers usually present short and thus superficial descriptions of the performed analyses, while the existing excellent books [131, 227, 259] cover a wide range of topics related to Empirical Software Engineering (ESE) and, therefore, do not focus on the joint analysis of closely related experiments.

Method

The effects of the TF programming practice were evaluated by conducting three experiments named ACCOUNTING (the experiment on the development of an accounting system), SUBMISSION (the experiment on the development of a paper submission and review system), and SMELLS&LIBRARY (the experiment on the development of both a tool for identifying bad smells in Java source code through the use of a set of software metrics and a library application). Those experiments, described in Chap. 4, were carried out in academic setting with over 200 graduate MSc students, using both between-groups (in Experiments ACCOUNTING and SUBMISSION) and repeated measures (in Experiment SMELLS&LIBRARY) experimental designs. Furthermore, the Pair Programming (PP) practice was used along with the TF programming practice in the first experiment to check whether there is a synergy between both XP practices. The data were collected with the help of different measurement tools. Some of them (Judy, Aopmetrics, ActivitySensor and SmartSensor Eclipse plugins) have been developed especially for the sake of the experiments. The statistical analysis of experiments has been described in Chap. 5, 6 and 7, while the meta-analysis has been performed in Chap. 9. A selective analysis and selective meta-analysis have been carried out to minimize threats to the validity (e.g. process conformance threat). Effect sizes were reported and interpreted with respect to their practical importance.

Results

The main result observed on the basis of the meta-analysis of Experiments ACCOUNTING SUBMISSION and SMELLS&LIBRARY is that programmers using Test-First Solo Programming (TFSP) technique produce a code that is significantly less coupled ($\chi^2(2k) = \chi^2(6) = 33.71$ where $k = 3$ is the number of the meta-analysed experiments, two-tailed $p < 0.01$) than that produced by programmers using Test-Last Solo Programming (TLSP) technique. This finding has also been confirmed by the selective analysis of Experiments SUBMISSION and SMELLS&LIBRARY ($\chi^2(4) = 19.90$, two-tailed $p = 0.00$). Furthermore, the mean effect size represents a medium (but close to large) effect on the basis of meta-analysis of all the experiments ($\overline{ES} = 0.43$, 95% confidence interval: 0.14 to 0.63), as well as selective meta-analysis ($\overline{ES} = 0.44$, 95% confidence interval: -0.13 to 0.79), which is a substantial finding. It suggests a better modularization (i.e. a more modular design), easier reuse and testing of the developed software products [43] due to the TF programming practice.

However, the superiority of the TF practice in the investigated context was not confirmed with respect to the two remaining areas of investigation. The mean value of weighted methods per class (WMC$_{Mean}$) was not significantly affected by the TF programming practice according to the meta-analysis ($\chi^2(6) = 8.10$, two-tailed $p = 0.46$), as well as selective meta-analysis ($\chi^2(4) = 5.08$, two-tailed $p = 0.56$), while the mean effect size represents a small effect according to the meta-analysis ($\overline{ES} = 0.04$, 95% confidence interval: -0.15 to 0.23), as well as the selective meta-analysis ($\overline{ES} = -0.02$, 95% confidence interval: -0.27 to 0.24).

The mean value of response for a class (RFC$_{Mean}$) was not significantly affected by the TF practice based on Fisher's method of combining p-values (meta-analysis: $\chi^2(6) = 14.35$, two-tailed $p = 0.052$; selective meta-analysis: $\chi^2(4) = 6.20$, two-tailed $p = 0.37$). The mean effect size represents a small effect according to meta-analysis ($\overline{ES} = 0.18$, 95% confidence interval: -0.04 to 0.39) as well as selective meta-analysis ($\overline{ES} = 0.09$, 95% confidence interval: -0.20 to 0.38).

Moreover, the results revealed that the TF practice does not have a statistically significant impact, neither on the percentage of acceptance tests passed (PATP), which is an indicator of external code quality (meta-analysis: $\chi^2(6) = 10.02$, two-tailed $p = 0.25$; selective meta-analysis: $\chi^2(4) = 5.38$, two-tailed $p = 0.50$), nor on the number of acceptance tests passed per development hour (NATPPH), which is an indicator of development speed (meta-analysis: $\chi^2(6) = 12.53$, two-tailed $p = 0.10$; selective meta-analysis: $\chi^2(4) = 7.88$, two-tailed $p = 0.19$). The mean effect size of TF on the percentage of acceptance tests passed (PATP) represents a small effect (meta-analysis: $\overline{ES} = -0.11$, 95% confidence interval: -0.30 to 0.08; selective meta-analysis: $\overline{ES} = -0.05$, 95% confidence interval: -0.29 to 0.21).

The mean effect size of TF on the number of acceptance tests passed per hour (NATPPH) represents a small effect (meta-analysis: $\overline{ES} = -0.11$, 95% confidence interval: -0.35 to 0.15; selective meta-analysis: $\overline{ES} = -0.08$, 95% confidence interval: -0.48 to 0.35), too.

Furthermore, the effect of the TF practice on unit tests was measured by branch coverage (BC) and mutation score indicator (MSI), which are indicators of the thoroughness and the fault detection effectiveness of unit tests, respectively. Relying on the preliminary results, BC was not significantly higher in the TFSP ($Mdn = 0.68$) than in the TLSP ($Mdn = 0.57$) group ($U = 31.00$, $p = 0.28$, $r = 0.26$). However, the effect size was medium in size and therefore the effect of TF on branch coverage is a substantive effect. TLSP ($Mdn = 0.16$) and TFSP ($Mdn = 0.15$) did not significantly differ in MSI ($U = 40.00$, $p > 0.05$, $r = 0.09$) and the effect size was small.

Limitations

The threats to the validity of the conducted experiments (e.g. relevance to industry) are thoroughly discussed in Sect. 10.5. The generalization of results is limited, since the analysed TF practice was applied to develop systems smaller than 10,000 lines of code. Further experimentation (e.g. in industrial context) is needed to establish evidence.

Conclusions

The results reinforced the evidence regarding the superiority of the TF practice over the Test-Last Programming (TL) practice, with respect to the lower coupling between classes (CBO_{Mean}). However, the superiority of the TF programming practice in the investigated context was not supported with respect to the percentage of acceptance tests passed (PATP), the number of acceptance tests passed per development hour (NATPPH), weighted methods per class WMC_{Mean} and response for a class (RFC_{Mean}).

Glossary

Between-groups (independent groups) experimental design Between-groups (independent groups or between-subjects) experimental designs take advantage of separate groups of subjects for each of the treatments in the experiment and each subject is tested only once (see Sect. 1.2.2.4).

Branch coverage (BC) BC reports whether Boolean expressions tested in the decision points (such as an `if` statement or a `case` statement) evaluated to both true and false (see Sect. "Thoroughness of Unit Tests" (p. 34)).

Case study A case study is a study of project, individual, group, organization, situation, etc., or a small number of related cases, taking its context into account (see Sect. "Case Studies" (p. 7)).

95% confidence interval Confidence interval is a pair of values which define a range within which there is 95% probablility that the parameter will fall.

Confounding variable A confounding variable is any variable which changes systematically over the levels of the IV. With a confounding variable it is difficult to conclude whether the results of an experiment are due to the IV alone, confounding variable alone or due to some interaction between those variables.

Coupling between object classes (CBO) CBO measure is included in the CK metrics suite [43] and is defined as the number of classes to which a class is coupled. Two classes are coupled when methods declared in one class use methods or instance variables defined by the other class (see Sect. 3.3.2.2).

Degrees of freedom Degrees of freedom equals to the number of independent observations, which is the number of original observations minus the number of parameters (e.g. the means of the experimental groups) estimated from them [55, 68, 249].

Dependent (or response) variable (DV) The dependent variable is measured to see the effect of the changes in the independent variables (IVs) [259].

Effect size (ES) Effect size is a name given to indicators that measure the magnitude of a treatment effect (see Sect. 4.7.5).

Experiment A formal experiment is a controlled, rigorous investigation of an activity, where independent variables (IVs) are manipulated to document their effects on dependent variables (DVs) (see Sect. "Experiments" (p. 6)).

Experimental design Experimental design is a term used to describe the way in which an experiment is conducted (e.g. between-groups or repeated measures). The aim of the experimental design is to minimize the chance that irrelevant variables (i.e. other than the independent and the dependent variables) become confounding variables.

eXtreme Programming (XP) XP can be seen from various perspectives as: a mechanism for social change, a software development methodology, a constant path to perfection, an attempt to bring together humanity and productivity in software development [248]. XP is founded on five abstract but universal values (communication, simplicity, feedback, courage, respect) and tangible practices (e.g. test-first programming, pair programming) that are bridged together by certain principles (e.g. mutual benefit) [23]. According to Beck [23], values are the large-scale criteria we use to judge what we see, what we think, what we do; values also underlie our immediate and intuitive recognition of what we accept and what we reject in a given situation. Making values explicit is important, as, without values, practices (which are extremely situated) lose their purpose and direction. However, there is a gap between values and practices, since values are too abstract to directly guide development. Therefore, principles act as a bridge between values and practices. A detailed description of XP is given by Beck [23]. According to DeMarco, "The movement called Extreme Programming is to my mind the most encouraging trend in software development today. It focuses us all on the real essentials: talent, discipline without dogma, teamwork, risk-taking, and light process. It poses a particular challenge to the manager, since it pushes control downward (managing people who are empowered to make decisions and even make their own mistakes is a lot harder than managing people who are obliged to shut up and do what you tell them to).".

Hypothesis Hypothesis is a statement expressing the expected relationship between two or more variables.

Independent (or factor) variable (IV) The independent (or factor) variable is the variable that is systematically manipulated and controlled by the experimenter [259]. Each value of the IV is called a level.

Measurement method Measurement method is a logical sequence of operations, described generically, used in quantifying an attribute with respect to a specified scale [86, 117].

Measurement Measurement is defined as "a mapping from the empirical world to the formal, relational world" [74] (see Sect. 1.3).

Measure "A measure is the number or symbol assigned to an entity... in order to characterize an attribute" [74] (see Sect. 1.3).

Mutation score indicator (MSI) Mutation score (also called mutation adequacy) is a kind of quantitative measurement of test quality [271] and is defined as the ratio of the number of killed mutants to the total number of non-equivalent mutants. The total number of non-equivalent mutants results from a difference between the total number of mutants and the number of equivalent mutants. The latter always produce the same output as the original program, so they cannot be killed. Determining which mutants are equivalent to the original program is a very tedious and error-prone activity, so even ignoring equivalent mutants is sometimes advised [198]. In such case, we accept the lower bound on mutation score called mutation score indicator [160, 161] (see Sect. "Fault Detection Effectiveness of Unit Tests" (p. 35)).

Number of acceptance tests passed per hour (NATPPH) The number of acceptance tests passed (NATP) per hour denoted as NATPPH is a measure of development speed (see Sect. 3.3.2.3).

Pair programming (PP) / solo programming (SP) PP constitutes a software development practice in which two distinct roles are usually identified by researchers, i.e. the role of a driver and a navigator [14, 161, 254, 258]. They contribute to the synergy of the individuals in a pair working together at one computer and collaborating on the same development tasks (e.g. design, test, code). The driver types on the keyboard and focuses on the details of the production code or tests. The navigator observes the work of the driver, reviews the code, proposes test cases, considers the strategic implications [254, 258] and looks for tactical and strategic defects or alternatives [14]. In the case of solo programming, both activities are performed by a single programmer.

Percentage of acceptance tests passed (PATP) The percentage of acceptance tests passed (PATP) is NATP normalized by the number of acceptance tests (NAT), i.e. PATP = NATP/NAT (see Sect. 3.3.2.1).

Refactoring Refactoring is a disciplined technique for reorganising an existing body of code in such a way that it improves its internal structure yet does not alter the external behaviour [81].

Repeated measures (within-subjects) experimental design In repeated measures (within-subjects) experimental designs, each subject is exposed to all of the treatments in the experiment, so that two or more measures are collected for each subject (see Sect. 1.2.2.4).

Response For a Class (RFC) RFC measure is included in the CK metrics suite [43] and is defined as the number of methods that can potentially be executed in response to a message received by an object of that class.

Subject Subjects (or participants) are people who take part in an experiment.

Survey A survey is a retrospective investigation in which data are collected from a population, or a sample from that population, through some form of interviews or questionnaires aimed at describing accurately the characteristics of that population (see Sect. "Surveys" (p. 7)).

Test-first programming TF constitutes an incremental development, design and coding practice which is based on taking a requirement, specifying a piece of functionality as a test, ensuring that the test can fail, then writing the production code that will satisfy the test condition, refactoring (if necessary) to improve the internal structure of the code, and iterating the process, as shown in Fig. 3.2. The TF practice is not a testing or quality assurance practice per se, as it may appear. It is primarily, and very intentionally, a development, design and coding practice (guided by tests), with possible quality side effects. By writing the test first, you ensure that you write the code that embodies the requirements.

Test-last programming TL incremental development practice involves writing all the tests for a new system feature after, instead of before, the corresponding piece of the production code for that feature, as shown in Fig. 3.3. As a result, there is more of a chance that you will end up with the tests written to fit your production code, which may not accurately reflect the requirements.

Treatment A treatment is one particular value of an independent variable (or factor) [259].

Weighted methods per class (WMC) WMC measure is included in the CK metrics suite [43] and measures the complexity of an individual class. In accordance with [43], we consider all methods of a class to be equally complex, i.e. WMC is simply the number of methods defined in each class. This approach is commonly adopted for the sake of simplicity, and in order to avoid being somewhat arbitrary, since the choice of a method complexity metric is not fully specified in the CK metrics suite [19] (see Sect. 3.3.2.2).

Z-score Z-score expresses the distance of the experimental result from the most probable result as a number of standard deviations. The larger the value of z, the less probable the experimental result is due to chance.

References

1. ActivitySensor project – Wroclaw University of Technology, Software Engineering Society (Cited 1 Apr 2009). URL http://www.e-informatyka.pl/sens/Wiki.jsp?page=Projects.ActivitySensor
2. Ant project (Cited 1 Apr 2009). URL http://ant.apache.org/
3. Aopmetrics project – Wroclaw University of Technology, Software Engineering Society (http://www.e-informatyka.pl/sens/Wiki.jsp?page=Projects.AOPMetrics) (Cited 1 Apr 2009). URL http://aopmetrics.tigris.org
4. AspectJ project (Cited 1 Apr 2009). URL http://www.eclipse.org/aspectj/
5. Cactus project (Cited 1 Apr 2009). URL http://jakarta.apache.org/cactus/
6. Wiki (Cited 1 Apr 2009). URL http://en.wikipedia.org/wiki/Wiki
7. Aaron, B., Kromrey, J.D., Ferron, J.: Equating "r"-based and "d"-based effect size indices: Problems with a commonly recommended formula. In: FERA'98: 43rd Annual Meeting of the Florida Educational Research Association, pp. 1–13 (1998)
8. Abrahamsson, P., Hanhineva, A., Jäälinoja, J.: Improving business agility through technical solutions: A case study on test-driven development in mobile software development. In: R. Baskerville, L. Mathiassen, J. Pries-Heje, J.I. DeGross (eds.) IFIP TC8 WG 8.6 International Working Conference on Business Agility and Information Technology Diffusion, *IFIP International Federation for Information Processing*, vol. 180, pp. 1–17. Springer (2005). URL http://dx.doi.org/10.1007/0-387-25590-7_14
9. Al-Kilidar, H., Cox, K., Kitchenham, B.: The use and usefulness of the ISO/IEC 9126 quality standard. In: R. Jeffery, J. Verner, G.H. Travassos (eds.) ISESE'05: ACM/IEEE International Symposium on Empirical Software Engineering, pp. 126–132. IEEE (2005). URL http://dx.doi.org/10.1109/ISESE.2005.1541821
10. Alshayeb, M., Li, W.: An Empirical Validation of Object-Oriented Metrics in Two Different Iterative Software Processes. IEEE Trans. Softw. Eng. **29**(11), 1043–1049 (2003). URL http://dx.doi.org/10.1109/TSE.2003.1245305
11. Ambler, S.: Introduction to Test Driven Design (TDD) (Cited 1 Apr 2009). URL http://www.agiledata.org/essays/tdd.html
12. American Psychological Association: Publication manual of the American Psychological Association, 5th edn. American Psychological Association, Washington, DC, USA (2001)
13. Arisholm, E.: Empirical Assessment of Changeability in Object-Oriented Software. Ph.D. thesis, University of Oslo (2001). URL http://simula.no/research/engineering/publications/SE.3.Arisholm.2001/simula_pdf_file
14. Arisholm, E., Gallis, H., Dybå, T., Sjøberg, D.I.K.: Evaluating Pair Programming with Respect to System Complexity and Programmer Expertise. IEEE Trans. Softw. Eng. **33**(2), 65–86 (2007). URL http://dx.doi.org/10.1109/TSE.2007.17
15. Astels, D.: Test Driven Development: A Practical Guide. Prentice Hall (2003)
16. Atlassian Pty Ltd: Clover project (Cited 1 Apr 2009). URL http://www.atlassian.com/software/clover/

17. Baheti, P., Gehringer, E.F., Stotts, P.D.: Exploring the efficacy of distributed pair program-ming. In: D. Wells, L. Williams (eds.) XP'02: Second XP Universe and First Agile Universe Conference on Extreme Programming and Agile Methods – XP/Agile Universe 2002, Lecture Notes in Computer Science, vol. 2418, pp. 208–220. Springer, Berlin Heidelberg, DE (2002). URL http://dx.doi.org/10.1007/3-540-45672-4_20

18. Bansiya, J., Davis, C.G.: A hierarchical model for object-oriented design quality assess-ment. IEEE Trans. Softw. Eng. **28**(1), 4–17 (2002). URL http://dx.doi.org/ 10.1109/32.979986

19. Basili, V.R., Briand, L.C., Melo, W.L.: A Validation of Object-Oriented Design Metrics as Quality Indicators. IEEE Trans. Softw. Eng. **22**(10), 751–761 (1996). URL http://dx.doi. org/10.1109/32.544352

20. Basili, V.R., Caldiera, G., Rombach, H.D.: Encyclopedia of Software Engineering, Chap. The Goal Question Metric Approach, pp. 528–532. Wiley-Interscience (1994)

21. Bayley, L., Eldredge, J.: The Structured Abstract: An Essential Tool for Researchers. Hypothesis **17**(1), 11–13 (2003). URL http://gainweb.mercer.edu/ mla/research/hyp03v17n1.pdf

22. Beck, K.: Test Driven Development: By Example. Addison-Wesley, Boston, MA, USA (2002)

23. Beck, K., Andres, C.: Extreme Programming Explained: Embrace Change, 2nd edn. Addison-Wesley, Boston, MA, USA (2004)

24. Beck, K., Beedle, M., van Bennekum, A., Cockburn, A., Cunningham, W., Fowler, M., Grenning, J., Highsmith, J., Hunt, A., Jeffries, R., Kern, J., Marick, B., Martin, R.C., Mellor, S., Schwaber, K., Sutherland, J., Thomas, D.: Manifesto for Agile Software Development (Cited 1 Apr. 2009). URL http://www.agilemanifesto.org/

25. Beck, K., Fowler, M.: Planning Extreme Programming. Addison-Wesley, Boston, MA, USA (2000)

26. Benbasat, I., Zmud, R.W.: Empirical research in information systems: the practice of relevance. MIS Q. pp. 3–16 (1999). URL http://dx.doi.org/10.2307/249403

27. Berry, E., Coustére-Yakin, C., Grover, N.: The significance of non-significance. QJM: Int. J. Med. **91**, 647–653 (1998). URL http://qjmed. oxfordjournals.org/cgi/reprint/91/9/647.pdf

28. Bhat, T., Nagappan, N.: Evaluating the efficacy of test-driven development: indus-trial case studies. In: ISESE'06: ACM/IEEE International Symposium on Empirical Software Engineering, pp. 356–363. ACM Press, New York, NY, USA (2006). URL http://dx.doi.org/10.1145/1159733.1159787

29. Bipp, T., Lepper, A., Schmedding, D.: Pair programming in software development teams – An empirical study of its benefits. Inf. Softw. Technol. **50**(3), 231–240 (2008). URL http://dx.doi.org/10.1016/j.infsof.2007.05.006

30. Bøegh, J.: A new standard for quality requirements. IEEE Softw. **25**(2), 57–63 (2008). URL http://dx.doi.org/10.1109/MS.2008.30

31. Briand, L.C., Melo, W.L., Wüst, J.: Assessing the Applicability of Fault-Proneness Models Across Object-Oriented Software Projects. IEEE Trans. Softw. Eng. **28**(7), 706–720 (2002). URL http://dx.doi.org/10.1109/TSE.2002.1019484

32. Briand, L.C., Wüst, J.: Empirical Studies of Quality Models in Object-Oriented Systems. Adv. Comput. **59**, 97–166 (2002). URL http://squall.sce.carleton.ca/pubs/ journal/2002_Briand_Wuest.pdf

33. Briand, L.C., Wüst, J., Daly, J.W., Porter, D.V.: Exploring the relationships between design measures and software quality in object-oriented systems. J. Syst. Softw. **51**(3), 245–273 (2000). URL http://dx.doi.org/10.1016/S0164-1212(99)00102-8

34. Briand, L.C., Wüst, J., Ikonomovski, S.V., Lounis, H.: Investigating quality factors in object-oriented designs: An industrial case study. In: ICSE'99: International Conference on Software Engineering, pp. 345–354. IEEE Computer Society Press, Los Alamitos, CA, USA (1999). URL http://dx.doi.org/10.1145/302405.302654

35. Brown, S.: One-Tailed or Two-Tailed Hypothesis Test? (Cited 1 Apr 2009). URL http://www.tc3.edu/instruct/sbrown/stat/httails.htm
36. Burke, E.M., Coyner, B.M.: Java™ Extreme Programming Cookbook. O'Reilly (2003)
37. Cai, X., Lyu, M.R.: The Effect of Code Coverage on Fault Detection under Different Testing Profiles. SIGSOFT Softw. Eng. Notes 30(4), 1–7 (2005). URL http://dx.doi.org/10.1145/1082983.1083288
38. Canfora, G., Cimitile, A., Carballeira, F.G., Piattini, M., Visaggio, C.A.: Productivity of test driven development: A controlled experiment with professionals. In: J. Münch, M. Vierimaa (eds.) PROFES'06: Product Focused Software Process Improvement, Lecture Notes in Computer Science, vol. 4034, pp. 383–388. Springer, Berlin, Heidelberg (2006). URL http://dx.doi.org/10.1007/11767718_32
39. Canfora, G., Cimitile, A., Garcia, F., Piattini, M., Visaggio, C.A.: Confirming the influence of educational background in pair-design knowledge through experiments. In: SAC'05: ACM Symposium on Applied Computing, pp. 1478–1484. ACM Press, New York, NY, USA (2005). URL http://dx.doi.org/10.1145/1066677.1067013
40. Canfora, G., Cimitile, A., Garcia, F., Piattini, M., Visaggio, C.A.: Evaluating advantages of test driven development: a controlled experiment with professionals. In: ISESE'06: ACM/IEEE International Symposium on Empirical Software Engineering, pp. 364–371. ACM Press, New York, NY, USA (2006). URL http://dx.doi.org/10.1145/1159733.1159788
41. Carver, J., Jaccheri, L., Morasca, S., Shull, F.: Issues in using students in empirical studies in software engineering education. In: METRICS'03: 9th International Symposium on Software Metrics, pp. 239–249. IEEE Computer Society, Washington, DC, USA (2003). URL http://dx.doi.org/10.1109/METRIC.2003.1232471
42. Cazzola, W., Marchetto, A.: AOP HiddenMetrics: Separation, Extensibility and Adaptability in SW Measurement. J. Object Tech. 7(2), 53–68 (2008). URL http://www.jot.fm/issues/issue_2008_02/article3.pdf
43. Chidamber, S.R., Kemerer, C.F.: A Metrics Suite for Object Oriented Design. IEEE Trans. Softw. Eng. 20(6), 476–493 (1994). URL http://dx.doi.org/10.1109/32.295895
44. Clare, J., Hamilton, H.: Writing Research: Transforming Data Into Text. Elsevier, Amsterdam, The Netherlands (2003)
45. Cohen, J.W.: Statistical Power Analysis for the Behavioral Sciences, 2nd edn. Lawrence Erlbaum Associates, Hillsdale, New York, USA (1988)
46. Cohen, J.W.: A Power Primer. Psychol. Bull. 112, 155–159 (1992)
47. Cohen, J.W.: A new goal: Preventing Disease, Not Infection. Science 262, 1820–1821 (1993). URL http://dx.doi.org/10.1126/science.8266069
48. Cohn, M., Ford, D.: Introducing an Agile Process to an Organization. IEEE Comput. 36(6), 74–78 (2003). URL http://dx.doi.org/10.1109/MC.2003.1204378
49. Coleman, D., Ash, D., Lowther, B., Oman, P.: Using Metrics to Evaluate Software System Maintainability. IEEE Comput. 27(8), 44–49 (1994). URL http://dx.doi.org/10.1109/2.303623
50. Conover, W.J., Iman, R.L.: Rank Transformations as a Bridge Between Parametric and Nonparametric Statistics. Am. Stat. 35(3), 124–129 (1981)
51. Conover, W.J., Iman, R.L.: Analysis of Covariance Using the Rank Transformation. Biometrics 38(3), 715–724 (1982)
52. Cook, T.D., Campbell, D.T.: Quasi-Experimentation: Design and Analysis Issues. Houghton Mifflin Company, Boston, MA, USA (1979)
53. Cornett, S.: Code Coverage Analysis (Cited 1 Apr. 2009). URL http://www.bullseye.com/coverage.html
54. Corporation, A.: (Cited 1 Apr. 2009). URL http://www.answers.com/topic/rule-of-thumb

55. Dallal, G.E.: Degrees of Freedom (Cited 1 Apr. 2009). URL http://www.tufts.edu/~gdallal/dof.htm

56. Damm, L.O., Lundberg, L.: Results from introducing component-level test automation and Test-Driven Development. J. Syst. Softw. **79**(7), 1001–1014 (2006). URL http://dx.doi.org/10.1016/j.jss.2005.10.015

57. Damm, L.O., Lundberg, L.: Quality impact of introducing component-level test automation and test-driven development. In: P. Abrahamsson, N. Baddoo, T. Margaria, R. Messnarz (eds.) EuroSPI'07: Software Process Improvement, Lecture Notes in Computer Science, vol. 4764, pp. 187–199. Springer (2007). URL http://dx.doi.org/10.1007/978-3-540-75381-0_17

58. Davies, R.: Agile Requirements. Methods and Tools **13**(3), 24–30 (2005). URL http://www.methodsandtools.com/PDF/mt200503.pdf

59. DeMarco, T.: Controlling Software Projects: Management, Measurement, and Estimation. Yourdon Press, New York, NY, USA (1982)

60. DeMarco, T., Lister, T.: Peopleware: Productive Projects and Teams. Dorset House Publishing. New York, NY, USA (1999)

61. DeMillo, R.A., Lipton, R.J., Sayward, F.G.: Hints on Test Data Selection: Help for the Practicing Programmer. IEEE Comput. **11**(4), 34–41 (1978). URL http://dx.doi.org/10.1109/C-M.1978.218136

62. DerSimonian, R., Laird, N.: Meta-Analysis in Clinical Trials. Control. Clin. Trials **7**(3), 177–188 (1986)

63. Dmitrienko, A., Molenberghs, G., Chuang-Stein, C., Offen, W.: Analysis of Clinical Trials Using SAS: A Practical Guide. SAS Publishing (2005)

64. Dunlap, P.W., Cortina, J.M., Vaslow, J.B., Burke, M.J.: Meta-Analysis of Experiments with Matched Groups or Repeated Measures Designs. Psychol. Methods **1**(2), 170–177 (1996)

65. Dybå, T., Arisholm, E., Sjøberg, D.I.K., Hannay, J.E., Shull, F.: Are two heads better than one? on the effectiveness of pair programming. IEEE Softw. **24**(6), 12–15 (2007). URL http://dx.doi.org/10.1109/MS.2007.158

66. Edwards, S.H.: Rethinking computer science education from a test-first perspective. In: OOPSLA'03: Companion of the 18th Annual ACM SIGPLAN Conference on Object-Oriented Programming, Systems, Languages, and Applications, pp. 148–155. ACM, New York, NY, USA (2003). URL http://dx.doi.org/10.1145/949344.949390

67. Edwards, S.H.: Teaching software testing: automatic grading meets test-first coding. In: OOPSLA'03: Companion of the 18th Annual ACM SIGPLAN Conference on Object-Oriented Programming, Systems, Languages, and Applications, pp. 318–319. ACM, New York, NY, USA (2003). URL http://dx.doi.org/10.1145/949344.949431

68. Eisenhauer, J.G.: Degrees of Freedom. Teach. Stat. **30**(3), 75–78 (2008)

69. Elliott, A.C., Woodward, W.A.: Statistical Analysis Quick Reference Guidebook: With SPSS Examples. Sage Publications, Los Angeles, CA, USA (2006)

70. Emam, K.E., Benlarbi, S., Goel, N., Rai, S.N.: The confounding effect of class size on the validity of object-oriented metrics. IEEE Trans. Softw. Eng. **27**(7), 630–650 (2001). URL http://dx.doi.org/10.1109/32.935855

71. Emam, K.E., Melo, W.L., Machado, J.C.: The Prediction of Faulty Classes Using Object-Oriented Design Metrics. J. Syst. Softw. **56**(1), 63–75 (2001). URL http://dx.doi.org/10.1016/S0164-1212(00)00086-8

72. Erdogmus, H., Morisio, M., Torchiano, M.: On the Effectiveness of the Test-First Approach to Programming. IEEE Trans. Softw. Eng. **31**(3), 226–237 (2005). URL http://dx.doi.org/10.1109/TSE.2005.37

73. Evanco, W.M.: Comments on "The Confounding Effect of Class Size on the Validity of Object-Oriented Metrics". IEEE Trans. Softw. Eng. **29**(7), 670–672 (2003). URL http://dx.doi.org/10.1109/TSE.2003.1214331

74. Fenton, N., Pfleeger, S.L.: Software Metrics (2nd ed.): A Rigorous and Practical Approach. PWS Publishing Co., Boston, MA, USA (1997)

75. Field, A.: Meta-analysis of correlation coefficients: a Monte Carlo comparison of fixed- and random-effects methods. Psychol. Methods **6**(2), 161–180 (2001)
76. Field, A.: How to Design and Report Experiments. SAGE Publications, Los Angeles, CA, USA (2003)
77. Field, A.: Discovering Statistics Using SPSS. SAGE Publications, Los Angeles, CA, USA (2005)
78. Filho, F.C., Rubira, C.M.F., de A. Maranhão Ferreira, R., Garcia, A.: Aspectizing exception handling: A quantitative study. In: C. Dony, J.L. Knudsen, A.B. Romanovsky, A. Tripathi (eds.) ECOOP Workshops '06: Advanced Topics in Exception Handling Techniques, Lecture Notes in Computer Science, vol. 4119, pp. 255–274. Springer (2006). URL http://dx.doi.org/10.1007/11818502_14
79. Flohr, T., Schneider, T.: Lessons Learned from an XP Experiment with Students: Test-First Need More Teachings. In: J. Münch, M. Vierimaa (eds.) PROFES'06: Product Focused Software Process Improvement, Lecture Notes in Computer Science, vol. 4034, pp. 305–318. Springer, Berlin, Heidelberg (2006). URL http://dx.doi.org/10.1007/11767718_26
80. Fowler, M.: The New Methodology (Cited 1 Apr. 2009). URL http://www.martinfowler.com/articles/newMethodology.html
81. Fowler, M., Beck, K., Brant, J., Opdyke, W., Roberts, D.: Refactoring: Improving the Design of Existing Code. Addison-Wesley, Boston, MA, USA (1999)
82. Frankl, P.G., Weiss, S.N., Hu, C.: All-Uses vs Mutation Testing: An Experimental Comparison of Effectiveness. J. Syst. Softw. **38**(3), 235–253 (1997). URL http://dx.doi.org/10.1016/S0164-1212(96)00154-9
83. Freeman, P.R.: The Performance of the Two-Stage Analysis of Two-Treatment, Two-Period Crossover Trials. Stat. Med. **8**(12), 1421–1432 (1989)
84. Friedman, H.: Magnitude of Experimental Effect and a Table for its Rapid Estimation. Psychol. Bull. **70**, 245–251 (1968)
85. Gamma, E., Beck, K.: JUnit (Cited 1 Apr. 2009). URL http://www.junit.org/
86. García, F., Bertoa, M.F., Calero, C., Vallecillo, A., Ruíz-Sánchez, F., Piattini, M., Genero, M.: Towards a Consistent Terminology for Software Measurement. Inf. Softw. Technol. **48**(8), 631–644 (2006). URL http://dx.doi.org/10.1016/j.infsof.2005.07.001
87. George, B., Williams, L.: An initial investigation of test driven development in industry. In: SAC'03: ACM Symposium on Applied Computing, pp. 1135–1139. ACM, New York, NY, USA (2003). URL http://dx.doi.org/10.1145/952532.952753
88. George, B., Williams, L.A.: A Structured Experiment of Test-Driven Development. Inf. Softw. Technol. **46**(5), 337–342 (2004). URL http://dx.doi.org/10.1016/j.infsof.2003.09.011
89. Geras, A., Smith, M.R., Miller, J.: A Prototype Empirical Evaluation of Test Driven Development. In: IEEE METRICS'2004: IEEE International Software Metrics Symposium, pp. 405–416. IEEE Computer Society (2004). URL http://dx.doi.org/10.1109/METRICS.2004.2
90. Glass, G.V., Mcgaw, B., Smith, M.L.: Meta-Analysis in Social Research. Sage Publications, Beverly Hills, CA, USA (1981)
91. Grigori Melnik and Frank Maurer: A cross-program investigation of students' perceptions of agile methods. In: ICSE'05: International Conference on Software Engineering, pp. 481–488 (2005). URL http://dx.doi.org/10.1145/1062455.1062543
92. Grissom, R.J., Kim, J.J.: Effect Sizes for Research: A Broad Practical Approach. Psychology Press, Indianapolis, Indiana, USA (2005)
93. Grizzle, J.E.: The Two-Period Change-Over Design and Its Use in Clinical Trials. Biometrics **21**(2), 467–480 (1965)
94. Gupta, A., Jalote, P.: An experimental evaluation of the effectiveness and efficiency of the test driven development. In: ESEM'07: International Symposium on Empirical Software

Engineering and Measurement, pp. 285–294. IEEE Computer Society, Washington, DC, USA (2007). URL http://dx.doi.org/10.1109/ESEM.2007.20

95. Gyimothy, T., Ferenc, R., Siket, I.: Empirical validation of object-oriented metrics on open source software for fault prediction. IEEE Trans. Softw. Eng. **31**(10), 897–910 (2005). URL http://dx.doi.org/10.1109/TSE.2005.112

96. Hamlet, R.G.: Testing Programs with the Aid of a Compiler. IEEE Trans. Softw. Eng. **3**(4), 279–290 (1977)

97. Hammell, T., Gold, R., Snyder, T.: Test-Driven Development: A J2EE Example. Apress, Berkeley, CA, USA (2004)

98. Hayward, R.S.A., Wilson, M.C., Tunis, S.R., Bass, E.B., Rubin, H.R., Haynes, R.B.: More Informative Abstracts of Articles Describing Clinical Practice Guidelines. Ann. Intern. Med. **118**(9), 731–737 (1993). URL http://www.annals.org/cgi/content/abstract/118/9/731

99. Hedges, L.V., Olkin, I.: Statistical Methods for Meta-Analysis. Academic Press, Orlando, Florida, USA (1985)

100. Hedges, L.V., Vevea, J.L.: Fixed- and Random-Effects Models in Meta-Analysis. Psychol. Methods **3**(4), 486–504 (1998)

101. Heiberg, S., Puus, U., Salumaa, P., Seeba, A.: Pair-programming effect on developers productivity. In: M. Marchesi, G. Succi (eds.) XP'03: Extreme Programming and Agile Processes in Software Engineering, Lecture Notes in Computer Science, vol. 2675, pp. 215–224. Springer (2003). URL http://dx.doi.org/10.1007/3-540-44870-5_27

102. Hochberg, Y.: A Sharper Bonferroni Procedure for Multiple Tests of Significance. Biometrika **75**, 800–802 (1988)

103. Hoffman, K., Eugster, P.: Towards reusable components with aspects: An empirical study on modularity and obliviousness. In: ICSE'08: International conference on Software engineering, pp. 91–100. ACM, New York, NY, USA (2008). URL http://dx.doi.org/10.1145/1368088.1368102

104. Holm, S.: A Simple Sequential Rejective Multiple Test Procedure. Scand. J. Stat. **6**, 65–70 (1979)

105. Hommel, G.: A Stagewise Rejective Multiple Test Procedure on a Modified Bonferroni Test. Biometrika **75**, 383–386 (1988)

106. Höst, M., , Wohlin, C., Thelin, T.: Experimental context classification: Incentives and experience of subjects. In: ICSE'05: International Conference on Software Engineering, pp. 470–478. ACM Press, New York, NY, USA (2005). URL http://dx.doi.org/10.1145/1062455.1062539

107. Höst, M., Regnell, B., Wohlin, C.: Using Students as Subjects – A Comparative Study of Students and Professionals in Lead-Time Impact Assessment. Empir. Softw. Eng. **5**(3), 201–214 (2000). URL http://dx.doi.org/10.1023/A:1026586415054

108. Huang, L., Holcombe, M.: Empirical Investigation Towards the Effectiveness of Test First Programming. Inf. Softw. Technol. **51**(1), 182–194 (2009). URL http://dx.doi.org/10.1016/j.infsof.2008.03.007

109. Huisman, M., Iivari, J.: Current Findings from Research on Structured Abstracts. J. Med. Libr. Assoc. **92**(3), 368–371 (2004)

110. Huitema, B.E.: The Analysis of Covariance and Alternatives. Wiley, New York, NY, USA (1980)

111. Hulkko, H., Abrahamsson, P.: A multiple case study on the impact of pair programming on product quality. In: ICSE'05: International Conference on Software Engineering, pp. 495–504. ACM Press, New York, NY, USA (2005). URL http://dx.doi.org/10.1145/1062455.1062545

112. Hunter, J.E., Schmidt, F.L.: Methods of Meta-analysis: Correcting Error and Bias in Research Findings, 2nd edn. SAGE Publications, Thousand Oaks, CA, USA (2004)

113. IEEE: IEEE Std 610.12-1990, IEEE standard glossary of software engineering terminology. Institute of Electrical and Electronics Engineers, Inc. (1990)

114. ISO: ISO/IEC 14598-5, Information Technology – Software product evaluation – Part 5: Process for evaluators. International Organization for Standardization (1998)
115. ISO: ISO/IEC 14598-1, Information Technology – Software Product Evaluation – Part 1: General Overview. International Organization for Standardization (1999)
116. ISO: ISO/IEC 14598-4, Software Engineering – Product Evaluation – Part 4: Process for Acquirers. International Organization for Standardization (1999)
117. ISO: ISO/IEC 14598, Software Engineering – Product Evaluation – Parts 1–5. International Organization for Standardization (1999)
118. ISO: ISO/IEC 14598-2, Software Engineering – Product Evaluation – Part 2: Planning and Management. International Organization for Standardization (2000)
119. ISO: ISO/IEC 14598-3, Software Engineering – Product Evaluation – Part 3: Process for Developers. International Organization for Standardization (2000)
120. ISO: ISO/IEC 14598-6, Software Engineering – Product Evaluation – Part 6: Documentation of Evaluation Modules. International Organization for Standardization (2001)
121. ISO: ISO/IEC 9126-1, Software Engineering – Product Quality – Part 1: Quality Model. International Organization for Standardization (2001)
122. ISO: ISO/IEC 9126-2, Software Engineering – Product Quality – Part2: External Metrics. International Organization for Standardization (2002)
123. ISO: ISO/IEC 9126-3, Software Engineering – Product Quality – Part3: Internal Metrics. International Organization for Standardization (2002)
124. ISO: ISO/IEC 9126-4, Software Engineering – Product Quality – Part4: Quality In Use metrics. International Organization for Standardization (2002)
125. ISO: ISO/IEC 25000, Software Engineering – Software product Quality Requirements and Evaluation (SQuaRE) – Guide to SQuaRE. International Organization for Standardization (2005)
126. Janzen, D., Saiedian, H.: Does Test-Driven Development Really Improve Software Design Quality? IEEE Softw. 25(2), 77–84 (Mar.–Apr. 2008). URL http://dx.doi.org/10.1109/MS.2008.34
127. Jedlitschka, A., Pfahl, D.: Reporting guidelines for controlled experiments in software engineering. In: R. Jeffery, J. Verner, G.H. Travassos (eds.) ISESE'05: ACM/IEEE International Symposium on Empirical Software Engineering, pp. 95–104. IEEE (2005). URL http://dx.doi.org/10.1109/ISESE.2005.1541818
128. Jeffries, R., Melnik, G.: Guest Editors' Introduction: TDD – The Art of Fearless Programming. IEEE Software 24(3), 24–30 (2007). URL http://dx.doi.org/10.1109/MS.2007.75
129. Jeffries, R.E., Anderson, A., Hendrickson, C.: Extreme Programming Installed. Addison-Wesley, Boston, MA, USA (2000)
130. Jørgensen, M.: Software Quality Measurement. Adv. Eng. Softw. 30(12), 907–912 (1999). URL http://dx.doi.org/10.1016/S0965-9978(99)00015-0
131. Juristo, N., Moreno, A.M.: Basics of Software Engineering Experimentation. Kluwer, Dordrecht, The Netherlands (2001)
132. Juristo, N., Moreno, A.M. (eds.): Lecture Notes on Empirical Software Engineering. World Scientific Publishing Co., Inc., River Edge, NJ, USA (2003)
133. Kampenes, V.B., Dybå, T., Hannay, J.E., Sjøberg, D.I.K.: Systematic review: A systematic review of effect size in software engineering experiments. Inf. Softw. Technol. 49(11-12), 1073–1086 (2007). URL http://dx.doi.org/10.1016/j.infsof.2007.02.015
134. Kampenes, V.B., Dybå, T., Hannay, J.E., Sjøberg, D.I.K.: Systematic review: A systematic review of effect size in software engineering experiments. Inf. Softw. Technol. 49(11-12), 1073–1086 (2007). URL http://dx.doi.org/10.1016/j.infsof.2007.02.015
135. Kan, S.H.: Metrics and Models in Software Quality Engineering. Addison-Wesley, Boston, MA, USA (2002)

136. Kaner, C.: Software Negligence and Testing Coverage. In: STAR'96: International Conference, Software Testing, Analysis and Review, pp. 299–327. Orlando, USA (1996)
137. Kerievsky, J.: Refactoring to Patterns, 1st edn. Addison-Wesley, Westford, MA, USA (2004)
138. Kerr, A.W., Hall, H.K., Kozub, S.: Doing Statistics with SPSS, 1st edn. Sage Publications Ltd, London, UK (2002)
139. Kitchenham, B.: Software Metrics. Measurement for Software Process Improvement. Blackwell Publishers Inc. (1996)
140. Kitchenham, B.: Procedures for Performing Systematic Reviews. Tech. Rep. Technical Report TR/SE-0401, Keele University (2004)
141. Kitchenham, B., Brereton, P., Owen, S., Butcher, J., Jefferies, C.: Length and Readability of Structured Software Engineering Abstracts. IET Softw. **2**(1), 37–45 (2008). URL http://dx.doi.org/10.1049/iet-sen:20070044
142. Kitchenham, B., Pfleeger, S.L., Pickard, L., Jones, P., Hoaglin, D.C., Emam, K.E., Rosenberg, J.: Preliminary Guidelines for Empirical Research in Software Engineering. IEEE Trans. Softw. Eng. **28**(8), 721–734 (2002). URL http://dx.doi.org/10.1109/TSE.2002.1027796
143. Kitchenham, B.A., Dybå, T., Jørgensen, M.: Evidence-Based Software Engineering. In: ICSE'04: International Conference on Software Engineering, pp. 273–281. IEEE Computer Society (2004)
144. Koskela, L.: Test Driven: Practical TDD and Acceptance TDD for Java Developers. Manning Publications, Greenwich, CT, USA (2007)
145. Kramer, S.H., Rosenthal, R.: Effect sizes and significance levels in small-sample research. In: R.H. Hoyle (ed.) Statistical Strategies for Small Sample Research. SAGE Publications, Thousand Oaks, CA, USA (1999)
146. Laddad, R.: AspectJ in Action: Practical Aspect-Oriented Programming. Manning Publications, Greenwich, CT, USA (2003)
147. Langr, J.: Pair Programming Observations (Cited 1 Apr. 2009). URL http://www.langrsoft.com/articles/pairing.shtml
148. Law, K.S., Schmidt, F.L., Hunter, J.E.: Nonlinearity of Range Corrections in Meta-Analysis: Test of an Improved Procedure. J. Appl. Psychol. **79**(3), 425–438 (1994)
149. Levesque, R.: SPSS Programming And Data Management: A Guide for SPSS And SAS Users. SPSS Inc. (2005)
150. Li, W., Henry, S.: Object Oriented Metrics that Predict Maintainability. J. Syst. Softw. **23**(2), 111–122 (1993). URL http://dx.doi.org/10.1016/0164-1212(93)90077-B
151. Lipsey, M.W., Wilson, D.B.: Practical Meta-Analysis. Sage Publications, California, USA (2001)
152. Littell, J.H., Coracoran, J., Pillai, V.: Systematic Reviews and Meta-Analysis. Oxford University Press, New York, USA (2008)
153. Loftus, C., Ratcliffe, M.: Extreme Programming Promotes Extreme Learning? SIGCSE Bull. **37**(3), 311–315 (2005). URL http://dx.doi.org/10.1145/1151954.1067531
154. Ma, Y.S., Offutt, J., Kwon, Y.R.: MuJava: An Automated Class Mutation System. Softw. Test., Verif. Reliab. **15**(2), 97–133 (2005). URL http://dx.doi.org/10.1002/stvr.v15:2
155. MacCormack, A., Rusnak, J., Baldwin, C.Y.: The Impact of Component Modularity on Design Evolution: Evidence from the Software Industry. Research Paper No. 08-038, Harvard Business School – Technology & Operations Management Unit (2007). URL http://ssrn.com/abstract=1071720
156. Maciaszek, L., Liong, B.L.: Practical Software Engineering. A Case-Study Approach. Addison-Wesley, Boston, MA, USA (2004)
157. Madeyski, L.: Preliminary Analysis of the Effects of Pair Programming and Test-Driven Development on the External Code Quality. In: K. Zieliński, T. Szmuc (eds.)

Software Engineering: Evolution and Emerging Technologies, Frontiers in Artificial Intelligence and Applications, vol. 130, pp. 113–123. IOS Press (2005). URL http://madeyski.e-informatyka.pl/download/Madeyski05b.pdf

158. Madeyski, L.: Is External code quality correlated with programming experience or feelgood factor? In: P. Abrahamsson, M. Marchesi, G. Succi (eds.) XP'06: Extreme Programming and Agile Processes in Software Engineering, Lecture Notes in Computer Science, vol. 4044, pp. 65–74. Springer (2006). URL http://dx.doi.org/10.1007/11774129_7. (http://madeyski.e-informatyka.pl/download/Madeyski06b.pdf)

159. Madeyski, L.: The impact of pair programming and test-driven development on package dependencies in object-oriented design – an experiment. In: J. Münch, M. Vierimaa (eds.) PROFES'06: Product Focused Software Process Improvement, Lecture Notes in Computer Science, vol. 4034, pp. 278–289. Springer, Berlin, Heidelberg (2006). URL http://dx.doi.org/10.1007/11767718_24. (http://madeyski.e-informatyka.pl/download/Madeyski06.pdf)

160. Madeyski, L.: On the Effects of pair programming on thoroughness and fault-finding effectiveness of unit tests. In: J. Münch, P. Abrahamsson (eds.) PROFES'07: Product Focused Software Process Improvement, Lecture Notes in Computer Science, vol. 4589, pp. 207–221. Springer (2007). URL http://dx.doi.org/10.1007/978-3-540-73460-4_20. (http://madeyski.e-informatyka.pl/download/Madeyski07.pdf)

161. Madeyski, L.: The Impact of Pair Programming on Thoroughness and Fault Detection Effectiveness of Unit Tests Suites. Softw. Process Improv. Pract. 13(3), 281–295 (2008). URL http://dx.doi.org/10.1002/spip.382. (http://madeyski.e-informatyka.pl/download/Madeyski08.pdf)

162. Madeyski, L.: The Impact of Test-First Programming on Branch Coverage and Mutation Score Indicator of Unit Tests: An experiment. Inf. Softw. Technol. 52(2), 169–184 (2010). URL http://dx.doi.org/10.1016/j.infsof.2009.08.007. (http://madeyski.e-informatyka.pl/download/Madeyski10c.pdf)

163. Madeyski, L., Radyk, N.: Judy – A Mutation Testing Tool for Java. IET Softw. 4(1), (2010). (accepted) URL http://dx.doi.org/10.1049/iet-sen.2008.0038. (http://madeyski.e-informatyka.pl/download/Madeyski10b.pdf)

164. Madeyski, L., Radyk, N.: Judy – Mutation Testing Tool for Java (Cited 1. Apr 2009). URL http://www.e-informatyka.pl/sens/Wiki.jsp?page=Projects.Judy

165. Madeyski, L., Stochmiałek, M.: Architectural Design of Modern Web Applications. J. Found. Comput. Decis. Sci. 30(1), 49–60 (2005). URL http://madeyski.e-informatyka.pl/download/23.pdf

166. Madeyski, L., Szała, Ł.: Impact of Aspect-Oriented Programming on Software Development Efficiency and Design Quality: An Empirical Study. IET Softw. 1(5), 180–187 (2007). URL http://dx.doi.org/10.1049/iet-sen:20060071. (http://madeyski.e-informatyka.pl/download/Madeyski07g.pdf)

167. Madeyski, L., Szała, Ł.: The impact of test-driven development on software development productivity – an empirical study. In: P. Abrahamsson, N. Baddoo, T. Margaria, R. Messnarz (eds.) EuroSPI'07: Software Process Improvement, Lecture Notes in Computer Science, vol. 4764, pp. 200–211. Springer (2007). URL http://dx.doi.org/10.1007/978-3-540-75381-0_18. (http://madeyski.e-informatyka.pl/download/Madeyski07d.pdf)

168. Mäntylä, M.: Bad Smells in Software – a Taxonomy and an Empirical Study (2003). MSc thesis, Helsinki University of Technology

169. Mäntylä, M., Vanhanen, J., Lassenius, C.: A taxonomy and an initial empirical study of bad smells in code. In: ICSM'03: International Conference on Software Maintenance, pp. 381–384. IEEE Computer Society (2003). URL http://dx.doi.org/10.1109/ICSM.2003.1235447

170. Marick, B.: How to misuse code coverage. In: Proceedings of the 16th International Conference on Testing Computer Software. Washington, USA (1999). URL http://www.exampler.com/testing-com/writings/coverage.pdf

171. Martin, R.C.: OO Design Quality Metrics: An Analysis of Dependencies (1994, Cited 1 Apr. 2009). URL http://www.objectmentor.com/resources/articles/oodmetrc.pdf

172. Martin, R.C.: Agile Software Development, Principles, Patterns, and Practices. Prentice Hall, Upper Saddle River, NJ, USA (2002)

173. Mattu, B., Shankar, R.: Test driven design methodology for component-based system. In: 1st Annual IEEE Systems Conference, pp. 1–7 (2007). URL http://dx.doi.org/10.1109/SYSTEMS.2007.374646

174. Maximilien, E.M., Williams, L.A.: Assessing Test-Driven Development at IBM. In: ICSE'03: International Conference on Software Engineering, pp. 564–569. IEEE Computer Society (2003). URL http://dx.doi.org/10.1109/ICSE.2003.1201238

175. Maxwell, J.A.: Qualitative Research Design : An Interactive Approach (Applied Social Research Methods). SAGE Publications, London, UK (2004)

176. Maxwell, K., Forselius, P.: Benchmarking Software-Development Productivity – Applied Research Results. IEEE Softw. **17**(1), 80–88 (2000). URL http://dx.doi.org/10.1109/52.820015

177. Maxwell, K.D.: Collecting Data for Comparability: Benchmarking Software Development Productivity. IEEE Software **18**(5), 22–25 (2001). URL http://dx.doi.org/10.1109/52.951490

178. Maxwell, S.E., Delaney, H.D.: Designing Experiments and Analyzing Data: A Model Comparison Perspective, 2nd edn. Lawrence Erlbaum, Mahwah (2004)

179. McBreen, P.: Questioning Extreme Programming. Addison-Wesley, Boston, MA, USA (2002)

180. Miller, R.G.: Beyond ANOVA: Basics of Applied Statistics. CRC Press, Boca Raton, FL, USA (1997)

181. Montgomery, D.C.: Design and Analysis of Experiments, 5th edn. Wiley, New York, NY, USA (2001)

182. Mudholkar, G.S., George, E.O.: The logit method for combining probabilities. In: Symposium on Optimizing Methods in Statistics, pp. 345–366 (1979)

183. Müller, M.M.: Are Reviews an Alternative to Pair Programming? In: EASE'03: Conference on Empirical Assessment In Software Engineering, pp. 3–12 (2003)

184. Müller, M.M.: Are Reviews an Alternative to Pair Programming? Empir. Softw. Eng. **9**(4), 335–351 (2004). URL http://dx.doi.org/10.1023/B:EMSE.0000039883.47173.39

185. Müller, M.M.: Two Controlled Experiments Concerning the Comparison of Pair Programming to Peer Review. J. Syst. Softw. **78**(2), 166–179 (2005). URL http://dx.doi.org/10.1016/j.jss.2004.12.019

186. Müller, M.M.: The Effect of Test-Driven Development on Program Code. In: XP'06: Extreme Programming and Agile Processes in Software Engineering, 7th International Conference, XP 2006, Oulu, Finland, June 17-22, 2006, pp. 94–103. Springer (2006). URL http://dx.doi.org/10.1007/11774129_10

187. Müller, M.M., Hagner, O.: Experiment About Test-First Programming. IEE Proc-Softw. **149**(5), 131–136 (2002). URL http://dx.doi.org/10.1049/ip-sen:20020540

188. Müller, M.M., Höfer, A.: The Effect of Experience on the Test-Driven Development Process. Empir. Softw. Eng. **12**(6), 593–615 (2007). URL http://dx.doi.org/10.1007/s10664-007-9048-2

189. Munnelly, J., Fritsch, S., Clarke, S.: An aspect-oriented approach to the modularisation of context. In: PERCOM'07: IEEE International Conference on Pervasive Computing and Communications, pp. 114–124. IEEE Computer Society, Washington, DC, USA (2007).

URL http://dx.doi.org/10.1109/PERCOM.2007.7

190. Munson, J.C.: Software Engineering Measurement. Auerbach Publications, Boca Raton, FL, USA (2003)

191. Myers, G.J.: The art of software testing. Wiley, New York, NY, USA (1979)

192. Nagappan, N., Maximilien, E.M., Bhat, T., Williams, L.: Realizing quality improvement through test driven development: results and experiences of four industrial teams. Empir. Softw. Eng. **13**(3) (2008). URL http://dx.doi.org/10.1007/s10664-008-9062-z

193. Nawrocki, J.R., Jasiński, M., Olek, L., Lange, B.: Pair Programming vs. Side-by-Side Programming. In: I. Richardson, P. Abrahamsson, R. Messnarz (eds.) EuroSPI'05: Software Process Improvement, Lecture Notes in Computer Science, vol. 3792, pp. 28–38. Springer (2005). URL http://dx.doi.org/10.1007/11586012_4

194. Nawrocki, J.R., Wojciechowski, A.: Experimental evaluation of pair programming. In: ESCOM'01: European Software Control and Metrics, pp. 269–276. London, UK (2001). URL http://www.agilealliance.org/system/article/file/1215/file.pdf

195. Newkirk, J.W., Vorontsov, A.A.: Test-driven development in Microsoft .Net. Microsoft Press, Redmond, WA, USA (2004)

196. Nosek, J.T.: The Case for Collaborative Programming. Commun. ACM **41**(3), 105–108 (1998). URL http://dx.doi.org/10.1145/272287.272333

197. Offutt, A.J., Pan, J., Tewary, K., Zhang, T.: An Experimental Evaluation of Data Flow and Mutation Testing. Softw., Pract. Exper. **26**(2), 165–176 (1996)

198. Offutt, A.J., Untch, R.H.: Mutation Testing for the New Century, Chap. Mutation 2000: Uniting the Orthogonal, pp. 34–44. Kluwer Academic Publishers, Norwell, MA, USA (2001)

199. Olejnik, S.F., Algina, J.: Parametric ANCOVA vs. rank transform ANCOVA when assumptions of conditional normality and homoscedasticity are violated. In: Annual Meeting of the American Educational Research Association (67th, Montreal, Quebec, Apr. 11–15, 1983) (1983)

200. Pai, G.J., Dugan, J.B.: Empirical Analysis of Software Fault Content and Fault Proneness Using Bayesian Methods. IEEE Trans. Softw. Eng. **33**(10), 675–686 (2007). URL http://dx.doi.org/10.1109/TSE.2007.70722

201. Pančur, M., Ciglarič, M., Trampuš, M., Vidmar, T.: Towards empirical evaluation of test-driven development in a university environment. In: EUROCON'03: International Conference on Computer as a Tool, pp. 83–86 (2003). URL http://dx.doi.org/10.1109/EURCON.2003.1248153

202. Perneger, T.V.: What's wrong with Bonferroni adjustments. BMJ **27**, 1236–1238 (1998)

203. Pfleeger, S.L., Fenton, N., Page, S.: Evaluating Software Engineering Standards. Computer **27**(9), 71–79 (1994). URL http://dx.doi.org/10.1109/2.312041

204. Piechowiak, A., Madeyski, L.: Project 2006 – Submission System: User Stories (2006). Power Media S.A. (Cited 1 Apr 2009). URL http://madeyski.e-informatyka.pl/download/project2006/SUBMISSION.pdf

205. Poppendieck, M.: Software Development Productivity. URL http://www.poppendieck.com/pdfs/SoftwareDevelopmentProductivity.pdf

206. Poppendieck, M., Poppendieck, T.: Lean Software Development: An Agile Toolkit. Addison-Wesley, Boston, MA, USA (2003)

207. Power Media S.A.: Project 2007/P4: Requirements (2007). Power Media S.A. (Cited 1 Apr 2009). URL http://download.e-informatyka.pl/project2007/requirements.pdf

208. Power Media S.A.: Project 2007/P4: User Stories (2007). Power Media S.A. (Cited 1 Apr 2009). URL http://download.e-informatyka.pl/project2007/project_4_us_1.pdf

209. Raab, G.M., Day, S., Sales, J.: How to Select Covariates to Include in the Analysis of a Clinical Trial. Control. Clin. Trials **21**, 330–342 (2000)
210. Robson, C.: Real World Research: A Resource for Social Scientists and Practitioner-Researchers. Blackwell Publishing Limited (2002)
211. Rosenthal, R.: An attempt at the experimental induction of the defence mechanism of projection. Ph.D. thesis, University of California, Los Angeles, CA, USA (1956)
212. Rosenthal, R.: Meta-analytic Procedures for Social Research, 2nd edn. SAGE Publications (1991)
213. Rosenthal, R., Rubin, D.B.: r Equivalent: A Simple Effect Size Indicator. Psychol. Methods **8**, 492–496 (2003)
214. Rosnow, R.L., Rosenthal, R.: Computing Contrasts, Effect Sizes, and Countermills on Other People's Published Data: General Procedures for Research Consumers. Psychol. Methods **1**(4), 331–340 (1996)
215. Rubin, A., Babbie, E.R.: Research Methods for Social Work, 5th edn. Thomson, Belmont, CA, USA (2004)
216. Runeson, P.: Using students as Experiment subjects – An analysis of graduate and freshmen student data. In: EASE'03: Empirical Assessment and Evaluation in Software Engineering, pp. 95–102. British Computer Society (2003)
217. Sanchez, J.C., Williams, L., Maximilien, E.M.: On the sustained use of a test-driven development practice at ibm. In: AGILE'07: Conference on Agile Software Development, pp. 5–14. IEEE Computer Society, Washington, DC, USA (2007). URL http://dx.doi.org/10.1109/AGILE.2007.43
218. Sarkar, S.K., Chang, C.K.: The Simes Method for Multiple Hypothesis Testing with Positively Dependent Test Statistics. J. Am. Stat. Assoc. **92**(440), 1601–1608 (1997). URL http://dx.doi.org/10.1109/TSE.2007.4
219. Scholfield, P.: Post Hoc Paired Comparisons after Kruskal-Wallis (Cited 1 Apr. 2009). URL http://privatewww.essex.ac.uk/~scholp/kw_posthoc.htm
220. Schwaber, K.: Agile Project Management with Scrum. Microsoft Press, Redmond, WA, USA (2004)
221. Schwaber, K., Beedle, M.: Agile Software Development with Scrum. Prentice Hall PTR, Upper Saddle River, NJ, USA (2001)
222. Senn, S.: Cross-over Trials in Clinical Research. Wiley, Indianapolis, Indiana, USA (2002)
223. Senn, S.: Within-patient studies: Cross-over Trials and n-of-1 Trials (Chap. 6). In: M.B. Max, J. Lynn (eds.) Symptom Research: Methods and Opportunities. National Institutes of Health, Bethesda, MD 20892-2190 (2008). URL http://symptomresearch.nih.gov/chapter_6/index.htm
224. Seshadri, G.: Understanding JavaServer Pages Model 2 architecture – Exploring the MVC design pattern (1999). URL http://www.javaworld.com/javaworld/jw-12-1999/jw-12-ssj-jspmvc.html
225. Shadish, W.R., Cook, T.D., Campbell, D.T.: Experimental and Quasi-Experimental Designs for Generalized Causal Inference. Houghton Mifflin, Boston, MA, USA (2002)
226. Shirley, E.A.C.: A Distribution-Free Method for Analysis of Covariance Based on Ranked Data. Appl. Stat. **30**(2), 158–162 (1981)
227. Shull, F., Singer, J., Sjøberg, D.I.K.: Guide to Advanced Empirical Software Engineering. Springer, London, UK (2008)
228. Simes, J.R.: An Improved Bonferroni Procedure for Multiple Tests of Significance. Biometrika **73**, 751–754 (1986)
229. Simpson, E.H.: The Interpretation of Interaction in Contingency Tables. J. Royal Stat. Soc. **B**(13), 238–241 (1951)
230. Siniaalto, M., Abrahamsson, P.: A Comparative Case Study on the Impact of Test-Driven Development on Program Design and Test Coverage. In: ESEM'07: International Symposium on Empirical Software Engineering and Measurement, pp. 275–284. IEEE Computer Society (2007). URL http://dx.doi.org/10.1109/ESEM.2007.2

231. Slinger, S.: Code Smell Detection in Eclipse (2005). URL `http://swerl.tudelft.nl/twiki/pub/Main/StefanSlinger/CodeNose-thesis.pdf`. MSc thesis, Delft University of Technology

232. Slyngstad, O.P.N., Li, J., Conradi, R., Rønneberg, H., Landre, E., Wesenberg, H.: The impact of test driven development on the evolution of a reusable framework of components - an industrial case study. In: ICSEA'08: International Conference on Software Engineering Advances, pp. 214–223. IEEE Computer Society, Washington, DC, USA (2008). URL `http://dx.doi.org/10.1109/ICSEA.2008.8`

233. van Solingen, R., Berghout, E.: The Goal/Question/Metric Method: A Practical Guide for Improvement of Software Development. McGraw-Hill, London, UK (1999)

234. Sørumgård, L.S.: Verification of Process Conformance in Empirical Studies of Software Development. Ph.D. thesis, The Norwegian University of Science and Technology (1997). URL `http://www.idi.ntnu.no/grupper/su/publ/phd/sorumgard_thesis.pdf`

235. Stevens, J.P.: Applied Multivariate Statistics for the Social Sciences, 4th edn. Lawrence Erlbaum, Mahwah, NJ, USA (2002)

236. Stouffer, S., Suchman, E.A., DeVinney, L.C., Star, S.A., Robin M. Williams, J.: The American soldier: adjustment during army life. Princeton University Press, Princeton, NJ, USA (1949)

237. Stout, D.E., Ruble, T.L.: Assessing the Practical Significance of Empirical Results in Accounting Education Research: The Use of Effect Size Information. J. Account. Educ. **13**(3), 281–298 (1995). URL `http://dx.doi.org/10.1016/0748-5751(95)00010-J`

238. Subramanyam, R., Krishnan, M.S.: Empirical Analysis of CK Metrics for Object-Oriented Design Complexity: Implications for Software Defects. IEEE Trans. Softw. Eng. **29**(4), 297–310 (2003). URL `http://dx.doi.org/10.1109/TSE.2003.1191795`

239. Svahnberg, M., Aurum, A., Wohlin, C.: Using students as subjects - an empirical evaluation. In: ESEM'08: ACM-IEEE International Symposium on Empirical Software Engineering and Measurement, pp. 288–290. ACM, New York, NY, USA (2008). URL `http://doi.acm.org/10.1145/1414004.1414055`

240. Tabachnick, B.G., Fidell, L.S.: Using Multivariate Statistics, 5th edn. Allyn & Bacon, Inc., Needham Heights, MA, USA (2006)

241. Thode, H.C.: Testing for normality. Marcel Dekker, New York, NY, USA (2002)

242. Tichy, W.F.: Hints for Reviewing Empirical Work in Software Engineering. Empir. Softw. Eng. **5**(4), 309–312 (2000). URL `http://dx.doi.org/10.1023/A:1009844119158`

243. Urdan, T.C.: Statistics in Plain English, 2th edn. Routledge, Oxon, UK (2005)

244. Vanhanen, J., Lassenius, C.: Effects of pair programming at the development team level: an experiment. In: ISESE'05: ACM/IEEE International Symposium on Empirical Software Engineering, pp. 336–345. IEEE (2005). URL `http://dx.doi.org/10.1109/ISESE.2005.1541842`

245. Venners, B.: Test-Driven Development. A Conversation with Martin Fowler, Part V (Cited 1 Apr 2009). URL `http://www.artima.com/intv/testdrivenP.html`

246. Vincent Massol and Ted Husted: JUnit in Action, 1st edn. Manning Publications, Greenwich, CT, USA (2003)

247. Wake, W.C.: Extreme Programming Explored, 1st edn. Addison-Wesley, Boston, MA, USA (2001)

248. Wake, W.C.: Overview of XP Explained, 2nd edn (Cited 1 Apr. 2009). URL `http://xp123.com/xplor/xp0502/index.shtml`

249. Walker, H.: Degrees of Freedom. J. Educ. Psychol. **31**(4), 253–269 (1940). URL `http://courses.ncssm.edu/math/Stat_Inst/PDFS/DFWalker.pdf`. Transcription by Chris Olsen with errata

250. Walsh, P.J.: A Measure of Test Case Completeness. Ph.D. thesis, University of New York (1985)

251. Wang, Y., Erdogmus, H.: The role of process measurement in test-driven development. In: C. Zannier, H. Erdogmus, L. Lindstrom (eds.) XP/Agile Universe'04: Extreme Programming and Agile Methods, Lecture Notes in Computer Science, vol. 3134, pp. 32–42. Springer (2004). URL http://dx.doi.org/10.1007/b99820

252. Williams, L.: The Collaborative Software Process. Ph.D. thesis, University of Utah (2000). URL http://collaboration.csc.ncsu.edu/laurie/Papers/dissertation.pdf

253. Williams, L., Kessler, R.: Pair Programming Illuminated. Addison-Wesley, Boston, MA, USA (2002)

254. Williams, L., Kessler, R.R., Cunningham, W., Jeffries, R.: Strengthening the Case for Pair Programming. IEEE Softw. **17**(4), 19–25 (2000)

255. Williams, L., Maximilien, E.M., Vouk, M.: Test-driven development as a defect-reduction practice. In: ISSRE'03: International Symposium on Software Reliability Engineering, pp. 34–48. IEEE Computer Society, Washington, DC, USA (2003). URL http://dx.doi.org/10.1109/ISSRE.2003.1251029

256. Williams, L., Shukla, A., Antón, A.I.: An initial exploration of the relationship between pair programming and Brooks' Law. In: ADC'04: Agile Development Conference, pp. 11–20. IEEE Computer Society, Washington, DC, USA (2004). URL http://dx.doi.org/10.1109/ADEVC.2004.6

257. Williams, L., Upchurch, R.L.: In support of student pair-programming. In: SIGCSE'01: SIGCSE Technical Symposium on Computer Science Education, pp. 327–331. ACM Press, New York, NY, USA (2001). URL http://dx.doi.org/10.1145/364447.364614

258. Williams, L.A., Kessler, R.R.: All I really need to know about pair programming I learned in kindergarten. Commun. ACM **43**(5), 108–114 (2000). URL http://dx.doi.org/10.1145/332833.332848

259. Wohlin, C., Runeson, P., Höst, M., Ohlsson, M.C., Regnell, B., Wesslén, A.: Experimentation in Software Engineering: An Introduction. Kluwer Academic Publishers, Norwell, MA, USA (2000)

260. Wójcicki, P.: Test-Driven Development (in Polish) (2008). Wroclaw University of Technology, MSc Thesis supervised by Lech Madeyski

261. Wójcicki, P.: Project 2007/P1: Eclipse plug-in which supports the developer during the process of creating unit tests (2007). Wroclaw University of Technology (Cited 1 Apr. 2009). URL http://download.e-informatyka.pl/project2007/project_1_requirements.pdf

262. Wójcicki, P.: Project 2007/P2: Transforming HTML into XHTML (2007). Wroclaw University of Technology (Cited 1 Apr. 2009). URL http://download.e-informatyka.pl/project2007/project_html_requirements.pdf

263. Wójcicki, P.: Project 2007/P3: Bad Smells Specification (2007). Wroclaw University of Technology (Cited 1 Apr. 2009). URL http://download.e-informatyka.pl/project2007/project_3_code_metrics_and_bad_smells.pdf

264. Wójcicki, P., Madeyski, L.: Project 2007/P3: Bad Smells Requirements and User Stories (2007). Wroclaw University of Technology (Cited 1 Apr. 2009). URL http://download.e-informatyka.pl/project2007/project_badsmells_requirements.pdf

265. Wójcicki, P.: Project 2007/P4: User Stories Set 2 (2007). Wroclaw University of Technology (Cited 1 Apr. 2009). URL http://download.e-informatyka.pl/project2007/project_4_us_2.pdf

266. Xu, S., Rajlich, V.: Empirical validation of test-driven pair programming in game development. In: ICIS-COMSAR'06: 5th IEEE/ACIS International Conference

on Computer and Information Science and 1st IEEE/ACIS International Workshop on Component-Based Software Engineering,Software Architecture and Reuse, pp. 500–505. IEEE Computer Society, Washington, DC, USA (2006). URL http://dx.doi.org/10.1109/ICIS-COMSAR.2006.34

267. Yin, R.K.: Case Study Research: Design and Methods, 3rd edn. SAGE Publications, Thousand Oaks, CA, USA (2003)

268. Ynchausti, R.A.: Integrating unit testing into A software development team's process. In: M. Marchesi, G. Succi (eds.) XP'01: Extreme Programming and Flexible Processes in Software Engineering, pp. 84–87. Sardinia, Italy (2001). URL http://www.agilealliance.org/system/article/file/1072/file.pdf

269. Yule, G.U.: Notes on the Theory of Association of Attributes in Statistics. Biometrika **2**, 121–134 (1903). URL http://dx.doi.org/10.1093/biomet/2.2.121

270. Zhou, Y., Leung, H.: Empirical Analysis of Object-Oriented Design Metrics for Predicting High and Low Severity Faults. IEEE Trans. Softw. Eng. **32**(10), 771–789 (2006). URL http://dx.doi.org/10.1109/TSE.2006.102

271. Zhu, H., Hall, P.A.V., May, J.H.R.: Software Unit Test Coverage and Adequacy. ACM Comput. Surv. **29**(4), 366–427 (1997). URL http://dx.doi.org/10.1145/267580.267590

Index